100
Nineteenth-Century
Rhyming
Alphabets
in English

From the Library of RUTH M. BALDWIN

SOUTHERN ILLINOIS UNIVERSITY PRESS
Carbondale and Edwardsville

Feffer & Simons, Inc.
London and Amsterdam

Designed by Gary Gore

International Standard Book Number 0–8093–0509–7
Library of Congress Catalog Card Number 79–132482

To mama and papa

Preface

LESS THAN twenty years ago I received in the fall as a birthday gift from my parents who were in England a handful of chapbooks, and, being properly appreciative of these quaint volumes, throughout the winter small packages of other old children's books. From this beginning started the great adventure of developing a library of nineteenth-century children's books in English to which I have added more than a thousand volumes a year. The story of the building of any library is a fascinating one—particularly to the builder—and considerable discipline is required to resist the telling.

Since in the early years books seemed scarce and money more so, I collected anything available to me that was a children's book in English before 1900, and I learned to prefer an inscribed copy definitely read and used by children. After all, a real children's book is not only one written for children but one used by them as well, and if the collector does not prefer worn and frequently tattered volumes he must become resigned to them or else limit his collection to those rare volumes which never fell into a child's hands. As a teacher this I could not do. Defensively at first, if a choice was to be made, I took the unknown and forgotten book rather than the classic, the common edition rather than the limited one. Great libraries which could afford them would see to the preservation of the others.

As the years have gone by I have never ceased to be amazed at the endless quantity and variety of children's books which one century produced. In the spring of 1968 I purchased from Ben Tighe of Athol, Massachusetts, some two hundred and fifty nineteenth-century alphabets rhyming and otherwise. It was almost a reluctant purchase because, although these books exemplified the very thing I was trying to preserve, they were for the most part, being in paper covers, in what seemed to be a miserable condition. However, this collection gave impetus to this book and has furnished about half the examples in it.

This book is by no means a definitive collection. In fact it may contain only a small portion of all the rhyming alphabets in English produced for children in the nineteenth century. It does not even contain a majority of my own examples many of which have been eliminated, many acquired since this volume was selected, and many more not even found. Dozens of children's magazines and annuals which ran for many years are probably full of them. Only a few of these have been used here. Two of these were serialized in children's magazines in twelve monthly parts a few letters at a time. Most remarkable perhaps is the fact that neither the alphabets nor their illustrations were commonly reprinted from one book to another as the stories so frequently were. With few exceptions each one that turned up was new and different. However, two examples in this book use the same pictures with different verses. One was an English edition and an American edition, the other two American editions.

Making a choice was most difficult. The best illustrations sometimes had rhymes without content or form, while the best poetry was occasionally attached to insignificant pictures. A paramount decision was not to use only those which would reproduce well or even to limit the collection to those which could be reproduced at all. Many originally in color are in black and white, and many of those made from hand-colored pictures show clearly that the painter did not stay within the lines. Yellowed paper, bleeding ink, foxing, and grubby finger prints may show up as well. Some plates have not been reproduced, and occasionally it can be noted that the poet or rhymer has made reference to pictures obviously missing. However, as can be seen in this collection even where the book has been reproduced in its entirety the plates in the original text do not always show what they were purported to.

In the earlier alphabets the letters *I* and *J* and *U* and *V* were not differentiated. However, when it suited the purpose of the author the practice seems to have been continued long after it was the custom. Occasionally other letters have been skipped over and sometimes ignored completely. All kinds of excuses were used in the treatment of the hard letters such as *X* and *Z*. The challenge of the alphabet was not in getting off to a good start but in coming up with a good conclusion.

Included in this group are a few famous alphabets and a few famous authors or, more frequently, artists, but most are completely anonymous and unknown. And several of the most famous which have been reprinted elsewhere are not included here. Because of the nature of the books the bibliographical notations may be challengeable. The paper cover frequently serves as a title page with the limited amount of information woven into the picture. In many of these when a separate title page does exist it does not agree with the cover. About half are undated and little effort has been made to establish the exact date of the books much less the edition or chronological sequence, since to do this properly would be almost impossible. A simple bibliography of all the nineteenth-century rhyming alphabets would be a book in itself. Without authors or artists, as most of these are, an alphabetical arrangement or index is meaningless. Therefore, an effort has been made to group like alphabets together or those on a similar theme. That authors were not always faithful to the themes they had chosen is frequently clear. The

collection after an "Invitation" starts with those alphabets based on the familiar "A was an Apple Pie" followed by longer poems on the apple pie. The use of a child's name for each letter of the alphabet and then themes around a single name or person follow. Nature, animals, birds, farm life, gardening and flowers are the next groups. Alphabets of trades and the ones beginning with the famous lines "A was an Angler" or, what is known as the Tom Thumb Alphabet with its variants, "A was an Archer," are next. Goodness and scripture, which formed such a large part of the original collection, and my whole library for that matter, are, even after great elimination, a large group here, too. Travel and peoples follow. The remainder of the book consists of miscellaneous alphabets with a single thought for each letter followed by those where each letter represents many things. Several themes have undoubtedly been inadequately represented. Some have been eliminated altogether including some types of humorous, fanciful and absurd, and all those printed to advertise patent medicines and other products. With these exceptions, however, if there is an imbalance in this selection it reflects the imbalance in my own library.

It is difficult to conceive of all the people who made this book possible. It is highly unlikely that any author, illustrator, publisher, or anyone else involved in the distribution of the alphabets in their original form still lives. However, to all the living who found the books, sold them to me, and especially to those who are now involved in publishing them again in this volume, I am grateful.

Baton Rouge, Louisiana   Ruth M. Baldwin
January 1972

One Hundred Nineteenth-Century
Rhyming Alphabets in English

The Invited Alphabet, or, Address of A to B; containing his Friendly Proposal for the Amusement and Instruction of Good Children. By R. R. London: W. Darton, Jun., [ca. 1810–30]. Pp. 11 preface, pp. [26] text. 13.5 x 12.6 cm.

1

THE

INVITED ALPHABET,

OR,

ADDRESS OF

A TO B;

containing his

FRIENDLY PROPOSAL

FOR THE

Amusement and Instruction of Good Children.

Virginibus Puerisque canto.   Hor.
I sing for Girls and Boys.

By R. R.

LONDON:
PUBLISHED BY W. DARTON, JUN.
JUVENILE AND SCHOOL LIBRARY, 58, HOLBORN HILL.

A said to B, Come here to me,

| A a | *A a* | B b | *B b* |

The whole designed by R. R. and Engraved by Charles Knight.

And we will go and Call on C;

D will not dilatory be

In helping to Enquire for E;

Then, finding E, I fancy we

Shall not be long in getting G;

And, though some say, H is no letter, *
I think, he cannot do much better,

Than herd with us; and after I,

Inviting J, will jointly try, †

J j   J j
J j   J j
J j

If K will be so kind to tell,

K k   K k
K k   K k
K k

Where we shall light on lounging L,

L l   L l
L l   L l
L l

M next will meet us; N and O,

M m   M m
M m   M m
M m

Though sometimes known to answer no,

N n   N n
N n   N n
N n

Will, when we summon them, come on;

O o   O o
O o   O o
O o

And P his part will play anon;

P p   P p
P p   P p
P p

Q will not quarrel with our views,

Q q   Q q
Q q   Q q
Q q

And R, I'm sure, will not refuse.

R r   R r
R r   R r
R r

S, it is true, is apt to *hiss*, ‡
But will not take our Scheme amiss;

T will accompany us too,

And talk of it to useful U;

Our Visit V will no way Vex;

W will Welcome us; and X,

Though backward to *begin*, I know, ‖
Will still a good eXample show;

Y will say Yes, with much applause,

And Z be Zealous in our cause.

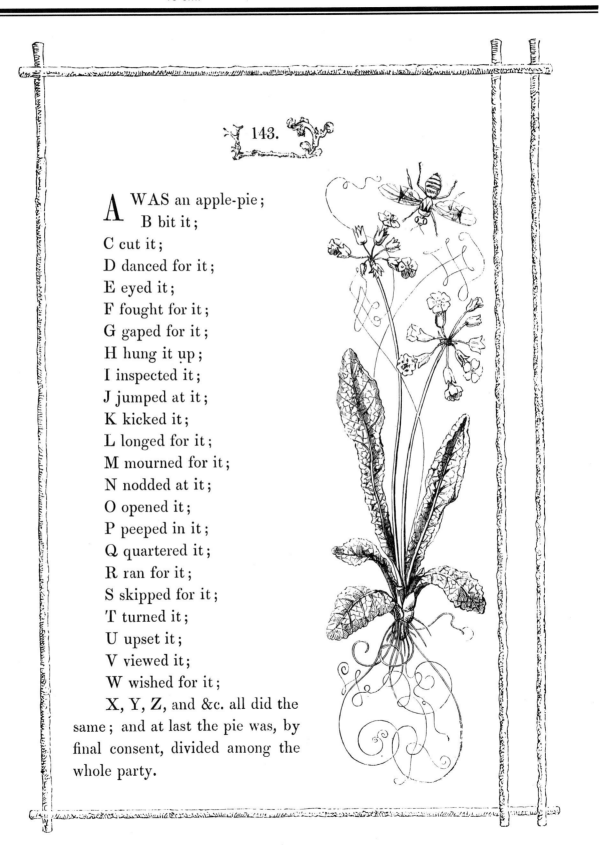

143.

A WAS an apple-pie;
　B bit it;
C cut it;
D danced for it;
E eyed it;
F fought for it;
G gaped for it;
H hung it up;
I inspected it;
J jumped at it;
K kicked it;
L longed for it;
M mourned for it;
N nodded at it;
O opened it;
P peeped in it;
Q quartered it;
R ran for it;
S skipped for it;
T turned it;
U upset it;
V viewed it;
W wished for it;
X, Y, Z, and &c. all did the same; and at last the pie was, by final consent, divided among the whole party.

The History of an Apple Pie. New York: McLoughlin Bro's. Publishers. P. [8].
Hand-colored plates. 19.4 x 11.8 cm.

5

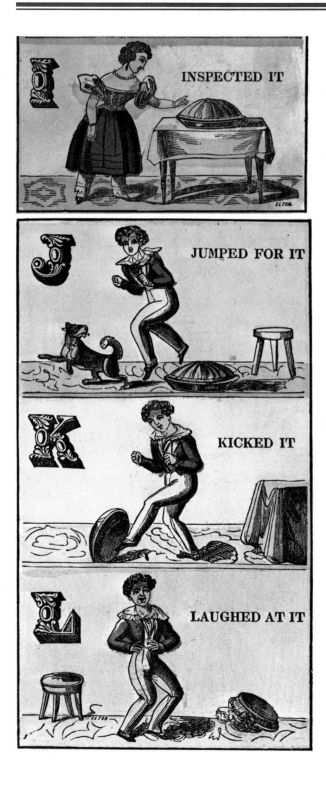

INSPECTED IT

JUMPED FOR IT

KICKED IT

LAUGHED AT IT

MOURNED FOR IT

NODDED FOR IT

OPENED IT

PEEPED IN IT

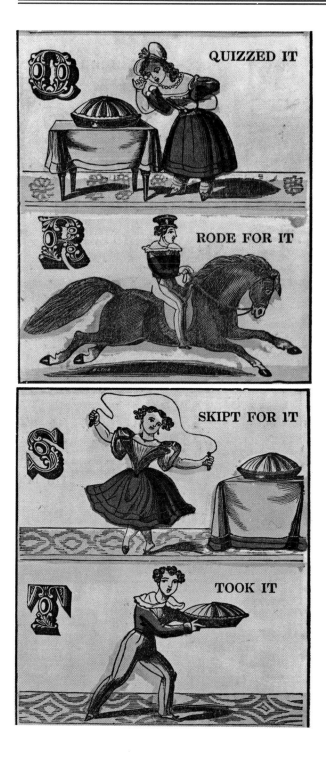

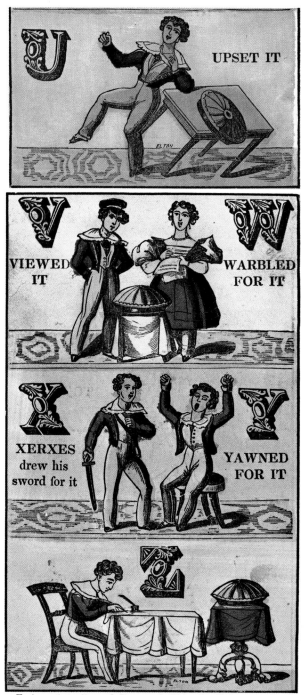

Zealous that all good Boys and Girls should be acquainted with his Family, sat down and wrote the History of it.

Picture Alphabet of Birds. London and Edinburgh: Thomas Nelson and Sons, [1874]. Pp. [8], including 4 pages of colored plates. 28.4 x 22 cm.

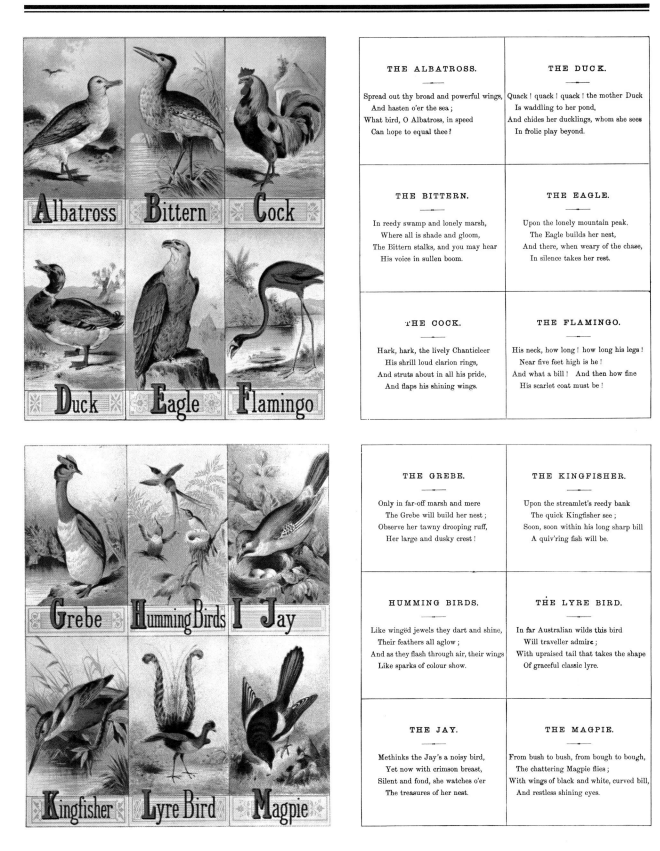

THE ALBATROSS.

Spread out thy broad and powerful wings,
    And hasten o'er the sea ;
What bird, O Albatross, in speed
    Can hope to equal thee ?

THE DUCK.

Quack ! quack ! quack ! the mother Duck
    Is waddling to her pond,
And chides her ducklings, whom she sees
    In frolic play beyond.

THE BITTERN.

In reedy swamp and lonely marsh,
    Where all is shade and gloom,
The Bittern stalks, and you may hear
    His voice in sullen boom.

THE EAGLE.

Upon the lonely mountain peak.
    The Eagle builds her nest,
And there, when weary of the chase,
    In silence takes her rest.

THE COCK.

Hark, hark, the lively Chanticleer
    His shrill loud clarion rings,
And struts about in all his pride,
    And flaps his shining wings.

THE FLAMINGO.

His neck, how long ! how long his legs !
    Near five feet high is he !
And what a bill ! And then how fine
    His scarlet coat must be !

THE GREBE.

Only in far-off marsh and mere
    The Grebe will build her nest ;
Observe her tawny drooping ruff,
    Her large and dusky crest !

THE KINGFISHER.

Upon the streamlet's reedy bank
    The quick Kingfisher see ;
Soon, soon within his long sharp bill
    A quiv'ring fish will be.

HUMMING BIRDS.

Like wingëd jewels they dart and shine,
    Their feathers all aglow ;
And as they flash through air, their wings
    Like sparks of colour show.

THE LYRE BIRD.

In far Australian wilds this bird
    Will traveller admire ;
With upraised tail that takes the shape
    Of graceful classic lyre.

THE JAY.

Methinks the Jay's a noisy bird,
    Yet now with crimson breast,
Silent and fond, she watches o'er
    The treasures of her nest.

THE MAGPIE.

From bush to bush, from bough to bough,
    The chattering Magpie flies ;
With wings of black and white, curved bill,
    And restless shining eyes.

THE NIGHTINGALE.

Of all the songsters of the grove,
  The minstrels of the dale,
None has a strain so sweet and rich
  As the famed Nightingale.

THE QUAIL.

When come the leaves and buds of spring
  Then comes the swift-winged Quail;
But ever quits our western lands
  Before the winter pale.

THE OSTRICH.

O'er desert sands the Ostrich skims,
  Beneath a burning sky;
Swift as the swiftest horse he runs,
  But has no wings to fly.

THE ROBIN.

The Robin is our winter guest,
  And trips across the snow
To peck the frequent crumbs our hands
  Are well-pleased to bestow.

THE PELICAN.

On river banks, on shores of lakes,
  Or marge of sounding sea,
The Pelican, in quest of fish,
  Roams uncontrolled and free.

THE SWALLOW.

Now hovering on rapid wing,
  Now down to earth, now high,
And circling round in airy ring
  To chase the painted fly.

THE THRUSH.

How gaily sounds the Thrush's voice
  In liquid notes and fast,
As if to bid the vales rejoice
  That winter stern is past!

THE XEMA.

In far-off lands, 'neath northern skies,
  And on the surfy shore,
Lives the lone Xema, and delights
  In ocean's thunder roar.

THE VULTURE.

On rugged rock the Vulture waits
  To scent its carrion prey,
When down into the plains below
  It takes its rapid way.

THE YELLOWHAMMER.

Who does not know this fav'rite bird
  With spotted yellow breast?
Of moss and roots and hair, with skill
  He weaves his curious nest.

THE WREN.

A tiny bird the modest Wren,
  Yet pleasant is his song;
His little nest he loves to build
  The hawthorn bowers among.

THE OUZEL.

The Ouzel is a songster sweet
  As you could wish to hear,
And in the woodland echoes far
  His note both rich and clear.

"Country Alphabet" (12 pp., including 6 colored plates), from *Aunt Louisa's Alphabet Book.* Comprising Nursery Alphabet, Country Alphabet, London Alphabet, Alphabet of Games & Sports. With Twenty Four Pages of Illustrations. Printed in Colours by Kronheim. London: Warne and Co., [1875]. 27 x 22.6 cm.

10

ACORNS.

Acorns that grow on the great oak tree
Make nice little cups for Grace and me;
We fill them with dew at early morn,
And make tiny rolls of seeds of corn.

BARN.

The *Barn's* a capital place for play,
When we are warm on a Summer's day;
The pigeons sit on the roof and coo,
While cows are breathing a drowsy "M-o-o!"

COWS.

Cows are delightful creatures, I think;
They give us such fresh, sweet milk to drink,
When the buttercups are golden bright,
And Summer meadows with daisies white.

DUCKS.

Ducks sail all day on the shining pond;
Of water they must be very fond,
But though their feathers upon it rest,
It does not wet their beautiful breast.

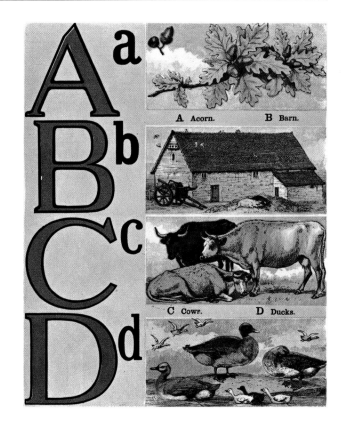

A Acorn.   B Barn.

C Cows.   D Ducks.

EGGS.

To seek in the nests *Eggs* clean and white,
Is Sister Grace's and my delight;
The basket is full of those we found,
And three besides we laid on the ground.

FARM.

Grandmamma's *Farm* is a charming place,
And very happy am I and Grace,
When we go to see her with Mamma,
And walk in the fields with dear Papa.

GATE.

There is John looking over the *Gate;*
For Granny always thinks we are late,
And waits in the porch for our return,
And says, "To be punctual we must learn."

HORSES.

Here are the *Horses,* Dobbin and Joe,
Who backwards and forwards meekly go,
Dragging the plough o'er the stubborn soil,
Winning us bread by their patient toil.

INN.

At the village *Inn* the stage-coach waits,
For here his horses the coachman baits,
And while they drink and get a short rest,
Calls for "a glass of the landlord's best."

E Eggs.   F Farm.   G Gate.

H Horses.   I Inn.

JACKDAWS.

Jackdaws build on the highest steeple;
They are disliked by many people,
Because when they can they always steal,
Or things they cannot want, conceal.

KITE.

John has a *Kite* which flies very high,
It seems quite lost in the dark blue sky:
If I could sit on its paper tail,
Up to the snowy clouds I would sail.

LADDER.

Here is the *Ladder* the gardener brings
To mount the trees where the blackbird sings,
And gather cherries for Grace and me;
They're beautifully ripe and red, you see.

MILL.

This is the *Mill*, where the wheel goes round,
And wheat into nice white flour is ground.
The Miller sings when his work is done:
To be a Miller must be great fun:

J Jackdaws.   K Kite.

L Ladder.   M Mill.

NUTTING.

Nutting's the best of country pleasures;
To strip the green boughs of their treasures
Delights all children, both rich and poor,
Who eagerly share the squirrels' store.

ORCHARD.

Johnny and I in the *Orchard* play,
And gather apples and pears to-day;
Nothing the rosy beauty can match,
Of those in my little apron I catch.

PLOUGH.

The *Plough* cuts deep furrows, long and straight
While close beside it the sparrows wait,
To pick up the worms on ev'ry side,
And thus for their little broods provide.

QUARRY.

In the *Quarry* men are hewing stone;
A piece of rock by their side is thrown.
They dig out gravel and snowy chalk:
It is dangerous on the edge to walk.

N Nutting.   O Orchard.

P Plough.   Q Quarry.

RABBITS.

These *Rabbits* look very much afraid;
I think from their warren they have strayed,
To have in the field a game of play;
Should they see us they will run away.

STILE.

This is the *Stile* that we cannot climb;
Mamma says we shall do it in time;
Now we creep under the lower railing,
Taking firm hold of the nearest paling.

TEAM.

The *Team* goes homeward at set of sun,
Its daily labour over and done;
We hope the carter off Dobbin won't slip,
As he waves and cracks his long thick whip.

R Rabbits.   S Stile.

T Team.   U Urchin.

URCHIN.

This *Urchin* belongs to the gipsy band
Who pitch their tents on Grandmamma's land;
He is resting awhile his weary feet,
And listening to chimes far off, but sweet.

VINE.

The *Vine* looks pretty upon the wall;
From its stem the purple clusters fall.
Could you think, when you look at a Vine,
Such little berries would make strong wine?

WAGGON.

The *Waggon* moves slowly up the road;
The horses find it a heavy load,
For it is full of all sorts of things,
That home from market the carter brings.

X. YEW.

The sails of the Mill make an *X*, you see,
And down below grows an old *Yew* tree;
To eat its berries be afraid.
Bows from its wood long ago were made.

ZIG-ZAG.

Zig-zag goes the path up the steep hill,
Past the old yew tree, under the mill.
We have not time up its turns to run,
For our country visit now is done.

V Vine.   W Waggon.

Y Yew-tree.   Z Zig-zag.

Alphabet of Trades. Dean's Untearable Cloth Children's Coloured Toy Books.
London: Dean & Son, Juvenile Book Publishers, [1850]. Pp. [8], hand-colored.
25 x 16.5 cm.

13

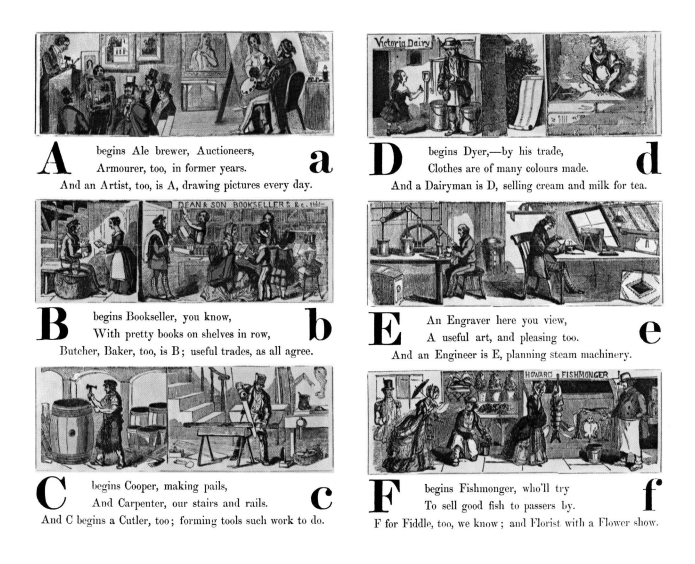

A begins Ale brewer, Auctioneers,
Armourer, too, in former years.
And an Artist, too, is A, drawing pictures every day. **a**

B begins Bookseller, you know,
With pretty books on shelves in row,
Butcher, Baker, too, is B; useful trades, as all agree. **b**

C begins Cooper, making pails,
And Carpenter, our stairs and rails.
And C begins a Cutler, too; forming tools such work to do. **c**

D begins Dyer,—by his trade,
Clothes are of many colours made.
And a Dairyman is D, selling cream and milk for tea. **d**

E An Engraver here you view,
A useful art, and pleasing too.
And an Engineer is E, planning steam machinery. **e**

F begins Fishmonger, who'll try
To sell good fish to passers by.
F for Fiddle, too, we know; and Florist with a Flower show. **f**

G begins Grocer, selling nice
Tea and sugar, plums, and spice. **g**
G begins a Glazier, too, mending windows broken through.

K begins Knife-maker, that's a trade
By which both knives and forks are made. **k**
K a Knitter, too, may be, knitting cuffs for you and me.

H begins Hatter, Hawker, too,
And will for Haberdasher do. **h**
H a Horse dealer,—what a show, of pretty ponies in a row.

L for Letter-founder stands;
Lace-maker, too, with nimble hands. **l**
And Locksmith begins with L; Linen-draper, too, as well.

IJ begins Ironmonger,—make he can
A stove, a kettle, or a pan. **ij**
J as Jeweller behold; selling diamonds, pearls, and gold.

M begins Milliner, so fine,
And Miner, working in a Mine, **m**
And for Merchant, with his store, trading to a foreign shore.

N n   begins Nurse, without whose care
Our baby folks would badly fare.
And a Newsman, too, is N, sending out his boys and men.

Q q   for a Quarry-man is found,
Heaving stones from under-ground.
Q is a Quack-doctor's pill; it may not cure, but make us ill.

O o   begins Oilman, and Orange as well,
And Optician, who magic-lanterns sell.
O begins an Omnibus, which the coach-builder makes for us.

R r   is a Rope-maker, by whose trade,
All sorts of Rope and string are made,
R begins Rider, too; so R is training horses near and far.

P P   For P I'm sure you'll quickly look,
For P begins a Pastry-cook;
And pray remember, it is true, P begins Physician, too.

S S   you'll find begins Shoemaker,
Shipwright, Scavenger, and Slater;
Surgeon, Sawyer, Saddler, too; and for Smith will also do.

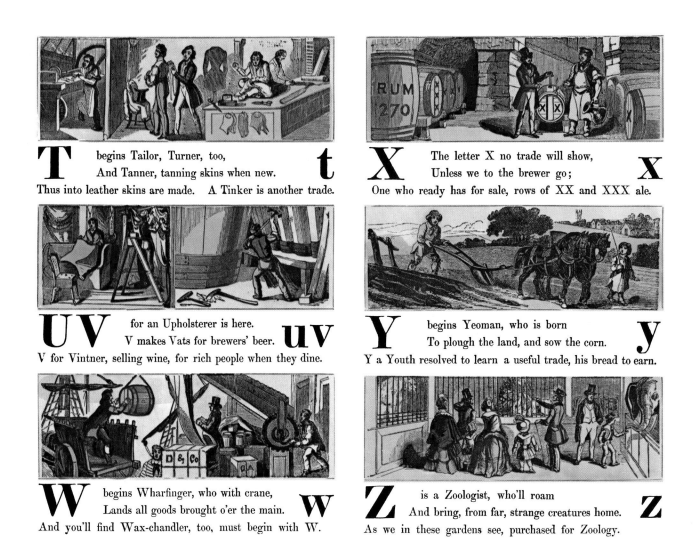

T begins Tailor, Turner, too,
And Tanner, tanning skins when new. **t**
Thus into leather skins are made.   A Tinker is another trade.

UV for an Upholsterer is here.
V makes Vats for brewers' beer. **uv**
V for Vintner, selling wine, for rich people when they dine.

W begins Wharfinger, who with crane,
Lands all goods brought o'er the main. **w**
And you'll find Wax-chandler, too, must begin with W.

X The letter X no trade will show,
Unless we to the brewer go; **X**
One who ready has for sale, rows of XX and XXX ale.

Y begins Yeoman, who is born
To plough the land, and sow the corn. **y**
Y a Youth resolved to learn a useful trade, his bread to earn.

Z is a Zoologist, who'll roam
And bring, from far, strange creatures home. **Z**
As we in these gardens see, purchased for Zoology.

"The Nursery Rhyme Alphabet" (pp. 10, including 8 colored plates), from *The Girl's Nursery Gift.* Comprising Nursery Rhyme Alphabet. Nursery Lullabies. Nursery Numbers. The Tiny Tea Party. With Thirty-Two Pages of Illustrations, Printed in Colours. London: Frederick Warne and Co. New York: Scribner, Welford and Armstrong [1875]. 24.5 x 18 cm.

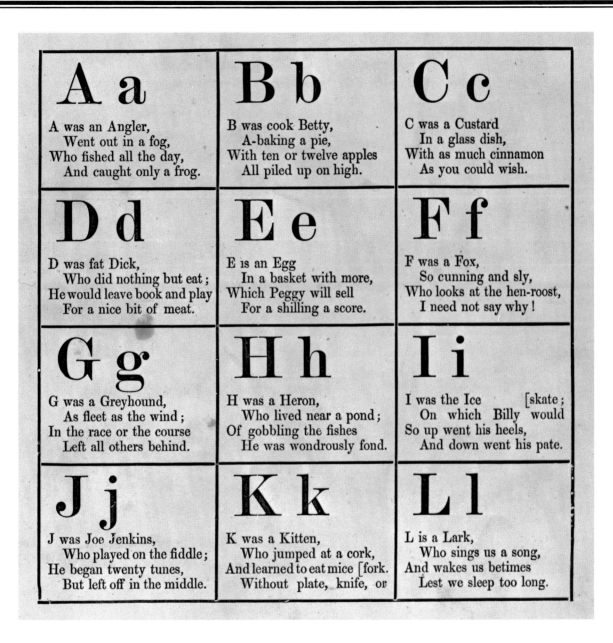

A a

A was an Angler,
    Went out in a fog,
Who fished all the day,
    And caught only a frog.

B b

B was cook Betty,
    A-baking a pie,
With ten or twelve apples
    All piled up on high.

C c

C was a Custard
    In a glass dish,
With as much cinnamon
    As you could wish.

D d

D was fat Dick,
    Who did nothing but eat;
He would leave book and play
    For a nice bit of meat.

E e

E is an Egg
    In a basket with more,
Which Peggy will sell
    For a shilling a score.

F f

F was a Fox,
    So cunning and sly,
Who looks at the hen-roost,
    I need not say why!

G g

G was a Greyhound,
    As fleet as the wind;
In the race or the course
    Left all others behind.

H h

H was a Heron,
    Who lived near a pond;
Of gobbling the fishes
    He was wondrously fond.

I i

I was the Ice   [skate;
    On which Billy would
So up went his heels,
    And down went his pate.

J j

J was Joe Jenkins,
    Who played on the fiddle;
He began twenty tunes,
    But left off in the middle.

K k

K was a Kitten,
    Who jumped at a cork,
And learned to eat mice [fork.
    Without plate, knife, or

L l

L is a Lark,
    Who sings us a song,
And wakes us betimes
    Lest we sleep too long.

M m
M was Miss Molly,
    Who turned in her toes,
And hung down her head
    Till her knees touched her
        nose.

N n
N is a Nosegay
    Sprinkled with dew,
Pulled in the morning,
    And presented to you.

O o
O is an Owl,   [wise;
    Who looks wondrously
But he's watching a mouse
    With his large round eyes.

P p
P is a Parrot,
    With feathers like gold,
Who talks just as much,
    And no more, than he's
        told.

Q q
Q is the Queen
    Who governs the land,
And sits on a throne
    Very lofty and grand.

R r
R is a Raven,
    Perched on an oak,
Who, with a gruff voice,
    Cries, Croak, croak, croak!

S s
S is the Sheep,
    Cropping grass on the lea:
Their owner has marked
    On their backs a large D.

T t
T is a Trumpeter,
    Blowing his horn,
Who tells us the news
    As we rise in the morn.

U u
U is a Unicorn,
    Who, as it is said,
Wears an ivory bodkin
    On his forehead.

V v
V is a Vulture
    Who eats a great deal,
Devouring a dog
    Or a cat at a meal.

W w
W was a Watchman,
    Who guarded the street,
Lest robbers or thieves
    Good people should meet.

X x
X was King Xerxes,
    Who, if you don't know,
Reigned over Persia
    A great while ago.

Y y
Y for a Yacht
    Sailing far out to sea;
If you were on board,
    How nice it would be!

Z z
Z is a Zebra,   [before;
    Whom you've heard of
So here ends my rhyme
    Till I find you some more.

"A Apple Pie" (pp. 128–39), from *Mother Goose's Nursery Rhymes. A Collection of Alphabets, Rhymes, Tales and Jingles.* With illustrations by Sir John Gilbert, R. A., John Tenniel, Harrison Weir, Walter Crane, W. McConnell, J. B. Zwecker and others. London: George Routledge and Sons, 1891. Pp. 288. 21.2 x 14 cm.

A Apple Pie.
B bit it.
C cut it.
D dealt it.

N nodded at it.
O opened it.
P peeped at it.
Q quartered it.

E eat it.
F fought for it.
G got it.
H hid it.

R ran for it.
S stole it.
T tried for it.
V viewed it.

J jumped for it.
K kept it.
L longed for it.
M mourned for it.

X Y Z &
   Amperse-and,
   All wished for
   A piece in hand.

"A Apple Pie" (2 pp.), from *Old Nursery Rhymes from Mother Goose*. New York: McLoughlin Bros. 26.5 x 20 cm.

A Apple Pie

A was an apple pie

B bit it.

C cut it,

D dealt it;

E eat it,

F fought for it,

G got it,

H had it.

J joined it.

K kept it,

L longed for it,

M mourned for it.

N nodded for it,

O opened it,

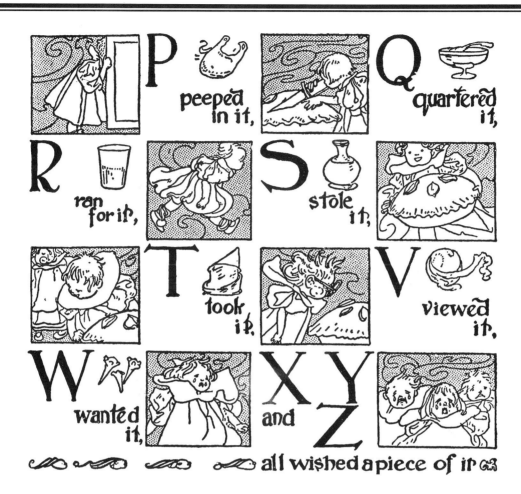

"A Apple Pie" (p. 14, unillustrated), from *The Picturesque Primer*. London: Griffith, Farran, Okeden & Welsh (Successors to Newbery and Harris). New York: E. P. Dutton, [1880]. Pp. 30. 29.6 x 23.3 cm.

A apple pie.
B bit it.
C cried for it.
D danced for it.
E eyed it.
F fiddled for it.
G gobbled it.
H hid it.
I inspected it.

J jumped over it.
K kicked it.
L laughed at it.
M mourned for it.
N nodded for it.
O opened it.
P peeped into it.
Q quaked for it.
R rode for it.

S skipped for it.
T took it.
U upset it.
V viewed it.
W warbled for it.
X Xerxes drew his sword for it.
Y yawned for it.
Z zealous that all good boys and girls should be acquainted with his family, sat down and wrote the history of it.

Apple Pie A, B, C. New York: McLoughlin Bro's., 1890. Pp. [16]. 21 x 16 cm.

APPLE PIE A, B, C.

A was an Apple Pie ever so nice,
   Seasoned with plenty of sugar and spice.

B was the Baker who rolled the crust thin,
   And also the Butter he had to put in.

C stands for Charlie who went to the shelf
   And cut out a very big piece for himself.

D Danced around it for nearly an hour,
   And then down he sat the whole Pie to devour.

E stands for Ellen who sat at the table,
   And tried to eat more than she really was able.

F had a Fight with his sisters and brothers,
   Declaring he would not divide with the others.

APPLE PIE A, B, C.

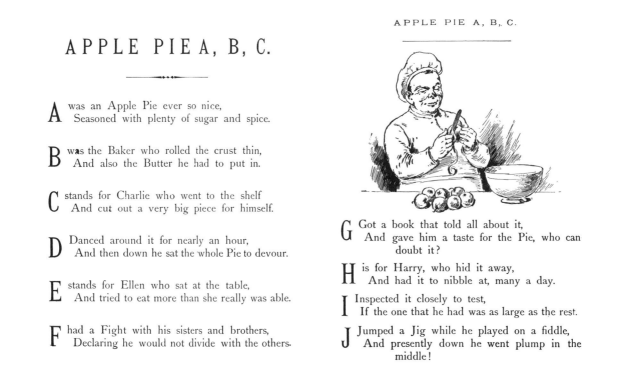

G Got a book that told all about it,
   And gave him a taste for the Pie, who can doubt it?

H is for Harry, who hid it away,
   And had it to nibble at, many a day.

I Inspected it closely to test,
   If the one that he had was as large as the rest.

J Jumped a Jig while he played on a fiddle,
   And presently down he went plump in the middle!

APPLE PIE A, B, C.

K Knelt beside it for more than a minute,
 Trying in vain to find out what was in it.

L Longed for it so she no longer could wait,
 But made her appearance with knife, fork
 and plate.

M Mourned: for, having been naughty, Oh fie!
 To bed he was sent without tasting the Pie.

N Nodded her head, and shook out her curls,
 And said "Apple Pie is for good boys
 and girls."

APPLE PIE A, B, C.

O Opened the Pie in a bit of a flurry,
 And then shut the lid down again in a hurry.

P Peeped through the door, and exclaimed with
 a sigh.
"Dear me! I could eat up the whole of that Pie!"

Q Quailed when he saw all the guests crowding in,
 For he knew that his slice would be narrow
 and thin.

R Ran for the knife in exceeding great haste,
 To cut up the Pie he was eager to taste.

APPLE PIE A, B, C.

S Stood on a chair, and with serious air
 Made a sensible speech to the relatives there.

T Took it away, but they got on his track,
 And made the young thief bring the Apple
 Pie back.

U Understood well she could have but one slice
 And it wasn't polite to be helped to it twice.

V Viewed it with wonder and joy in his eyes,
 And quietly noted its very great size.

APPLE PIE A, B, C.

W Weighed it with critical air,
 And said that he thought it would only
 be fair

If **X**—Extra—on the Pie as a sign
 Of goodness were put—'t was certainly fine.

Y is the Youth who had all he could eat,
 And grew so in girth that his belt wouldn't
 meet.

Z is for Zero, the share that was doled
 To poor Zachariah, left out in the cold.

"A. Apple Pie" (12 pp.), from *Aunt Louisa's Children's Gift.* Comprising A. Apple Pie. Dick Whittington. Pussy's London Life. With Full-Page Illustrations from Original Designs. Printed in Colours by Kronheim. London: Frederick Warne and Co., [1875]. 26 x 21.5 cm.

A was an Apple Pie, juicy and sweet,
For very good children, a very great treat.

B is young Bertie, who bit at the pie,
And took care to do it when no one was by.

C stands for Charlie, who cut for the others,
And handed it round to his sisters and brothers.

D Danced so gaily before the great Pie,
And showed her delight by the glance of her eye.

J Jumped twenty times with a face full of joy,
So eager to taste it was this little boy.

K Kept it, and thought that she looked very grand,
As she sat by its side with a rod in her hand.

L Longed for the Pie, and she wanted it soon,
For her plate was quite ready, and so was her spoon.

M Mourned; for Mamma had just sent him to bed,
For tasks left undone, and for lessons unsaid.

R Ran for a knife, as he wanted to try
How much he could eat of this large Apple Pie.

S Stood by the table and picked at the crust;
You'll not be so sly or so greedy, I trust.

T Took up with pleasure so splendid a gift,
But found it too hot and too heavy to lift.

V Viewed the big Pie and admired its figure,
For Grandmama's spectacles made it look bigger.

E is eating her Pie, with the plate on her knees,
Such a good little girl, and so easy to please.

F Fought for this largest and sweetest of Pies,
With another rude boy nearly double his size.

G Got at the Pie, and then bore it away,
To be laid on the shelf and be eaten next day.

H Hid the great Pie under grandmama's table,
And thought that to find it she would not be able.

N Nodded her head when she stood on the chair,
And shook all the curls of her pretty brown hair.

O Opened the Pie, just to see what was in it,
And lifted the crust up in less than a minute.

P Peeped at the Pie, which she thought very nice.
So she asked her Papa for a very large slice.

Q Quaked; for he thought that it looked rather small,
And he feared there might not be enough for them all.

W Wished for some more, but was ready to cry
When she heard that the servants had finished the Pie.

X expected his dear little sister would grieve,
So he brought her some pudding, her mind to relieve.

Y Yielded the point, and was cheerful about it,
Saying, " If the Pie's gone, we must all do without it."

Z Zealously tried little Winnie to cheer,
Like a good elder sister, so kind and sincere.

"Alphabet of Children," by Isabel Frances Bellows (pp. 112–17), from *Baby World Stories, Rhymes and Pictures for Little Folks*. Compiled from *St. Nicholas* by Mary Mapes Dodge. New York: The Century Co., 1884. Pp. xvi, 303. 26.3 x 19 cm.

27

A is for Apt little Annie,
Who lives down in Maine with her grannie.
Such pies she can make!
And such doughnuts and cake!
Oh, we like to make visits to Grannie!

B is for Bad little Bridget,
Who is morn, noon, and night in a fidget.
Her dresses she tears,
And she tumbles down-stairs,
And her mother's most worn to a midget.

C is for Curious Charlie,
Who lives on rice, oatmeal, and barley.
He once wrote a sonnet
On his mother's best bonnet;
And he lets his hair grow long and snarley.

D is for Dear little Dinah,
Whose manners grow finer and finer.
She smiles and she bows
To the pigs and the cows,
And she calls the old cat Angelina.

E is for Erring young Edward,
Who never can bear to go bedward.
Every evening at eight
He bewails his hard fate,
And they're all quite discouraged with
 Edward.

F is for Foolish Miss Florence,
Who of spiders has such an abhorrence
That she shivers with dread
When she looks overhead,
For she lives where they're plenty—at
 Lawrence.

G is for Glad little Gustave,
Who says that a monkey he *must* have;
But his mother thinks not,
And says that they've got
All the monkey they care for in Gustave.

H is for Horrid young Hannah,
Who has the most shocking bad manner.
Once she went out to dine
With a party of nine,
And she ate every single banana.

I is for Ignorant Ida,
Who does n't know rhubarb from cider.
Once she drank up a quart,
Which was more than she ought,
And it gave her queer feelings inside her.

J is for Jovial young Jack,
Who goes to the balls in a hack.
He thinks he can dance,
And he'll caper and prance
Till his joints are half ready to crack.

M is for Mournful Miss Molly,
Who likes to be thought melancholy.
She's as limp as a rag
When her sisters play tag,
For it's vulgar, she says, to be jolly.

N is for Naughty young Nat,
Who sat on his father's best hat.
When they asked if he thought
He had done as he ought,
He said he supposed 't was the cat!

K is for Kind little Katy,
Who weighs 'most a hundred and eighty;
But she eats every day,
And the doctors all say
That's the reason she's growing so weighty.

L is for Lazy young Lester,
Who works for a grocer in Chester;
But he says he needs rest,
And he finds it is best
To rest very often, does Lester.

O 's Operatic Olivia,
Who visits her aunt in Bolivia.
She can sing to high C—
But, between you and me,
They don't care for that in Bolivia.

P is for Poor little Paul,
Who does n't like study at all.
But he's learning to speak
In Latin and Greek,
And is going to take German next fall.

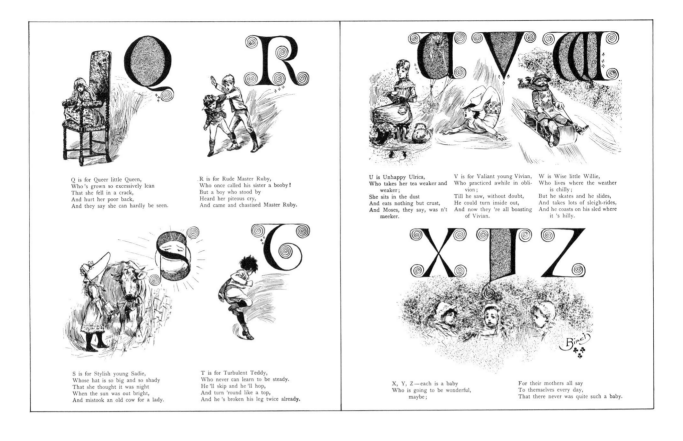

Q is for Queer little Queen,
Who's grown so excessively lean
That she fell in a crack,
And hurt her poor back,
And they say she can hardly be seen.

R is for Rude Master Ruby,
Who once called his sister a booby!
But a boy who stood by
Heard her piteous cry,
And came and chastised Master Ruby.

U is Unhappy Ulrica,
Who takes her tea weaker and
  weaker;
She sits in the dust
And eats nothing but crust,
And Moses, they say, was n't
  meeker.

V is for Valiant young Vivian,
Who practiced awhile in obli-
  vion;
Till he saw, without doubt,
He could turn inside out,
And now they 're all boasting
  of Vivian.

W is Wise little Willie,
Who lives where the weather
  is chilly;
But he skates and he slides,
And takes lots of sleigh-rides,
And he coasts on his sled where
  it 's hilly.

S is for Stylish young Sadie,
Whose hat is so big and so shady
That she thought it was night
When the sun was out bright,
And mistook an old cow for a lady.

T is for Turbulent Teddy,
Who never can learn to be steady.
He 'll skip and he 'll hop,
And turn 'round like a top,
And he 's broken his leg twice already.

X, Y, Z — each is a baby
Who is going to be wonderful,
  maybe;

For their mothers all say
To themselves every day,
That there never was quite such a baby.

Uncle John's Panorama New Pictorial Alphabet. Philadelphia: C. G. Henderson & Co., 1854. Hand-colored plates. Pp. [26], including covers. 14.5 x 11.2 cm.

UNCLE JOHN'S PANORAMA.
NEW PICTORIAL ALPHABET.

A is Ann, with milk from the cow.

B is Benjamin, making a bow.

C is Charlotte, gathering flowers.

D is Dick, who is one of the mowers.

E is Eliza, feeding a hen.

F is Frank who is mending his pen.

G is Georgiana, shooting an arrow.

H is Harry, wheeling a barrow.

I is Isabella, gathering fruit.

J j K k L l

J is John, who is playing the flute.

K is Kate, nursing her dolly.

L is Lawrence, feeding poor Polly.

M m N n O o

M is Maja, learning to draw.

N is Nicholas, with a jackdaw.

O is Octavius, riding a goat.

P p Q q R r

P is Penelope, sailing a boat.

Q is Quintus, armed with a lance.

R is Rachel, learning to dance.

S s T t U u

S is Sarah, talking to cook.

T is Teddy, reading a book.

U is Urban, rolling the green.

V v W w X x

V is Victoria.   Britain's great Queen.

W is Walter, flying his kite.

X is Xerxes; a boy of great might.

Y y Z z

Y is Miss Youthful, eating her bread.

and Z is Zachariah, going to bed.

"Pretty Name Alphabet" (pp. 38–64), from *The Child's Picture Story Book.* With Four Hundred Illustrations by Sir John Gilbert, R. A., J. D. Watson, W. M'Connell, W. Harvey, Harrison Weir and others. Engraved by the Brothers Dalziel. London: George Routledge and Sons, inscribed June 27, 1886, earlier ed. dated 1856. Pp. 320. 20.6 x 16.5 cm.

PRETTY NAME ALPHABET.

A is for A-MY; pray look at her doll,
  Which is dress-ed in pink mus-lin, and call-ed lit-tle Poll.

B is for BRI-AN; I'm sor-ry to say,
  He took a young bird from its warm nest one day.

C is for CA-RO-LINE, grace-ful and tall,
  With her fan and bou-quet, just dress-ed for the ball.

D is for DA-VID, the dunce of the school,
  Who wears the fool's cap while he stands on a stool.

E is for EM-MA, who left her dull room
  To cull the bright ro-ses when they were in bloom.

F is for FRANK, who a sail-or would be,
  So in new hat and jack-et he starts for the sea.

G is for GER-TRUDE, in-dus-tri-ous and wise,
Who helps sis-ter ANN to make pud-dings and pies.

H is for HAR-RY, so kind and so good,
  Who took lit-tle JANE to pull flow-ers in the wood.

I is for Is-a-bel, learn-ing to ride
On a qui-et old don-key, with John
by her side.

J is for James, to all mis-chief a-live,
Who was stung by the bees when he
lift-ed the hive.

K is for Kate, who is puz-zled, you see,
How to catch the young par-rot she
chanc-ed to set free.

L is for Lew-is, who went to the fair,
And scream-ed like a cow-ard at
sight of the bear.

M is for Min-na, who gives her dog Gip
A bowl of rich cream, for the beauty to sip.

N is for No-el, who soon did his task,
To a-muse his young cou-sins by
wear-ing a mask.

O for O-li-vi-a, a good lit-tle maid,
Who work-ed ve-ry hard her poor
pa-rents to aid.

P is for Pa-trick, the wild I-rish boy,
Whose blun-ders and fun all the
school-boys en-joy.

Q is for Quas-hee, a poor lit-tle slave,
Whom kind heart-ed chil-dren would
pi-ty and save.

R is for RICH-ARD, both ge-ne-rous and good,
Who gave his last pen-ny to poor BES-SY WOOD.

S is for SU-SAN, who sat on the ground,
To watch her tame spar-row that hop-ped round and round.

T is for THO-MAS, a spoil-ed lit-tle boy,
Who cri-ed for the Moon, as he would for a toy.

U is for UR-SU-LA, live-ly and quick,
Who at shut-tle-cock al-ways could beat bro-ther DICK.

V is for VIN-CENT, with trum-pet and gún,
Who thinks a great bat-tle is cap-i-tal fun.

W for WIN-NY, who pi-ties the poor,
And leads the blind boy to his own cot-tage door.

X for XI-ME-NA, a young girl of Spain,
Whose sweet songs we ask for a-gain and a-gain.

Y for you all, and I hope you may see,
When next Christ-mas comes, this grand Christ-mas tree.

Z is for ZO-E, with sweet smil-ing look,
Who bids you good bye, as you close up the book.

Girls and Boys Name A B C. New York: McLoughlin Bro's., 1889. Pp. [20] including cover in color. 30 x 25.5 cm.

A stands for ALFRED, an Archer is he,
So fond of his bow and his Arrow,
That Arthur cries out, "What are you about?
I hope you don't think I'm a sparrow!"

B is for BELLA—a beauty indeed—
Who dresses in silks and fine laces,
And never plays Ball with Bertha at all,
Or joins in the Bicycle races.

C is for CLARA who lives on a farm,
Where the Cows roam through fields of sweet clover,

And how you would laugh to see the young Calf
Go frisking and frolicking over.

D is for DAVID who beats on a Drum,
With a rub-a-dub-dub—and a rattle;
While Dora and all the Ducks within call
March off as if going to battle.

E stands for EMMA who landed an Eel
One day, when with Edwin out fishing,
She gave a great shriek, and when she could speak,
Said it wasn't for that she was wishing.

F is for FREDDIE who carried the Flag,
That Florence and Fanny had brought him;
And he waved it about, both indoors and out,
In the way that his Father had taught him.

G stands for GEORGE who rigged himself up
As a Ghost, with a great deal of laughter,
But one look at his face, so frightened poor Grace,
That she cried for a week or two after.

H is for HELEN, who day after day,
In a Hammock was sure to be found;
But once the rope broke, dear me! 'twas no joke,
For she came with a bump to the ground.

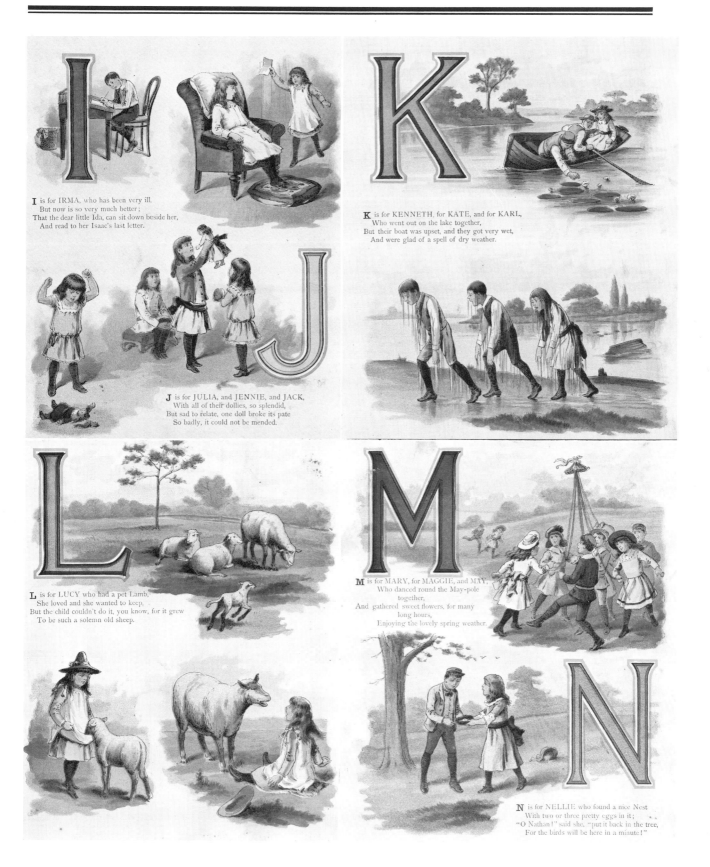

I is for IRMA, who has been very ill,
But now is so very much better;
That the dear little Ida, can sit down beside her,
And read to her Isaac's last letter.

J is for JULIA, and JENNIE, and JACK,
With all of their dollies, so splendid,
But sad to relate, one doll broke its pate
So badly, it could not be mended.

K is for KENNETH, for KATE, and for KARL,
Who went out on the lake together,
But their boat was upset, and they got very wet,
And were glad of a spell of dry weather.

L is for LUCY who had a pet Lamb,
She loved and she wanted to keep,
But the child couldn't do it, you know, for it grew
To be such a solemn old sheep.

M is for MARY, for MAGGIE, and MAY,
Who danced round the May-pole
together,
And gathered sweet flowers, for many
long hours,
Enjoying the lovely spring weather.

N is for NELLIE who found a nice Nest
With two or three pretty eggs in it;
"O Nathan!" said she, "put it back in the tree,
For the birds will be here in a minute!"

O is for OLIVE who went to the land
  Where Oranges grew in such plenty,
That she ate all she chose, as you may suppose,
  And took off a dozen or twenty.

P is for PETER and pretty PAULINE,
  Who danced to the tune of the fiddle,
Now forward and back, then on a side track,
  And all hands around in the middle.

Q is for QUEENIE, who went out to walk
  Whenever the nurse-maid would take her,
She wore a long cloak, and a queer-looking poke,
  And looked like a dear little Quaker.

R is for ROBERT, and RACHEL, who love
  To gather the sweet smelling roses;
They spend the whole day in the garden at play,
  Delighting their dear little noses.

S is for SUSIE who sits in the Swing,
  Dreamily, dozily, rocking,
While Sam, and a swarm of his school-mates perform
  On the See-saw in ways that are shocking!

T is for TILLIE, for TOMMY, and TED,
  Three little folks so delightful,
Who dressed up as Turks with trousers and dirks,
  And looked very savage and frightful.

U is for UNA, who went out one day
And carried a great big Umbrella,
She enquired the way to Botany Bay,
But there wasn't a soul who could tell her.

W is for WANDA, who went to the woods
With WILLIE; and somebody found them
At night, fast asleep beneath a great heap
Of leaves, they had gathered around them.

V is for VINNIE, and VIOLET, too,
Both very vain little misses,
Who care more for clothes, for ribbons and bows,
Than they do for cakes, candies, or kisses.

X is the EXTRA. The EXTRA! along
The streets all the news-boys will cry it;
And the folks will run out of the houses about,
In a very great hurry to buy it!

Z is for ZOE, and ZILLAH, who come
With smiles their bright faces adorning,
At the first break of day, or when darkness ho..
To whisper GOOD NIGHT or GOOD MORNING!

Y is the YOUNGSTERS who went on a YACHT,
Never were children more jolly,
But they shipped a big sea, and then, oh, dear me,
They loudly lamented their folly.

"My Primer" [alphabet], (pp. 5–13), from *My Primer*. Edited by Uncle Herbert. Philadelphia: J. B. Lippincott & Co., 1877. Pp. 48. 20 x 14.6 cm.

MY PRIMER.

A
Is for Albert, tired of play;

B
Is for Bertha, happy and gay.

C
Is for Carrie, afraid of a spider;

D
Is for Dolly, with Dora to ride her.

E
Is for Emma, grandpapa's pet;

F
Is for Fannie, who's getting wet.

G
Is for Gerty, with lessons all done;

H
Is for Hattie, who has not begun.

I
Is for Ida, who's grandma's joy;

J
Is for Johnny, poor fatherless boy.

K
Is for Katie, whose hands are cold;

L
Is for Lulu, just three years old.

M
Is for Morgan, awake with the sun;

N
Is for Nathan, out for a run.

O
Is for Oliver, poor crippled lad;

P
Is for Polly, reading to Thad.

Q
Is a queer looking boy in the snow;

R
Is for Rooster; hear him crow.

S
Is for Sally, with sand in her shoe;

T
Is for Tillie, out in the dew.

U
Is for Una, saying a prayer;

V
Is Victoria, pretty and fair.

W
Is for Willie, alone on the water;

X
I expect is a cross little daughter.

Y
Is young Freddie, not in bed yet;

Z
Is Zerlina, feeding her pet.

The Lu Lu Alphabet. New York: Samuel Raynor, 1850. Pp. [28], hand-colored.
11.8 x 9.5 cm.

For children small, both one and all,
This little book is made;
And if it teach as well as please,
I shall be well repaid.

THE LU LU

ALPHABET.

NEW YORK:
PUBLISHED BY SAMUEL RAYNOR,
No. 76 BOWERY.
1850.

A a
Stands for Alice,
So graceful and fair.

B b
For her Bridal,
And we were all there.

C c
For us Children,
As gay as e'er seen.

D d
The fine Dance
We had on the green.

E e
For Eliza,
Who joined us at that.

F f
The gay Feather
She wore in her hat.

G g
For the Grapes,
Much better than wine.

H h

For the Harp
Alice played on 'Lang syne.'

I i

For the Image
That stood in the hall.

J j

Is young James,
Who played with us all.

K k

For the Kite,
With colors so gay.

L l

For the Lady
In costly array.

M m

For the Melon,
Brought in by a friend.

N n

The bright Nosegay
The bridegroom did send.

O o

For the Oranges,
Delicious and sweet.

P p

For young Patty,
So cheerful and neat.

Q q

For the Quinces,
All set in a row,

R r

The large Raspberries;
O! what a show!

S s

For the Slipper,
One held in her hand.

T t

The great Trumpet,
That sounded so grand.

U u

For my Uncle,
Who blew the loud blast.

V v

The grand Villa,
In which this all passed.

W w

The Watch,
That dear Alice wore.

X x

For king Xerxes,
Who now lives no more.

Y y

For our Yeoman,
And with him did come,

"Bobby's Pocket" (pp. 109–11, unillustrated), from Wells, Carolyn, *The Jingle Book*. Pictured by Oliver Herford. New York: The Macmillan Company; London: Macmillan & Co., 1899. Pp. x, 124. 19.8 x 13 cm.

Z Z

The good Zebra,
To bring us all home.

Bobby's Pocket

OUR Bobby is a little boy, of six years old, or so;
And every kind of rubbish in his pocket he will stow.

One day he thought he'd empty it (so he again could stock it);
And here's an alphabet of what was found in Bobby's pocket.

A was a rosy Apple, with some bites out, here and there;
B was a bouncing rubber Ball that bounded in the air.

C was a crispy crusty Cake with citron on the top;
D was a dancing Donkey that could jump around and hop.

E was a little robin's Egg, all speckled blue and brown;
F was a fluffy Feather that was white and soft as down.

G was a lively Grasshopper, whose legs and wings were green;
H was a grimy Handkerchief that once perhaps was clean.

I was a plaster Image that had lost its plaster head;
J was a jolly Jumping-Jack all painted blue and red.

K was a keen and shining Knife, 'twould cut the toughest bark;
L was a little wooden Lion, strayed out of Noah's Ark.

M was a Marble, large and round, with colors bright and clear;
N was a bent and rusty Nail, of little use, I fear.

O was a tiny Oil-can, which was always upside down;
P was a Penny Bob had saved to spend some day in town.

Q was a Quilted ear-tab, which had lost its velvet mate;
R was a Ring with a glassy gem of wondrous size and weight.

S was a String, a piece of Soap, a Stone, a Sponge, a Stick;
T was a lump of Taffy, exceeding soft and thick.

U, an Umbrella-handle, of silver-mounted horn;
V was a comic Valentine, a little creased and worn.

W was some sticky Wax, lovely to pinch and mould;
X was an old Xpress receipt, worn out in every fold.

Y was a lot of Yellow Yarn, all bunched up like a mop;
Z was a jagged piece of Zinc, found in a plumber's shop.

All these are Bob's possessions; he loves every single thing;
And owning all these treasures he's as happy as a King!

"Alice's Alphabet," from *Babyland,* vol. 8 (Jan. pp. 13–14, Feb. p. 21, Mar. p. 29, Apr. p. 37, May p. 45, June p. 53, July p. 61, Aug. p. 71, Sept. p. 79, Oct. p. 85, Nov. pp. 94–95, Dec. pp. 102–3.) Boston: D. Lothrop & Co., Publishers, 1884. 24 x 19.5 cm.

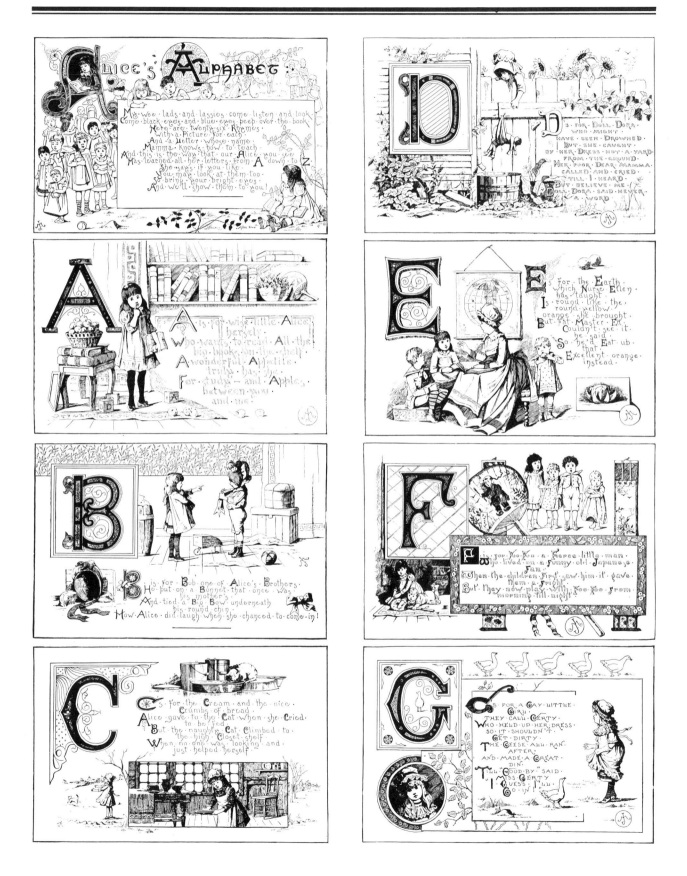

H for the Hay-field Heaped High
with sweet Hay
Where the children work Happily
all the Hot day
And the mischievous baby Helps
scatter the clover
Haly Hid by His big Hat the jolly young rover

L for the Lads and
the Lasses who Learn
Their Letters
and
Lessons
each one
in his
turn
The Lazy one, Laughing one,
Large ones, and small
And our own Little Lady
the Last of them all

I for that Innocent smooth
strip of Ice
That looked to poor Bob
so Inviting and nice
"Oho I will slide!"
he Imprudently cried
And he wished pretty soon
that he never
had tried

Come Alice
my merry
wee maiden
and tall
What M is
to stand for
you know very well
Not sister
nor
brother
Come think of
another!"
She waits just
a minute
why M's
for
my Mother!"

J's for the Jam Alice
found on the shelf
And Jumping for Joy
thought she'd Just
help herself
It took but a minute
For her to begin it
And when she had finished
the Jar
had none in it!

N's for that
Nimble
young Negro
Named Ned
Who Never
is tired
or sleepy
'tis said
But smiling and
bright
With a bow most
polite
He brings us the
news
every morning
and Night

K for a Kite - such a King
of a Kite!
Kind Mamma tied the string
in a Knot firm and tight
But the wind it blew hard and the
Kite flew away
And the boys wonder where it
is gone to this day

O for an Ocean
once made in
a pail
Where the poor ships
were all
Overturned by
a gale
The water leaked Out
and ran Over
the floor
And O! said the nurse
when she
Opened the door

P is for Pears, and for Peaches, like roses

For Pies, Pickles, Plum-cake,
For Pink, and for Posies,
For Parasols, Pretty,
for Pleasure and Play
In short, for a Picnic
we'll have one to-day!

T is—O dear can I tell
The sad Tale
For Ten little Toddlers
That Tearfully wail
What for do you think? Why
How not one of them knew
To count up to Twenty
or say
Two Times Two!

Q's for this Queer-looking
little Quartette Quaint
Who in Grandmama's
garret-chamber have met!
They Quarreled at first over
feather and frill
But made up Quite Quickly and
danced a Quadrille

U's for this
very Unruly
Umbrella
Which Tommy
think
must have found
in
the cellar
It shut Up
at once
when the wind
chanced to blow
Which was rather Unpleasant
for Tommy you know.
The Unruly Umbrella

R for a Rollicking Round
little Rover Who
Rode on a Rail through
the Red-clover
As he was Rash
for it broke with a crash
And away down the hill
he Rolled
over and over

V's for a Visit
this fine lady paid
Very Vain of her Velvet
and for him a Vnaid
But so shy were both
hostess and guest
I have heard
What they
quite lost their
Voices
and spoke
not a word.

S is for Somebody
Swaying
and Swinging
Out in the Sun
where the
robins
are Singing
A Spider
came
Spinning
her Soft
thread
of gray
And
Somebody
Screaming
ran Swiftly away.

W stands for a Wheelbarrow Wide
Which carried its load on a Wonderful ride
In the bright Winter weather they set out together
"Won't you jump in and go With us?" they cried

"The Schoolboys' Alphabet" (p. 2), from *Chatterbox,* November 20, 1886. 25 x 18.5 cm.

THE SCHOOLBOYS' ALPHABET.

FIRST, A must stand for Alphabet,
  The first in all the row;
And B for our Beginners here,
  The clever or the slow.

And C for all the Cramming hard,
  With all its botheration;
And D for Drawing, Dancing, Dates,
  And dreary dull Dictation.

And E for all our English tasks—
  We hail with joy their turn;
And F for all the hard French words
  We always hate to learn.

And G for all Geography,
  And Master's old Greek Grammar;
And H for all the History
  In our poor Heads He'd Hammer.

And I stands for the Ignorance
  He always does deplore;
And J the Jigs we dance for Joy
  When lesson-time is o'er.

And K the Kites we long to fly,
  When once the bell will ring;
And L for all the Latin books
  Our tutor bids us bring.

And M the Music that we strum
  And N the Notes we strike;
And O! we cry, when fingers feel
  The raps we all dislike.

And P for Poetry and Prose,
  And Q for puzzling Questions,
And R for Master's stinging Rod
  And all its grim suggestions.

And S for Sums upon the Slate,
  And eke the Solemn Scolding
Which Master gives, where everywhere
  Wrong figures he's beholding.

And T the Times and Tempers lost,
  The Tears we wept when crying;
And U the Use we might have made
  Of school, by more applying.

And V the verses that we made,
  And W the Writing,
And X the algebraic sign
  So dry and uninviting.

And Y the Yawns we all did give,
  And that without apology,
When Master said the letter Z
  Stands for our task—Zoology.

But hark! the joyful bell's ding-dong
  Proclaims our hour for playing,
And out the boys are rushing all
  With shouts and hip-hurrahing!

           EDITH C. RICKARDS.

"Mr. A's Dinner Party" (pp. 11–12), from *The Picture Book for Little Children.*
London: The Book Society, [1864]. Pp. 60. 31.5 x 24.5 cm.

MR. A.'S DINNER PARTY.

Mr. A. was head man in the small town of Al-pha. Some said he liked to be at the top of the tree; but I do not think he was a proud man. He was very kind to all, but all did not val-ue his kind-ness as they ought to have done: and he found that he could not please all. I will tell you what I was told a-bout twen-ty-six men who liv-ed near him, and who went to dine with him one day.

WAITING FOR THE PARTY.

Head of the Table: A—ask-ed all his friends to take what they lik-ed best:
  1 B—be-gan with roast Beef, and gave it no rest;
  2 C—chose some fine Chick-en made into a Pie;
  3 D—dear-ly loved Duck—so *that* he would try;
  4 E—eager-ly ate some boil-ed Eggs with his meat;
  5 F—fan-cied some Fruit, and thought it a treat;
  6 G—grasp-ing a Goose, fin-ish-ed all but the legs;
  7 H—help-ed him-self large-ly, to Ham and Fried Eggs;
 8, 9 I & J—join-ed to-ge-ther, ate Jel-ly and Ice;
 10 K—"knew no-thing so good as Cur-ry and Rice;"
 11 L—lov-ed a boil-ed lob-ster, that glow-ed in a dish;
 12 M—Mack-e-rel, told them, was the best of all fish;
 13 N—not lik-ing meat, took some Nuts fresh and sound;
 14 O—Oy-sters pre-ferr-ed—and plen-ty he found;
 15 P—prais-ed the roast Pig, and to eat it was able;
 16 Q—quite fond of Quails, ate all on the ta-ble;
 17 R—Rab-bit en-joy-ed, nor said ma-ny words;
 18 S—said that the Snipe was best of all birds;
 19 T—tast-ed some Tripe, and sipp-ed some nice Tea;
 20 U—ug-ly, ill-tem-per-ed, with none could a-gree;
 21 V—ven-tur-ed on Ven-i-son to dine, like a lord;
 22 W—wore out the pa-tience of all at the board;
 23 X—ex-pect-ed some pas-try, cross-ed his legs, and sat still;
 24 Y—yawn-ed, and said, " I have eat-en my fill;"
 25 Z—Za-ny-like, mim-ick-ed all at the ta-ble;
 26 &—said, " Rise from your seats, friends, while you're able."

Arthur's Alphabet. Aunt Mavor's Toy Books. London: Routledge, Warne & Routledge, [1877]. Pp. [8], hand colored. 24.6 x 17.5 cm.

A for ARTHUR, careful and good,
Learning his lesson, as little boys should.

B is BABY, cheerful and gay,
Too young to learn, but ready for play.

C is the CART, in which baby sits down,
Playing with Arthur at driving to town.

G for Gratitude; Arthur stands there,
Emma to thank for her kindness and care.

H for the Horses the carriage that drew,
In which Arthur is riding, and Baby went too.

I for the Indian, who comes from afar,
From a country in which there has often been war.

D is the Dinner brought up on a tray,
For which Master Baby's quite ready to-day.

E is Nurse Emma, who sits in her place,
Teaching dear Arthur how he should say grace.

F the Footman; this shows how he stood,
to say Mamma wants them if both have been good.

J is for Jug, by Baby o'erthrown;
Dear children, don't meddle with things not your own.

K for the Kiss Baby took with great joy,
When Mamma had forgiven her dear little boy.

L is the Lady Mamma went to see,
Who said: "Arthur and Baby must come and see me."

M for the Monkey, smartly arrayed,
That danced on the organ the Savoyard played.

N for the Nosegay of flowers so gay,
That Arthur brought home for Nurse Emma one day.

O for the Orange which Baby holds tight,
While Arthur cries for it;—dear boy, that's not right.

P for Papa, who came in and said,
If Arthur is greedy we'll send him to bed.

Q for the Quarrel that happened one day,
When Arthur took Baby's big bounce-ball away.

R is the Rod, that to Arthur was shown,
To teach him to leave poor Baby alone.

S is the Stool, on which Arthur must sit,
Till he has got over his covetous fit.

T for the Toys, with which he must not play,
For in well-earned disgrace is poor Arthur to-day.

U for Uncle, who came home from sea,
And Arthur, forgiven, here sits on his knee.

V is the Vessel, with sails all unfurled,
That has carried dear Uncle half over the world.

W is the Watch, Master Baby's great joy,
Which Mamma now holds up to amuse her dear boy.

X is for Xerxes, and Uncle has said:
"I'll tell you about him, but now go to bed."

Y is the Yawn, given by Arthur at last;
So they put him to bed, for his bed-time was past.

Z the Zoological Gardens must be,
Which Arthur and Baby were taken to see;
And when our young friends have learned this book through,
I think they deserve to be taken there too.

"Alphabet, No. 6" (pp. 140–42, unillustrated), from Lear, Edward, *Nonsense Botany, and Nonsense Alphabets,* Etc. Etc. Fifth Edition. London and New York: Frederick Warne & Co., 1889. Pp. 142. 22 x 17 cm.

A tumbled down, and hurt his Arm, against a bit of wood.

B said, "My Boy, O! do not cry; it cannot do you good!"

C said, "A Cup of Coffee hot can't do you any harm."

D said, "A Doctor should be fetched, and he would cure the arm."

E said, "An Egg beat up with milk would quickly make him well."

F said, "A Fish, if broiled, might cure, if only by the smell."

G said, "Green Gooseberry fool, the best of cures I hold."

H said, "His Hat should be kept on, to keep him from the cold."

I said, "Some Ice upon his head will make him better soon."

J said, "Some Jam, if spread on bread, or given in a spoon!"

K said, "A Kangaroo is here,—this picture let him see."

L said, "A Lamp pray keep alight, to make some barley tea."

M said, "A Mulberry or two might give him satisfaction."

N said, "Some Nuts, if rolled about, might be a slight attraction."

O said, "An Owl might make him laugh, if only it would wink."

P said, "Some Poetry might be read aloud, to make him think."

Q said, "A Quince I recommend,—a Quince, or else a Quail."

R said, "Some Rats might make him move, if fastened by their tail."

S said, "A Song should now be sung, in hopes to make him laugh!"

T said, "A Turnip might avail, if sliced or cut in half!"

U said, 'An Urn, with water hot, place underneath his chin!"

V said, "I'll stand upon a chair, and play a Violin!"

W said, "Some Whisky-Whizzgigs fetch, some marbles and a ball!"

X said, "Some double XX ale would be the best of all!"

Y said, "Some Yeast mixed up with salt would make a perfect plaster!"

Z said, "Here is a box of Zinc! Get in, my little master!
"We'll shut you up! We'll nail you down! We will, my little master!
"We think we've all heard quite enough of this your sad disaster!"

"The Picture Alphabet of Birds and Beasts for Little Naturalists" (pp. 2–14), from *Picturesque Primer*. London: Griffith, Farran, Okeden & Welsh (Successors to Newbery and Harris); New York: E. P. Dutton, [1880]. Pp. 30. 29.6 x 23.3 cm.

53

A stands for Ape: so greedy, you see,
He is stealing the cakes which were meant for our tea.

B is for Beaver, who builds without hands,
A home that even the water withstands.

C stands for Camel: he lives in the East:
A patient, a useful, and powerful beast.

D stands for Dog: see, he watches the Sheep;
And faithful and truly his guard he will keep.

E stands for Eagle: of birds called the king;
His eyesight is keen, and strong is his wing.

The Giraffe is so tall, he can nibble the leaves
That grow on the top of some very high trees.

The Fowls in the farmyard are pecking for food,
Seeking the grains for their pretty young brood.

The Horse is strong and patient too,
And heavy work he has to do.

i i

The Ichneumon kills snakes, rats, lizards,
and mice,
Sucks all kinds of eggs, and no doubt finds
them nice.

j j

J stands for Jaguar, so cat-like and slim,
But the natives, you see, are not frightened
by him.

m m

M stands for Monkey, the mischievous elf;
Full well he knows how to take care of
himself.

n n

The Nightingale sweetly sings in the wood,
When asleep and dreaming are girls that are
good.

k k

The Kangaroo timidly jumps out of sight,
With its young in a pocket secure from all
fright.

l l

L is for Lion: on guard he stands there,
And woe to the rash who go near his lair.

o o

O stands for Ostrich, so strong and so
fleet;
He can knock down a man with one of his
feet.

p p

Just look at the Piggy! so greedy and fat;
Be careful that you do not grow up like that.

Q stands for Quail : when roasted, so nice,
That most boys and girls would enjoy a small
    slice.

The Rabbit is always a favourite pet ;
But be careful to keep him from cold and
    from wet.

U stands for Urchin : perhaps if I tell
You his name is Hedgehog, you'll know him
    as well.

The Vampire Bat, with wings outspread,
Is oft to men a source of dread.

The Sheep from his back gives the wool for
    our clothes ;
And when dead becomes mutton, as every
    one knows.

The Turkey, with feathers all gold, blue,
    and green,
In farmyard and meadow may often be seen.

The Weasel sucks eggs, kills rabbits and
    rats,
And is not at all liked by dogs or by cats.

Xceedingly tough is the Elephant's hide,
And strong are his legs, trunk, and tusks
    beside.

A Wisehead is Owl: there he sits with his pen,
Looking as sage as the learned among men.

The Illustrated Alphabet of Animals. Boston: Crosby, Nichols and Company. Pp. [54]. 14.6 x 11.5 cm.

THE ANTELOPE.

A is an Antelope,
Airy and light.
Like a shaft from the bow,
Is his rapid flight.

THE BISON.

B is a Bison,
With a large hump and mane;
Far out in the west
He roams o'er the plain.

THE CAT.

C is a Cat,
Who pursues rats and mice;
And when she can catch them,
Eats them up in a trice.

THE DROMEDARY.

D is a Dromedary,
With a hump on his back;
He carries the Arab
O'er the desert's track.

THE ELEPHANT.

E is an Elephant,
Clumsy and wise,
He has very large ears.
And very small eyes

THE FISHER.

F is called a Fisher,
Though they say he don't fish,
But he thinks the wild rabbit
An excellent dish.

THE GIRAFFE.

G's a Giraffe,
Who eats leaves from the tree:
He can reach them quite well,
For a long neck has he.

THE HARE.

H is a Hare,
Who runs through the grass,
He would flee far away
If a child did but pass.

THE IBEX.

I is an Ibex,
  A kind of wild deer;
He flies from the hunters
  Approaching too near.

THE JAGUAR.

J is a Jaguar,
  A Brazilian beast;
On the flesh of wild deer
  He loves well to feast.

THE KANGAROO.

K is a Kangaroo,
  Brought from South Wales.
His family is famous
  For long leaps and long tails.

THE LLAMA.

L is a Llama,
  In Peru he is found,
Where he carries great burdens
  O'er smooth and rough ground.

THE MONKEY.

M is a Monkey,
  Who climbs the tall trees.
Among the long branches
  He sits at his ease.

THE NYL GHAU.

N is a Nyl Ghau,
  Half ox and half deer;
On the far plains of Hindostan,
  He roams without fear.

THE OCELET.

O is an Ocelet.
  This wild cat of Brazil,
Birds, rabbits, and squirrels,
  Rejoices to kill.

THE PRONGBUCK.

P is a Prongbuck,
  On the western plain,
He flies o'er the ground,
  Like a ship on the main.

THE QUAGGA.

Q is a Quagga,
  A sort of wild ass,
It lives in the forest,
  And feeds on the grass.

THE RABBIT.

R is a Rabbit,
When kept for a pet,
To give it fresh food,
We should never forget.

THE SQUIRREL.

S is a Squirrel,
Who lives in a tree.
In getting fresh nuts
Very active is he.

THE TIGER.

T is a Tiger,
From Asia's far shore,
Fierce and savage is he,
Madly thirsting for gore.

THE URUS.

U is a Urus,
Or Russian wild bull.
He scorns in the yoke
Of the farmer to pull.

THE VAMPIRE.

V is a Vampire,
A bloodsucking bat.
He's as large as a pigeon,
And bites like a rat.

THE WOODCHUCK.

W is a Woodchuck.
Fat and chunky is he;
And digs his deep hole
At the foot of a tree.

THE LETTER X.

X is a letter,
So cross and so odd,
That it stands for the name
Of no beast on the sod.

THE YAK.

Y is a Yak,
A wild ox. In the east
His tail makes a plume,
And his hump makes a feast.

THE ZEBRA.

Z is a Zebra,
Striped horse, that's so wild,
That he cannot be tamed,
E'en by harsh means or mild.

The A B C of Animals. New York: McLoughlin Bro's. Pp. [12], including 6 colored plates. 25.8 x 19.4 cm.

A animals. B bear. C cat. D dog.

E elephant.   F fox.   G goat.   H horse.

I ice.   J jackal.   K kangaroo.   L lion.

M for IS MOST MISCHIEVOUS HE

N is A from INDIA you SEE

O is FOR THAT SWIMS FAST AWAY

P For the WHO ARE eating ALL DAY

M monkey. N nylghau. O otter. P pigs.

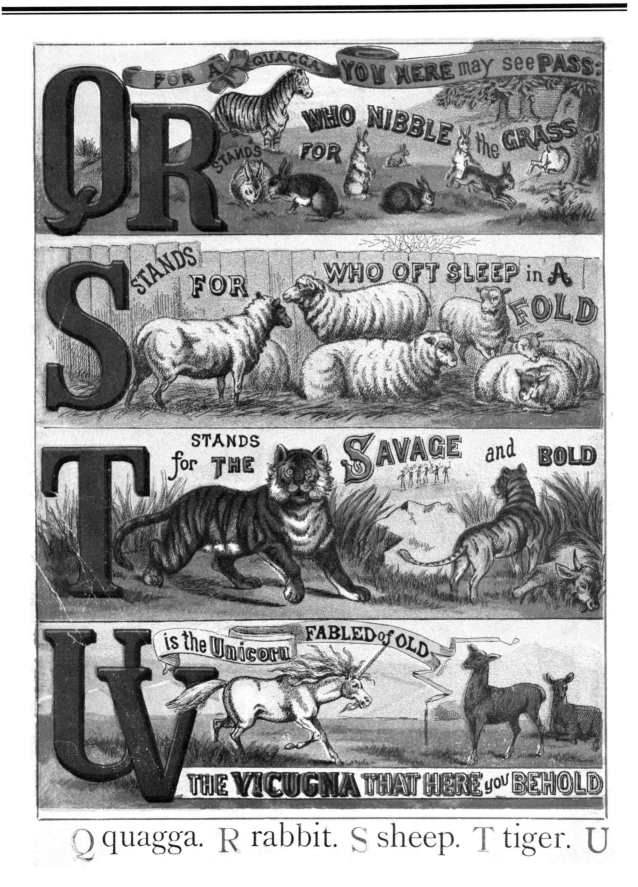

Q quagga. R rabbit. S sheep. T tiger. U

W wolf.　X ten.　Y yak.　Z zebra.

An Alphabet of Animals. By a Lady—Revised. London: Simpkin, Marshall & Co.; Leicester: Winks and Son. Pp. 30. 12 x 7.5 cm.

A—is the APE,
　Which some Monkey call;
He will swing on a rope,
　And toss up a ball.
He often is trying
　To do what we do,
But he can't say his lesson
　Like Lucy and you.

B—is the BEE,
　So busy and gay;
He is seeking for honey,
　Sweet honey, all day.
From him to be idle
　We learn to avoid—
How happy he is,
　For he's always employ'd.

C—is the Cow,
　Which so kindly brings
Nice milk for our supper,
　And twenty good things;
'Tis God who has made her
　For food for our race;
So when eating our meals,
　Let us think of His grace.

D—is the DOG;
　He is faithful and bold
In watching the house
　And guarding the fold.
Then come, faithful Keeper,
　You're honest and true,
And we'll try to be faithful
　And trusty like you.

E—is for EAGLE,
　Of birds he's the king;
With a very sharp eye,
　And a very strong wing,
He builds his rough nest
　On the rocks high away;
And there he is feeding
　His young ones with prey.

F—is the FROG;
　He will soon leap away;
How cruel to hurt him
　In sport or in play.
On ground and in ponds
　He can hop and can swim;
He is frighten'd at us;
　We'll be gentle to him.

G—is a Welsh GOAT,
　On the mountains so high
And you cannot catch her
　If all day you try.
But pat her and feed her,
　And then you may take
Good milk from her udder,
　Your breakfast to make.

H—is the HARE,
　So timid and fleet,
That she scarcely touches
　The ground with her feet,
When she takes her long leaps
　To get out of the way
Of the dogs that are coming
　To make her their prey.

I—is the IBEX,
　Which lives on the rocks,
And these cunning creatures
　Are very shy folks.
You cannot get near them,
　Or climb up so high;
And down you might tumble
　If once you did try.

J—is the JAY,
Which now comes in sight;
Its wings are all painted
With black, blue, and white;
It talks like the magpie,
And utters some words—
We love and admire you,
You nice pretty birds.

K—is our KITTEN,
Now grown to a cat;
There up in that tree
What would you be at?
You would catch that bird,
But I hope you will not;
Fly away, little bird,
With the wings you have got.

L—is the LAMB,
It is gentle and mild;
But the best of all lambs
Is a dutiful child.
And that gracious Shepherd,
The Saviour, we're told,
Calls all the good children
The Lambs of his fold.'

M—is the MOUSE,
With its pretty black eye;
We will not torment it,
But let it run by;
So, mouse, you may go,
And get out of the way,
That puss may not catch you
And make you her prey.

N—is the NEST
Which little birds form,
To lay their nice eggs in,
So snug and so warm;
We never will take them,
Nor climb where they're hung,
For that would be robbing
Poor birds of their young.

O—is the OX,
A very fine beast,
Whose flesh is so rich,
That it makes us a feast.
Roast beef and plum-pudding
We all like to eat;
Let us give some to others
And make them a treat.

P—is the PIGEON—
An emblem of peace;
The dove showed to Noah
The waters should cease;
For she hasten'd again
Her kind master to seek,
And took him an olive leaf
Safe in her beak.

Q—is the QUAIL—
In the Bible we read,
God sent Quails from heaven
His people to feed.
So let us think always
When eating our food,
'Tis God gives us all things,
Who is very good.

R—is the RABBIT—
What pains does she take,
For her poor helpless young ones
A shelter to make!
So we to our mothers
Our duty should pay,
Who feed and who watch us
By night and by day.

S—is the Squirrel;
Some wisdom he'll lend,
For in cracking his nuts
He marks the right end.
Now this is a lesson
To me and to you,
To mind and do right
In all that we do.

T—is the Thrush—
How these singing-birds gay,
All praise their Creator
As well as they may !
Then we will be learning
Our hymns to repeat,
That we may sing praises
With voices as sweet.

U—is the Unicorn ;
But some people say
It is the Rhinoceros ;
And perhaps it may.
It is a strong creature,
And often has torn
Other wild beasts to pieces
With its mighty horn.

V—is the Viper,
It lives in the brake ;
Can anything useful
Be learned from a snake ?
O yes, we may think
How the Saviour approves,
To be " wise as the serpent,
And harmless as doves."

W—is Wagtail,
Hopping about
Close by the water,
Picking things out.
Hopping and wagging
Its tail all day long,
But never giving us
One little song.

X

X—is not a letter
Beginning a word
For any one animal—
Fish, beast, or bird.
But there was one creature
With two legs like you,
That the Greeks called a Xany ;
Now mind what you do—
Or they'll call you a Xany
If you go to school,
And dont mind your lesson—
For Xany means fool !

AND NOW ABOUT YOU.

So now I have done
What I did intend ;
And I hope to dumb creatures
You will be a friend.

Never teaze or torment them,
For God made them all ;
And he always feeds them—
The great and the small.

But God has made you
Much better than they ;
And he will care for you
If to him you pray.

For Jesus, the Saviour,
Has died in your place,
And I'm sure he will bless you
If you seek his face.

Y—is Yellow-hammer ;
O look ! on that tree,
It is sitting and chirping
So happy and free !
You may fly through the air,
Lovely bird, we engage
That we never will snare you,
Or keep you in cage.

Z—is the Zebra—
And whence cometh he ?
He came from wild Africa
Far over the sea ;
So he is a pilgrim
And is made to roam ;
And we are all pilgrims
To heaven our home.

Picture Alphabet of Beasts. London and Edinburgh: Thomas Nelson & Sons. Pp. [8], including 4 pages of colored plates. 28.4 x 22 cm.

69

Giraffe

Hyena

Ichneumon

Jaguar

Kangaroo

Lion

Mandrill

Nylghau

Otter

Puma

Quagga

Rhinoceros

Stag

Tiger. U Virginian Opossum

Wolf

X Yak

Zebra

THE ASS. Forbear to vex the patient Ass, Its heaving sides to goad, And far and safe its useful back Will carry many a load.	**THE GIRAFFE.** Full seventeen feet the Giraffe tall Measures "from top to toe," And with his neck outstretched can reach The branch that bendeth low.	**THE MANDRILL.** In Africa the Mandrill lives, Full five feet tall he stands ; With furrowed cheek-bones, tufted hair, And hairy arms and hands.	**THE STAG.** O'er Scotland's heathery hills the Stag Pursues his rapid way, And tosses high his antlered head When he is brought to bay.
THE BEAR. In the cold countries of the North Lives the white Polar Bear, And 'mong the dreary ice-caves makes Its dark and dreadful lair.	**THE HYENA.** In Asia and in Africa The fierce Hyenas prowl, And oft at night the traveller starts To hear their savage howl.	**THE NYLGHAU.** In Hindustan's dense forest-depths, Among the tangled groves, With slender limbs but powerful frame The shapely Nylghau roves.	**THE TIGER.** Fiercest of all the beasts of prey, With eyes that glow like fire, And glossy hide, who does not dread The Tiger, yet admire ?
THE CAMEL. The Camel is a useful beast, Patient, and slow, and mild ; To man a blessing and a boon In Afric's sandy wild.	**THE ICHNEUMON.** A foe to birds and rats and mice, See the Ichneumon glide ! Oft, too, on reptiles or their eggs Its hungry teeth are tried.	**THE OTTER.** Upon the streamlet's rushy bank The Otter takes her rest, And dives into the water deep When by the hunters prest.	**THE VIRGINIAN OPOSSUM.** In hollow trees the Opossum lives, And slumbers through the day, But when the shades of night descend, Goes forth in search of prey.
THE DOE. Graceful and gentle is the Doe ; Its tawny coat how sleek ! How bright yet tender are its eyes ! Its glance how softly meek !	**THE JAGUAR.** The Jaguar haunts the forest-depths, And climbs each mighty tree ; The "Tiger of the New World" called, A crafty beast is he !	**THE PUMA.** The Lion of America, The Puma oft is called ; More like a cat it seems to be, With head so round and bald.	**THE WOLF.** Fierce is the wolf, and crafty too, And swift of foot is he ; In forest-depths and mountain-glens He loves to wander free.
THE ELEPHANT. To noble race, O Elephant, Thou surely dost belong ; So grave, and kind, and sadly wise, So gentle, yet so strong !	**THE KANGAROO.** The timid Kangaroo frequents The wild Australian brakes ; With long hind-legs and fore-legs short Tremendous leaps he takes.	**THE QUAGGA.** O'er Southern Africa's warm plains The Quagga gallops free ; With black-brown mane and white-barred A gallant beast is he ! [neck,	**THE YAK.** In Central Asia, far away, 'Mid Thibet's pastures green, With shaggy hide and bushy tail, The valued Yak is seen.
THE FOX. The Fox will skulk in ferny brake, Yet loves the haunts of men ; And prowls around the farm, to pounce On capon, goose, or hen.	**THE LION.** With tawny hide and flowing mane, And loud-resounding roar, Of animals the Lion's king, And all bow down before.	**THE RHINOCEROS.** Down to the water-side to drink,— Within the jungle's shade,— Has come the huge Rhinoceros, In knotty hide arrayed.	**THE ZEBRA.** As strong and swift as any horse, The Zebra skims the plain ; With glossy bands of deepest black, Long ears, and upright mane.

The Alphabet of Animals, by Ernest Griset. London: Frederick Warne & Co., [1875]. Pp. [12], including 6 colored plates. 25 x 19 cm.

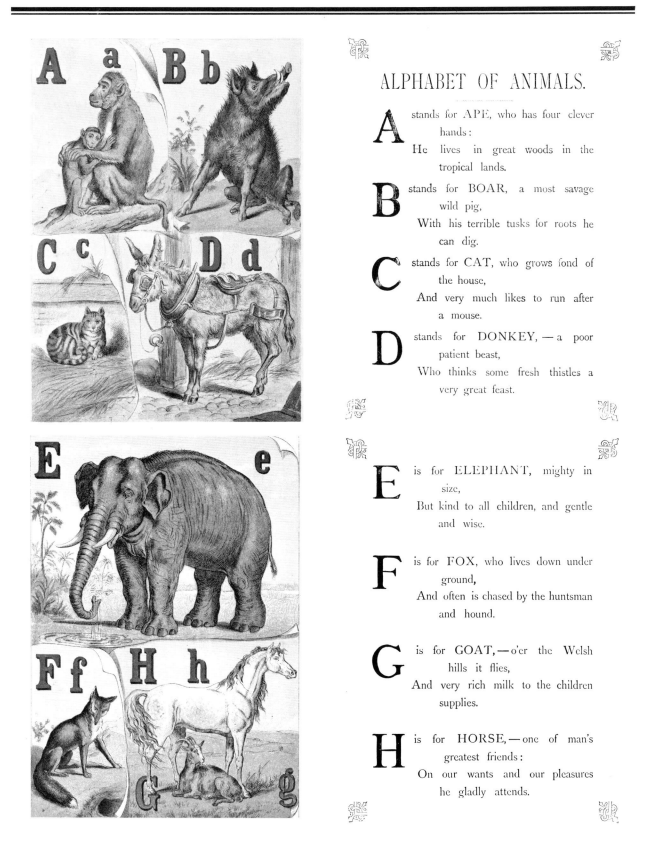

ALPHABET OF ANIMALS.

A stands for APE, who has four clever hands:
He lives in great woods in the tropical lands.

B stands for BOAR, a most savage wild pig,
With his terrible tusks for roots he can dig.

C stands for CAT, who grows fond of the house,
And very much likes to run after a mouse.

D stands for DONKEY, — a poor patient beast,
Who thinks some fresh thistles a very great feast.

E is for ELEPHANT, mighty in size,
But kind to all children, and gentle and wise.

F is for FOX, who lives down under ground,
And often is chased by the huntsman and hound.

G is for GOAT, — o'er the Welsh hills it flies,
And very rich milk to the children supplies.

H is for HORSE, — one of man's greatest friends:
On our wants and our pleasures he gladly attends.

I is for IBEX; a goat with long horns,
He lives on the mountains; the low lands he scorns.

J is for JAGUAR, a fierce beast of prey,
Who hides in American forests by day.

K is for KANGAROO: upright it keeps,
Except when it jumps o'er the ground in great leaps.

L stands for LYNX, clothed in fur thick and good,
Which finds home and food in the depths of the wood.

M is for MARMOT; its home's in the ground,
And good stores of nuts and corn in it are found.

N for NEWFOUNDLAND DOG, faithful and brave,
And ready from drowning dear children to save.

O is for OTTER, which lives in the streams,
And breakfasts on fish when the early dawn beams.

P is for PORCUPINE: up its quills stick,
If you touched him they surely would give you a prick.

Q is for QUAGGA,—o'er Africa's plains,
It gallops; or feeding in troops it remains.

R for RHINOCEROS, thick-skinned and strong,
To which two great horns on his hard nose belong.

S is for SQUIRREL, who sits on a tree;
When cracking his nuts very happy is he.

T for the Tiger, most savage of beasts,
Who on all living creatures most readily feasts.

U is for UNICORN, — well known in fable;
To find him alive I think no one is able.

V for VICUGNA; on mountains it lives,
And soft silky wool for the use of Man gives.

W for WALRUS; in cold Polar Seas,
It swims midst the icebergs with safety and ease.

X 'XTINCT ANIMAL !—You won't regret,
That creatures like this one no longer are met.

Y is for YAK, the wild ox of Thibet;
The Tartars are glad its long soft fleece to get.

Z is for ZEBRA — the brave desert steed,
Who flies o'er the African plains at full speed.

The Little Child's Alphabet in Rhyme. Providence: Geo. P. Daniels, 1843. Pp. [14], including paper covers. 10.8 x 6.8 cm.

77

A is an Avoset,
That wades about the marsh;

B is a Bittern,
whose cry is shrill and harsh.

C is a Condor,
The strongest bird that flies;

D is a Dove,
That is oft before your eyes.

E is an Eagle,
that gazes at the sun;

F is a Flamingo,
That quickly learns to run.

G is a Goshawk,
That whistles on the hill;

H is a Heron,
With slender legs and bill.

I is an Imber,
That lives in northern seas;

J is a Jackdaw,   [ease.
that oft is tamed with

K is a Kingfisher,
watching for his prey;

L is a Linnet,
That sings upon the spray.

M is a Marten,
That yearly does return

N is a Night Jar,
That breeds among the fern.

O is an Osprey,
That fishes in the streams

P is a Peacock,
That proudly struts and screams.

Q is a Quail,
That delights in fields of grain;

R is a Raven,
That preys upon the slain.

S is a Starling,
That roosts among the reeds;

T is a Tomtit,   [feeds.
That on small insects

V is a Vulture,
A cruel bird of prey;

W is a Wren,
That is innocent and gay.

Y is a Yellow Bird,
Perching on a bough;

Z is a Zebra,
and the end of the row.

"The Birds' Party" (pp. 45–47, unillustrated), from *The Alphabet in Rhyme.* Eight Illustrations in Oil Colors. New York: American News Company, 1869. Pp. 47. 18.5 x 13.5 cm.

THE BIRDS' PARTY.

—※—

A THE great Albatross wrote invitations;

B for the Bluebird who carried them round;

C for the Crow who brought all his relations;

D for the Duck waddling over the ground;

E for the Eagle who came with his daughter;

F the Flamingo with feathers so gay;

G for the Goose who swam up on the water;

H for the Hawk who came hoping for prey;

I for the Iris, quite tame and domestic;

J for the Jay who created much fun;

K for the Kingbird, so large and majestic;

L for the Lark who arose with the sun;

M for the Mockingbird sweet music trilling;

N for the Nightingale warbling so well;

O for the Owl with eyes round as a shilling;

P for the Peacock who cut quite a swell;

Q for the Quail who's so nice when he's roasted;

R for the Robin the sweetest of birds;

S for the long-legged Stork whom all toasted;

T for the Thrush sounding musical words;

U for the Union flags all were displaying;

V for the voices that filled all the glade;

W the waltzing, quadrilling, chassaing;

X the exertions that every one made;

Y for the young birds who kept up flirtations;

Z for the zeal which each songster displayed.

Birds of the Air A B C. Father Tuck's Nursery Tales Series A.B.C. New York, London, Paris: Raphael Tuck & Sons, Co., [1885]. Pp. [14], including 4 pages in color, printed on linen. 27.8 x 22 cm.

The Illustrated Alphabet of Birds. Boston: Crosby and Nichols. Pp. [54]. 14.6 x 11.5 cm.

THE AUK.

A is an Auk,

Of the Artic sea,

He lives on the ice,

Where the winds blow free.

THE BLUE BIRD.

B is a Blue Bird.

In early spring,

How sweet his songs

Through the forest ring.

THE CONDOR.

C is a Condor,

On the Andes' height,

He plumes his wings

For a lofty flight.

THE DUCK.

D is a Duck

Of the canvas back sort;

To shoot at a flock

Is considered fine sport.

THE EAGLE.

E 's a Bald Eagle,

So bold and so free;

On the flag of our country

He spans land sea.

THE FISH HAWK.

F is a Fish Hawk,

Who lives on the shore

He catches his prey

Mid the ocean's roar.

THE GOOSE.

G is a Goose;

His feathers we take

And put them in sacking

Our beds to make.

THE HUMMING BIRD.

H is a Humming Bird,

Sporting mid flowers

And brightly enjoying

The sunny hours.

THE IBIS.

I is an Ibis,
  Who wanders in bogs,
And lives upon lizards,
  And fishes and frogs.

THE JAY.

J is a Jay,
  With his blue and white coat,
With a crest on his head,
  And a ring round his throat.

THE KING BIRD.

K is a King Bird,
  Pugnacious and bold:
A hero in fight,
  And a terrible scold.

THE LARK.

L is a Lark,
  A sociable bird;
His song in the meadow
  Is frequently heard.

THE MAGPIE.

M is a Magpie,
  He lives at the west,
Steals and scolds and eats carrion;
  He's none of the best.

THE NIGHT HERON.

N is a Night Heron,
  Of fishes quite fond;
He looks for them now,
  As he stands by the pond.

THE OWL.

O is an Owl,
  Who hides through the day;
And comes out at night,
  To seek for his prey.

THE PIGEON

P is a Pigeon
  So rapid in flight,
That before you can shoot him
  He's gone out of sight.

THE QUAIL.

Q is a Quail,
  Who hides in a tree,
And whistles "Bob-White"
  With lively glee."

THE ROBIN.

R is the Robin,
    So kind and so good,
Who covered with leaves,
    The poor Babes in the Wood.

THE SWALLOW

S is the Swallow,
    She darts through the air
To catch little insects,
    Her favorite fare.

THE TURKEY.

T is a Turkey,
    A fine dashing beau,
By his fuming and strutting,
    His pride you may know.

THE UPUPA.

U 's the Upupa,
    Or Hoopoe. His crest
He can raise up or lower,
    As suits him best.

THE VULTURE.

V is a Vulture,
    Who feeds on the dead,
When the dark battle-field,
    With corpses is spread.

THE WOODPECKER.

W 's a Woodpecker,
    Who with his long bill,
Bores holes in a tree,
    And of worms eats his fill.

XANTHORNUS.

X is Xanthornus,
    Or Baltimore Bird.
Oft in our orchards,
    His music is heard.

THE YELLOW BIRD.

Y is a Yellow Bird,
    With feathers so bright,
Who sings all the day,
    And sleeps all the night.

THE LETTER Z, OR ROOST.

Z stands for none
    Of the feathered race.
It must serve as a roost,
    Or lose the last place.

Alphabet of Country Scenes. Aunt Louisa's Big Picture Series. New York: Mc-Loughlin Bros., [1885]. Pp. [12], including 6 pages of colored plates. 27 x 23.2 cm.

A stands for Arabian, with Neptune
    to guard ;
All saddled and bridled, the pet of
    our yard.

B for the Bees, that fly out here
    and there,
And bring to the hives the sweet
    honey with care.

C for the Cows, in the shade of the
    trees ;
They are chewing the cud, and seem
    quite at their ease.

D for Ducks, swimming, and play-
    ing together ;
They care not for rain nor the storm-
    iest weather.

E for the Eggs, which we find in
    the nest ;
They still feel quite warm, from the
    hen's downy breast.

F are the Fowls : the hens and the
    cocks.
Take care, my fine birdies, beware of
    the fox.

G is the Goat, with two kids young
    and gay ;
They run to their mother, then scam-
    per away.

H is the Horse, so sleek and so
    strong ;
He draws the hay-cart to the meadow
    along.

I is the Island, where Johnny doth wish
To sit on the bank, in the summer, and fish.

K are the Kittens, that live in the stable;
They will catch all the mice as soon as they're able.

L is for Lucy, who waits at the stile,
And puts down the pail, for she's resting awhile.

M is the Milk, which is good, Pussy thinks,
And so, uninvited and slyly, she drinks.

N stands for the Nuts; and when lessons are done,
Two boys can go nutting much better than one.

O for the Owl, that prowling at night,
Steals chicks from our barn in the quiet moonlight.

P for some Pigs, which have strayed from their sty,
But of course will return there to bed by-and-by.

Q stands for the Quince I have plucked from a tree,
To flavor the tart Mary's making for me.

R for the Rabbits, white, spotted, and gray;
Just see how that little one nibbles away.

S for the Sheep, with their coats of soft wool;
They stand in the meadows so pleasant and cool.

T for the Turkey, who stately doth sail,
With long sweeping wings and a wide-spreading tail.

U stands for Ursula, and V for the Vine
That yields her fine clusters in harvesting time.

W for Wheat, and for Whitey, the Calf,
Who nibbles away at the grain and the chaff.

X means on a Banknote, Ten Dollars, 'tis clear;
On a barrel, it stands for the strength of the beer.

Y stands for our Farm-yard, where chicks love to feed
On the oats, and the barley, and other good seed.

Z is for Zachary, shutting the gate;

So Good Night, little children; it's getting quite late.

''John Bull's Farm Alphabet'' (12 pp., including 6 colored plates), from *Aunt Louisa's Welcome Gift.* Comprising John Bull's Farm Alphabet. Tabby's Tea-Fight. Rover's Dinner Party. London Characters. With Twenty-Four pages of Illustrations, from Original Designs by Petherick, Henley &c. Printed in Colours by Kronheim. London: Frederick Warne and Co., [1875]. 27 x 22.6 cm.

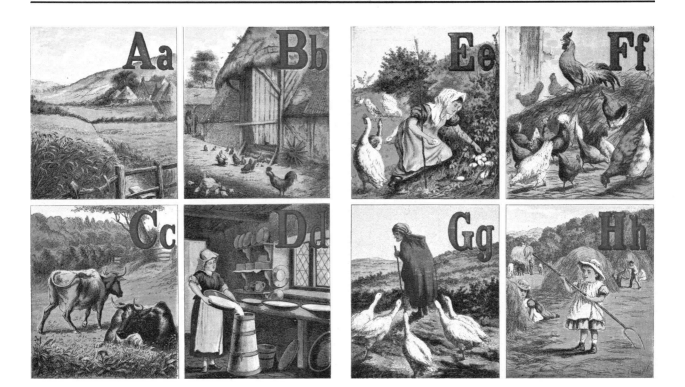

JOHN BULL'S
FARM ALPHABET.

A's Arable land, for ploughing and sowing:
Wheat, barley, and oats upon it are growing.

B stands for the Barn where we all our crops store;
The chickens pick up the fallen grains at the door.

C stands for our Cows, which give plenty of milk;
The coat of dear Colly is softer than silk.

D stands for the Dairy, where butter we make,
And very great care of our cheeses we take.

E stands for Eggs, which the poultry-girl finds;
The geese in the meadow this little lass minds.

F stands for Fowls, of which every kind,
From Cochin to Bantam, you'll at our farm find.

G stands for Geese—just see how they run!
To bite that poor woman they think will be fun.

H stands for Hay, which we all like to make;
Even dear little Norman a hayfork will take.

I stands for Ice, which the ploughman must break,
That he for the horses some water
may take.

J 's for John Bull, who this pretty
farm owns;
He's watching the women who
pick up the stones.

K 's the Knife-cutter which chops
up so neat,
The straw that in winter the cattle
must eat.

L 's for the Lambs, which so
merrily bound,
When spring-time is come, o'er
the daisy-starred ground.

M 's for the Milkmaid—a pretty
young lass,
Tripping with pail and stool over
the grass.

N stands for the Nag, that trots on
so well,
When John Bull goes to the market to sell.

O stands for Oats, which to horses
we give;
The carter is bringing them, here,
in a sieve.

P 's for the Plough, which must
win us our bread.
By means of the plough all the
nations are fed.

Q stands for Quinces; a nice jam
they make.
Mary would like a fine ripe one to
take.

R stands for Reapers, who cut down the wheat:
When harvest is over they all have a treat.

S is the Sow, with her litter of pigs:
See how she's grunting, and in the earth digs.

T stands for Turkeys; a fat one there'll be
When Christmas comes for my brothers and me.

U is for Useful things, such as the drill,
The harrow, the pitchfork, and what else you will.

V is the Vine which grows on the house wall;
The grapes are quite sweet, and not very small.

W's the Waggon which bears the wheat home,
For now near the end of the harvest we're come.

X is for Xcellent,—such is our mother,
Our father, our sisters, and dear little brother.

Y is the Youth who the bird scares away;
When his work's over he runs off to play.

Z's for what Yorkshiremen call our "zmall things,"
Which, at last, to its ending our Alphabet brings.

The Little Gardener ABC. Father Tuck's Nursery Tales Series A.B.C. Untearable Linen. New York, London, Paris: Raphael Tuck & Sons, Co., [1885]. Pp. [14], including 4 pages in color. 27.6 x 22 cm.

H is the Hawthorn,
the emblem of May,
The birds build their nests
in its branches so gay.

I and J are the best sort
of friend we can meet,
For the Ivy's so true and
the Jasmine's so sweet.

K, Kitchen garden, where
gooseberries grow,

Where for carrots, and cabbage, and salads we go.

L stands for Lilies,
some short and
some tall,
Be they big or quite
little we're fond of
them all.

M stands for Marguerites
seen everywhere,
And M for the Mignonette
scenting the air.

N stands for Nuts on
the hazel tree bough,
The squirrel he knows 'tis
his harvest time now.

O stands for Orchids the
hot-house contains,
For they've come from
the land where the
sun always reigns.

P is the Poppy, gay Princess in red,
Who lifts, in the corn-fields,

her proud little head.

Quinces

Q stands for Quince,
and as everyone knows
For "Queen-of the garden,
the **R**, that's the
Rose.

R

S is the Snowdrop
we all hold so dear,
Who comes to announce
that the Spring-time is
near.

Sweet
Peas

Sun-
flower

Snow
drop

Roses

Thistles

T is the Tulip, for
something to do
Ask a Dutch boy
to find you a Tulip
that's blue.

U for Utensils we call to
our aid,
The hoe and the trowel, the
rake and the
spade.

Tulip

Trumpet-
lily

V is the Violet, "Violets sweet!"
That are sold for a penny a bunch
in the street.

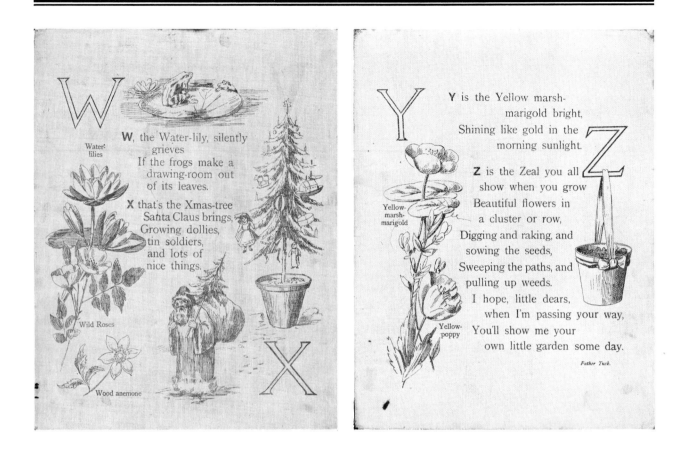

W, the Water-lily, silently
grieves
If the frogs make a
drawing-room out
of its leaves.

X that's the Xmas-tree
Santa Claus brings,
Growing dollies,
tin soldiers,
and lots of
nice things.

Water-
lilies

Wild Roses

Wood anemone

Y is the Yellow marsh-
marigold bright,
Shining like gold in the
morning sunlight.

Z is the Zeal you all
show when you grow
Beautiful flowers in
a cluster or row,
Digging and raking, and
sowing the seeds,
Sweeping the paths, and
pulling up weeds.
I hope, little dears,
when I'm passing your way,
You'll show me your
own little garden some day.

Yellow-
marsh-
marigold

Yellow-
poppy

Father Tuck.

An alphabet from *Little Buttercup's Picture Book.* New York: R. Worthington, 1880.
Pp. [14], including 7 pages of black-and-white illustrations. 24.8 x 18.5 cm.

Stands over APPLES,
So rosy and round.

Holds a Holly bush
Plucked by the root.

Begins the word BERRIES,
Which grow near the ground.

Is an Ivy vine,
It clings where it grows.

Commences CHERRIES,
They grow upon trees.

Is a Jessamine,
Most fragrant it blows.

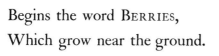

DATE-PALMS or DESERT,
Spell which word you please.

The rich Kidney bean,
Nutritious for food.

Twined by Evergreens,
They never fade.

Is the Lily,
An emblem of good.

Found in Fern-leaves,
Which grow in the shade.

Holds a Moss rose,
Covered with down.

Is a Grape-vine,
Bearing some fruit.

Stands for Walnuts,
In the woods they are found.

Is an Orange,
So juicy and sweet.

A Pine-apple,
Both are good to eat.

Quinces when ripe,
Have an excellent flavor.

The Rose when presented,
Is a sign of favor.

Strawberries in dish,
With sugar and cream.

Tomatoes as fine
As ever were seen.

Unicorn root,
Good at times for the health.

A beautiful Vine,
All alone by itself.

Wheat in the field,
Gently waved by the wind.

Xanthic flowers, which
Are a bright yellow kind.

To find these bright flags,
In the marsh you must hunt.

A Zigadenus flower,
Changing color each month.

Alphabet of Fruits. Aunt Louisa's London Toy Books. London: Frederick Warne & Co., Kronheim & Co., [1875]. Pp. [12], including 6 pages of colored plates. 26.5 x 23 cm.

A is for APPLES, so rosy and round,
Which the children delight to pick up
    from the ground.

B for the BLACKBERRY, open to all,
To the rich and the poor, to cottage
    and hall.

C is for CURRANTS, which Dora, you
    see,
Is picking for Tarts, from the red-
    currant tree.

D for the DAMSONS we make into
    Jam,
Which is often, in Germany, eaten
    with ham.

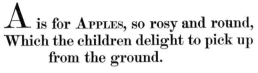

E for the ELDER, with berries so
    brown;
You may sell them for twopence a
    quart in the town.

F for the FIG, which in Italy grows,
All temptingly laid in a basket in rows.

G for the GRAPES which, beside the
    swift Rhine,
The peasant-girls gather to make into
    Wine.

H is the HAZEL-NUT, found in the
    copse,
Where the Squirrel from branch to
    branch playfully hops.

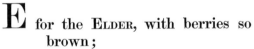

I IVY-BERRIES, both purple and blue;
You may not think them fruit, but
I'm sure the birds do.

J for the sweet russet JARGONELLE
PEAR,
Which on shelves in the store-room is
laid up with care.

K for the KERNEL that pays us so
well
For the trouble we've taken to open
the shell.

L is the fragrant and pale-coloured
LIME,
Growing ripe in the sun of a tropical
clime.

M for the MELON the Frenchwoman
sells,
By the arch within sound of the old
Minster bells.

N is the NECTARINE kind Jenny
took
To the sick girl who lived by the side
of the brook.

O is for ORANGE, so juicy and sweet,
Which Ellen has brought for the Baby
to eat.

P for the PEACHES, which little Ann's
ball,
To old William's dismay, has struck
down from the wall.

Q for the QUINCE, growing down in
the glade,
Of which Sarah the cook will make
nice Marmalade.

R for the RASPBERRIES, gathered at
dawn,
For the school-children's tea by-and-
by on the lawn.

S is for STRAWBERRY, brilliant and red,
Which we look for amongst the green
leaves of its bed.

T for the TAMARINDS brought from
the West,
With Ginger and Guava, in Mariner's
chest.

U and V have no fruit; but the
Grape-bearing VINE
Grows in Italy, Spain, and beside the
swift Rhine.

W for the WALNUTS at Christmas
we eat,
And make of the shells such a capital
fleet.

X, Y, Z I must leave; but you
may, if you please,
Call them FRUIT in the guise of "unknown quantities."

Grandmamma Easy's Pretty Poetry about Trees, Fruit, and Flowers. Boston: Brown, Bazin & Co. Nashua, N.H.: N. P. Greene & Co. Pp. [8], hand colored. 26 x 17 cm.

My little friend, this
book displays
The names of Trees
and flowers,
And fruits that grow in Summer days,
Watered by gentle showers.

The A stands first in Apple-
tree,
And Apricot so sweet ;
In Acorn, too, the A you 'll
see,
And Almonds, nice to eat.

In the Bluebell you 'll find
the B,
And Briar, sweet to smell ;
It 's also seen in Blackberry,
And Bilberry, as well.

The C commences Cherries
round,
And Currants, red or white ;
In Chestnut-tree and Crab 't is
found,
And yellow Cowslip bright.

In Dandelion and Daffodil
The D is always seen ;
In Daisy, too, o'er dale and
hill,
And on the village green.

The E is seen in Elder-tree,

To make nice Elder wine ;

It 's first in Elm of high degree,

And last in stately Pine.

The Filbert-tree the F displays,

And Fennel, green, also ;

And in the Fig it 's first, always,

With Flowers that ever blow.

In Gooseberry the G we see,

And in nice Grapes, also,

Of most delicious quality,

Which on the vine do grow.

The H in Honeysuckle
twines

Around the cottage door ;

In Hollyhock it well combines

The Hue of every flower.

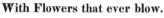

In Ivy green the I you see,

Which creeps round house
apace ;

It 's seen in Lime and Lupine-
tree,

And Lily's lovely face.

In Juice of fruit the J is seen,

To make nice Jam to eat ;

It stands the first in Jessamine,

That smells so very sweet.

The K you 'll find in King-
cup,

Like a bell upside down ;

In Kernel, too, of nut closed
up,

Whose shell is ever brown.

In Lemon-tree the L you
see,

The juice of which is tart,

It 's also found in Lilac-tree,

And Larkspur with its dart

In Melon round the M is found,
Whose pips again will grow,
In Mint, likewise, which scents the ground,
And Mulberry, also.

In Nonpareil and Nectarine,
The N stands first of all ;
And also in Narcissus fine,
With Nosegay large and small.

In Orange sweet, and Olive Oil,
Appears the letter O ;
In sturdy Oak that decks the soil
On which it 's found to grow.

The P is seen in Peach and Pear,
In Primrose of the Spring ;
In sweetest Pink for lady fair,
And Pippin, called a king.

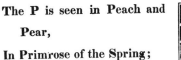

In Quickset-hedge is seen the Q,
On which red berries grow ;
And in nice Quince you 'll find it, too,
Whose blossoms pretty blow.

The R displays the Raspberry,
Fine fruit to make a pie ;
It 's first in Rose and Rosemary,
Also in Rush and Rye.

In Strawberry and Sunflower,
The S is always seen ;
In Sorrel, too, a plant that 's sour,
With Sage of darkest green.

The letter T the Tulip shows,
With Thistle for the ass ;
In Turk's-cap, too, which sweetly blows,
And Tares, a kind of grass.

The U is seen in Underwood,

And Unripe Fruit in May;

'T is also seen in soft Touch-
wood,

Which moulders fast away.

In Violet the V appears,

Most pleasing to the sight;

It 's first in Vine, which always bears

Nice grapes, both black and
white.

The W shows in Walnut-tree,

In Woodbine sweet to view;

It 's first in Willow-tree, you
see,

And Water-lily, too.

In Exotic the X you 'll find,

A plant from foreign lands,

It 's last in Box, so well de
signed

For garden walks, as bands

The sombre Yew displays
the Y;

'T is seen about the grave;

Y droops in Cyprus, mourn-
fully,

O'er old, and young, and
brave.

The Z is seen in Hazel-tree,

On which nice nuts do grow;

In Furze, also, the Z you 'll
see,

And Zephyr winds that blow.

A B C D E F G H I J
K L M N O P Q R S T U V W
X Y Z

a b c d e f g h i j k l m n o p
q r s t u v w x y z

"The Floral Alphabet" (pp. 260–61), from *Little Folks. A Magazine for the Young.* Vol. 2, no. 43. London, Paris & New York: Cassell, Petter & Calpin, [1871]. 21.1 x 16.2 cm.

THE FLORAL ALPHABET.

A IS the curious Arum,
    The merry children seek,
When they scamper through the
        meadows green
    In the pleasant Easter week.

B is the graceful Bluebell
    That cometh in the spring,
And rings its fairy peals, to call
    The welcome season in.

C is the golden Celandine,
    Catkin, and Cuckoo-flower,
The Cistus, and the Columbine,
    That dear old English flower.

D is the meek-eyed Daisy,
    So modest and so sweet,
  Bespangling the green carpet
    For sad and weary feet.

E is the fragrant Eglantine,
    Just by the summer bower;
  How pleasantly it scents the air
    In the cool evening hour.

F is the loved Forget-me-not,
    So simple and so true,
  Attired in graceful mantelet
    of pure celestial blue.

G the Germander Speedwell
    Gentian, and Guelder Rose,
  With its pure and snow-white clusters,
    The fairest flower that grows.

H is the flowering Hawthorn,
    To children all so dear,
  The queen of English hedgerows
    In the spring-time of the year.

I is the climbing Ivy,
    To the old church-tower clinging,
  As if it liketh much to hear
    The merry bells a-ringing.

J is the starry Jasmine,
    Sacred to memories dear
  Of loving hearts, and accents sweet,
    And eyes without a tear.

M is the fragrant Myrtle
    And Mignonette so sweet;
  And the bright-eyed Morning Glory
    You oft in summer greet.

N for the gay Nasturtium
    Climbing along the fence,
  Though to a fragrant odour
    It never makes pretence.

O is the spotted Orchis,
    The belle of hedge and field;
  And to its peerless beauty,
    All other wild flowers yield.

P is our favourite Pansy,
    Its many shades we pass;
  The Primrose fair, and Pimpernel,
    The poor man's weather-glass.

For *Q* we know no blossom,
    No gem in Flora's crown,
  So we offer our condolence,
    And leave poor *Q* alone.

R for the Roses, Roses
    Rich clusters, white and red,
  Pink, damask, cream, and wax-like,
    In border and in bed.

S for Starwort, Speedwell,
    Snapdragon, and Sweet Pea,
  And Snowdrop, with her drooping head,
    Sweetest of all to me.

T for the flaunting Tulip,
    Thistle, and Trumpet-flowers,
  And wild Thyme, on the breezy hills,
    The charm of summer hours.

V for the violet lowly,
    Liking to be unseen,
  As it hides its head securely
    Among its leaflets green.

Now for the Woodbine, lastly,
    To bind the flowers together;
  A bouquet sweetly welcome,
    Whatever be the weather.

THE PANSY.

"Alphabet of Flowers" (pp. 37–61, letters C, D, E, and F missing), from *The Boys' and Girls' Illustrated Gift Book.* With Upwards of Two Hundred and Fifty Illustrations by Wolf, Harrison Weir, Watson, Phiz, Alfred Crowquill, &c. &c. London: George Routledge and Sons, [1862]. Pp. 331. 17.6 x 13 cm. *The Flower Alphabet.* (Letters C, D, E, and F only.) Boston: Degen, Estes & Co. Pp. [40], hand-colored. 18 x 13.5 cm.

THE QUEEN OF THE MAY.

A for ANEMONES, telling of Spring,
And the gladness and brightness
gay colours bring.

B is the BLUE-BELL, that sparkles
with dew,
And carpets the ground with its flowers
of blue.

C for CONVOLVULUS, children's delight,
Which opens in day-time. and shuts up at
night.

D is the DAISY, that grows in the lanes,
Of which Jessie and Sarah make rosy-tipp'd
chains.

E is the EGLANTINE briar, so sweet,
Which Emily trains o'er the lattice-work
neat.

F is the FOX-GLOVE, which Tom stays to pop,
Though his mother has sent him for bread
to the shop.

G is the GRASS, which the sheep
love to eat,
And which makes for young Robert
so pleasant a seat.

H is the HEATHER, red, purple, and grey,
Which reminds the poor Swiss of his home far away.

I is the IVY, that gives the cool shade,
Where John eats the soup that his daughter has made.

J is the JONQUIL, that grows by the brook,
At which Ellen and Caroline longingly look.

K is the KING-CUP, as yellow as gold,
Which Katherine prizes as treasure untold.

L is the LILY, with leaves of bright
green,
Which we'll wreathe round the head of
our sweet Birthday Queen.

M is for MIGNONETTE, sweet-scented
weed,
Which Mary has raised in her garden
from seed.

N for NEMOPHILA, lovely of hue,
Like the sweet summer sky in
its delicate blue.

O OLEANDER, the Gardener's pride;
He thinks it the finest in all
England wide.

P is thè PRIMROSE, which comes in
the Spring,
When blackbirds, and thrushes, and
goldfinches sing.

Q for QUINCE-BLOSSOM, which
naughty young Ned
Pulls off, without minding what
Grandpapa said.

R is the ROSE-BUD, cherish'd by
all,
The pride of the cottage, the joy of
the hall.

S is the SNOW-DROP, drooping and
pale,
Which heeds not the snow-storm, but
bends to the gale.

T is the TULIP, which Eleanor fair,
Loving scarlet and orange, has placed in her hair.

V stands for VIOLETS, prized in the Spring,
When the birds of the grove are first heard to sing.

W WATER-LILIES, whereon Fairies delight,
And dance in the summer, when shines the moon bright.

X for EXOTICS, which Grandmamma sends,
That Fanny may garnish the room for her friends.

Y YELLOW-LILY, which John, with a crook, Is trying to reach from the bank of the brook.

Z is for ZINIA, which has carried away The prize at the Grand Show of Flowers to-day.

Flora's ABC. Philadelphia and New York: Turner & Fisher. Pp. [25] hand-colored accordion pages. 14.5 x 8.5 cm.

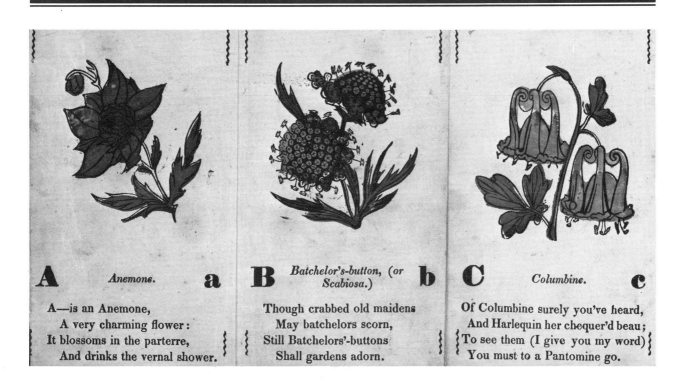

A   *Anemone.*   **a**

A—is an Anemone,
   A very charming flower:
It blossoms in the parterre,
   And drinks the vernal shower.

B   *Batchelor's-button, (or Scabiosa.)*   **b**

Though crabbed old maidens
   May batchelors scorn,
Still Batchelors'-buttons
   Shall gardens adorn.

C   *Columbine.*   **c**

Of Columbine surely you've heard,
   And Harlequin her chequer'd beau;
To see them (I give you my word)
   You must to a Pantomine go.

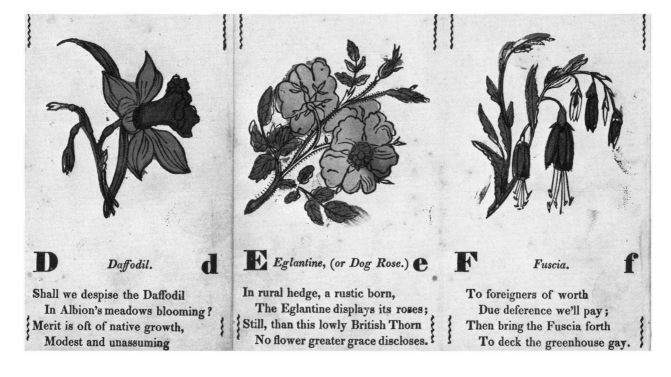

D   *Daffodil.*   **d**

Shall we despise the Daffodil
   In Albion's meadows blooming?
Merit is oft of native growth,
   Modest and unassuming

E *Eglantine, (or Dog Rose.)* **e**

In rural hedge, a rustic born,
   The Eglantine displays its roses;
Still, than this lowly British Thorn
   No flower greater grace discloses.

F   *Fuscia.*   **f**

To foreigners of worth
   Due deference we'll pay;
Then bring the Fuscia forth
   To deck the greenhouse gay.

G *Geranium.* **g**

Geraniums decorate the cot,
  And flourish in the mansion grand,
The noblest female scorneth not
To prune them with her ivory hand.

H *Honey-suckle, or Woodbine.* **h**

Come, Honey-suckle, from the glade
With gay festoons enrich my bower;
There be thy warmer tints display'd
Beneath the fost'ring sun of power.

I *Iris, or Fleur-de-lis.* **i**

The Iris fair, or Fleur-de-lis,
Of Frenchmen and frogs remind you,
Ye wealthy, then, who cross the sea,
O think on those you leave behind you

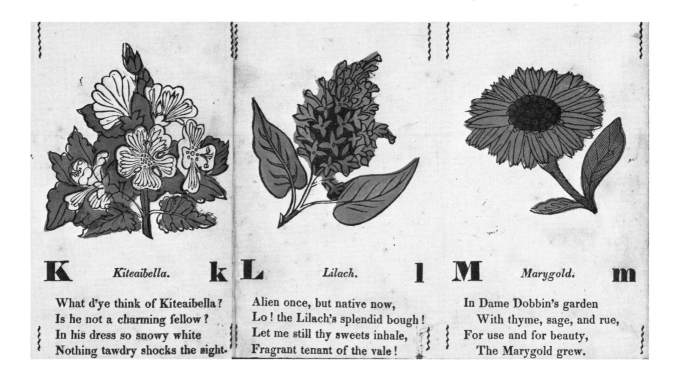

K *Kiteaibella.* **k**

What d'ye think of Kiteaibella?
Is he not a charming fellow?
In his dress so snowy white
Nothing tawdry shocks the sight.

L *Lilach.* **l**

Alien once, but native now,
Lo! the Lilach's splendid bough!
Let me still thy sweets inhale,
Fragrant tenant of the vale!

M *Marygold.* **m**

In Dame Dobbin's garden
  With thyme, sage, and rue,
For use and for beauty,
  The Marygold grew.

N   *Nightshade.*   **n**

Oh beware the Nightshade's berries,
  Tho' they're tempting to the eye :
From the pois'nous painted beauty,
  Dearest children, fly, oh, fly !

O   *Oxlip.*   **o**

Oxlip, come ! I love thee well,
  Come from out the mossy dell ;
In a flower-pot thou shalt grow,
  Child of spring,—I love thee so !

P   *Loving Idol.*   **P**

Pansey ! for heart's ease we roam,
  Loving Idols oft abound !
When I bear thee to my home,
  Both in one I shall have found.

Q *Quercus, or Common Oak.* **q**

The Oak is a Quercus,
  A Quercus the Oak is ,
The A-corn can't *B corn .
  My riddle no joke is.
     *be.

R   *Rocket.*   **r**

Sky-Rockets display their brief light
One moment, and then they expire ;
But *the Rocket of Gardens* is bright,
And gives you more time to admire.

S   *Sweet William.*   **S**

Sweet William, Sweet William's
  A flower so sweet,
I think he blooms sweetly
  Whenever we meet.

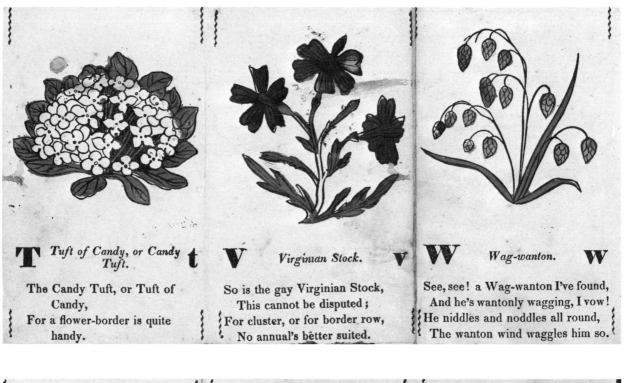

T *Tuft of Candy, or Candy Tuft.* **t**

The Candy Tuft, or Tuft of
  Candy,
For a flower-border is quite
  handy.

V *Virginian Stock.* **v**

So is the gay Virginian Stock,
  This cannot be disputed;
For cluster, or for border row,
  No annual's better suited.

W *Wag-wanton.* **W**

See, see! a Wag-wanton I've found,
  And he's wantonly wagging, I vow!
He niddles and noddles all round,
  The wanton wind waggles him so.

X *Xeranthemum* **x**

Xeranthemum's a hard word:
  Hard names are quite the go now,
And pedants many such afford
  To make a learned shew now!

Y *Yew.* **y**

Upon the ancient church-yard Yew
Some pretty crimson berries grew;
Poor Henry ate some out of pride,
But sicken'd soon, alas! and died.

Z *Zinnia.* **Z**

Tho' last, not least, the Zinnia tries
Good little children to invite
Into the path where merit flies
To pluck Fame's garland ever bright.

The Alphabet in Rhyme. New York: Kiggins & Kellogg. Pp. 16. 11.6 x 7.4 cm.

115

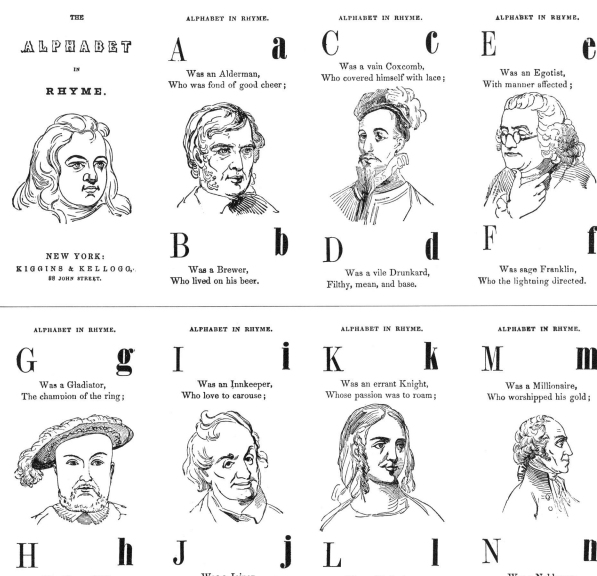

THE

ALPHABET

IN

RHYME.

NEW YORK:
KIGGINS & KELLOGG,
88 JOHN STREET.

ALPHABET IN RHYME.

A   a

Was an Alderman,
Who was fond of good cheer;

B   b

Was a Brewer,
Who lived on his beer.

ALPHABET IN RHYME.

C   c

Was a vain Coxcomb,
Who covered himself with lace;

D   d

Was a vile Drunkard,
Filthy, mean, and base.

ALPHABET IN RHYME.

E   e

Was an Egotist,
With manner affected;

F   f

Was sage Franklin,
Who the lightning directed.

ALPHABET IN RHYME.

G   g

Was a Gladiator,
The champion of the ring;

H   h

Was Henry VIII.,
A very wicked king.

ALPHABET IN RHYME.

I   i

Was an Innkeeper,
Who love to carouse;

J   j

Was a Joiner,
Who built a fine house.

ALPHABET IN RHYME.

K   k

Was an errant Knight,
Whose passion was to roam;

L   l

Was a fair Lady,
Who was much attached to home

ALPHABET IN RHYME.

M   m

Was a Millionaire,
Who worshipped his gold;

N   n

Was a Nobleman,
Who was haughty and cold.

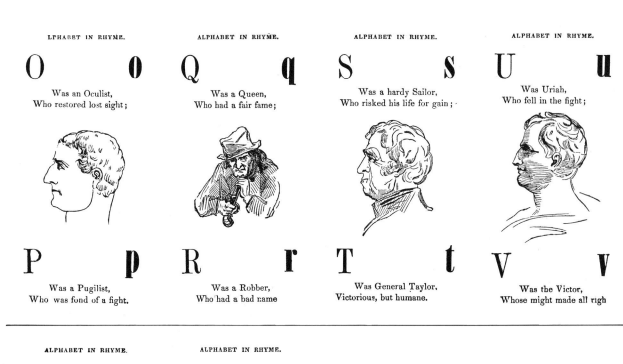

ALPHABET IN RHYME.

O **O**

Was an Oculist,
Who restored lost sight;

P **p**

Was a Pugilist,
Who was fond of a fight.

ALPHABET IN RHYME.

Q **q**

Was a Queen,
Who had a fair fame;

R **r**

Was a Robber,
Who had a bad name

ALPHABET IN RHYME.

S **s**

Was a hardy Sailor,
Who risked his life for gain;

T **t**

Was General Taylor,
Victorious, but humane.

ALPHABET IN RHYME.

U **u**

Was Uriah,
Who fell in the fight;

V **v**

Was the Victor,
Whose might made all right

ALPHABET IN RHYME.

W **W**

Was a great Wag,
Who was fond of his fun;

X **X**

Was Xpensive,
Whose race was soon run.

ALPHABET IN RHYME.

Y **y**

Was a Yankee,
Found every where;

Z **Z**

Was Zulemia,
Intelligent and fair.

Tom Thumb's Picture Alphabet; in Rhyme. New York: Kiggins & Kellogg. Pp. 8, including paper cover. 8.2 x 5.5 cm.

117

TOM THUMB'S

PICTURE ALPHABET;

IN RHYME.

NEW YORK:

KIGGINS & KELLOGG,
88 JOHN STREET.

THE

ALPHABET IN RHYME.

A is an Angler,
Young, but expert;

B is a Butcher,
Who wears a red shirt.

C is a Crabfish,
Who lives in a shell;

D is a Doctor,
Who gets sick folks well.

E is an Esquire,
With dignified brow;

F is a Farmer,
Who follows the plough.

G is the wide Gate,
Opened by Dennis;

H is the Horseman, who
Gave him some pennies.

I is an Iceboat,
Propelled by steam;

J is a Jockey,
Who drives a gay team.

K is the village Kirk,
With a very tall spire

L is a lazy Lout,
A loafer, and a liar.

M is a Miser,
Covetous and mean;

N is a Newsboy,
Bright, witty, and keen.

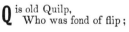

O is the farmer's Ox,
That is fattened for beef;

P is the Parson,
Whose sermons are brief.

Q is old Quilp,
Who was fond of flip;

R is a Rascal,
Who deserves the whip.

S is a large Ship,
That crosses the main;

T is a Tailor,
Who labors for gain.

U is an Umbrella,
That protects us from rain;

V is a Vagabond,
Vile, vicious, and vain.

W is a deep Well,
Dug no one knows when;

X is a letter, which
Often stands for T .

Y is a Yak,
A fourfooted beast;

Z is Zenobia,
The queen of the east.

Little Boys and Girls A B C. New York: McLoughlin Brothers, 1884. Pp. [10], including 8 pages of colored plates. 23 x 15 cm.

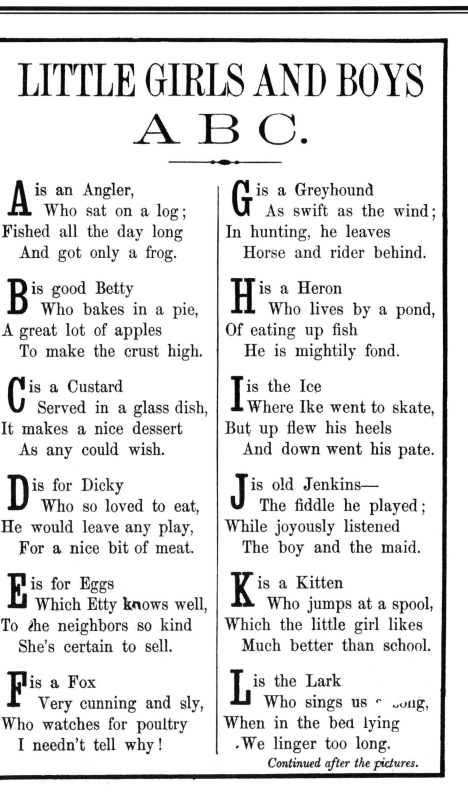

LITTLE GIRLS AND BOYS
A B C.

A is an Angler,
Who sat on a log;
Fished all the day long
And got only a frog.

B is good Betty
Who bakes in a pie,
A great lot of apples
To make the crust high.

C is a Custard
Served in a glass dish,
It makes a nice dessert
As any could wish.

D is for Dicky
Who so loved to eat,
He would leave any play,
For a nice bit of meat.

E is for Eggs
Which Etty knows well,
To the neighbors so kind
She's certain to sell.

F is a Fox
Very cunning and sly,
Who watches for poultry
I needn't tell why!

G is a Greyhound
As swift as the wind;
In hunting, he leaves
Horse and rider behind.

H is a Heron
Who lives by a pond,
Of eating up fish
He is mightily fond.

I is the Ice
Where Ike went to skate,
But up flew his heels
And down went his pate.

J is old Jenkins—
The fiddle he played;
While joyously listened
The boy and the maid.

K is a Kitten
Who jumps at a spool,
Which the little girl likes
Much better than school.

L is the Lark
Who sings us a song,
When in the bed lying
.We linger too long.

Continued after the pictures.

LITTLE GIRLS AND BOYS A B C.—Continued.

M is for Molly
 A nice mottled mare,
With fine flowing mane
 Of soft glossy hair.

N is a Nosegay
 Besprinkled with dew,
Picked in the morning
 And given to you.

O is a barn Owl
 Who looks very wise,
While watching a mouse
 With staring grey eyes.

P is a Parrot
 With feathers so gay,
We find him all colors
 Green, golden, and gray.

Q is a Queen
 Who governs the land,
Surrounded by courtiers
 Each kissing her hand.

R is a Robin
 Who sits on a limb,
He thinks the red cherries
 Grow only for him.

S is for Sheep
 Eating herbage you see,
The owner has marked
 On their wool a big D.

T is a Trumpeter
 Blowing his horn,
To wake up the soldiers
 Betimes in the morn.

U is a Unicorn
 Armed it is said,
With an ivory horn
 In front of   head.

V is a Vulture,
 Who eats a great deal,
And swallows a dog
 Or a cat at a meal.

W is a Watchman
 Who watches the street,
Lest thieves in the dark
 Good people should meet.

X is great Xerxes
 A king you must know,
Who reigned over Persia
 A long time ago.

Y is a Yacht
 Sailing out on the sea;
If we were on board
 How happy we'd be.

Z is the Zebra
 You've heard of before;
So here ends my rhyme
 Till I gather some more.

New Illuminated Alphabet: or, Pictorial Book. Concord, N.H.: Merriam & Merrill, 1854. Pp. [17], including paper cover. 21 x 15.2 cm.

A was an Angler, and fished in the stream.

B was a Barber, and will shave you quite clean.

C was a Cow, that gives us nice milk.

D was a Duchess, all dressed in rich silk.

E was an Elephant, of monstrous size.

F was a Friar, learned and wise.

G was a Goose, swims on the lake.

H was a Horse, works hard for our sake.

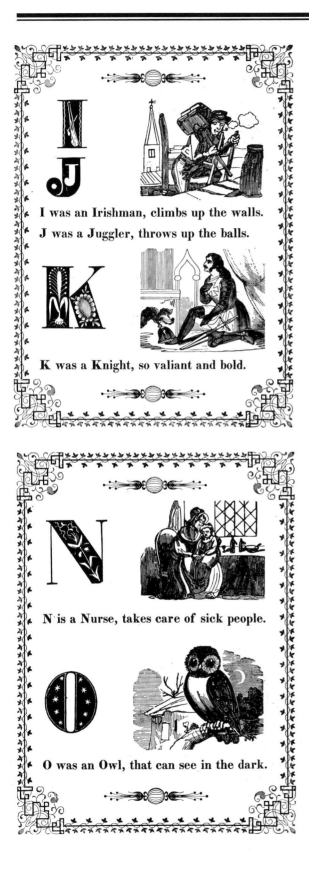

I was an Irishman, climbs up the walls.

J was a Juggler, throws up the balls.

K was a Knight, so valiant and bold.

L was a Lamb that strayed from the fold.

M is a Martin, flies over the steeple.

N is a Nurse, takes care of sick people.

O was an Owl, that can see in the dark.

P was a Ploughman, that will rise with the lark.

Q was a Queen, over England doth reign.

R was a Reaper, that cuts down the grain.

S was a Stag, at the brook drinking water.

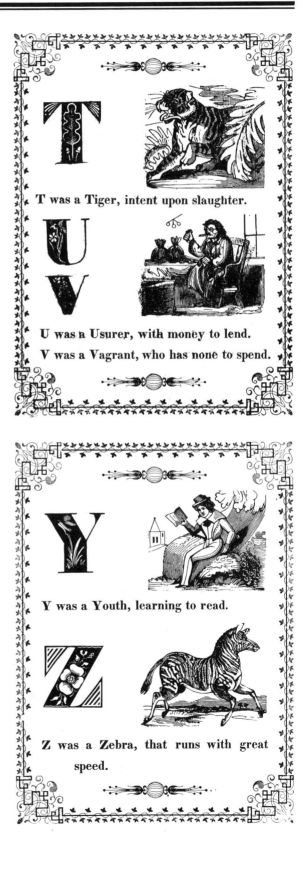

T was a Tiger, intent upon slaughter.

U was a Usurer, with money to lend.

V was a Vagrant, who has none to spend.

W was a Well, at the end of the path.

X on the mile-stone shows the distance from home.

Y was a Youth, learning to read.

Z was a Zebra, that runs with great speed.

"Little Harry's ABC" (pp. 2–8), from Heaton, Mrs. Charles, *Routledge's Album for Children*. With One Hundred and Ninety Illustrations by Birket Foster, John Gilbert, J. E. Millais, J. Wolf, J. B. Zwecker. London: George Routledge and Sons, inscribed December 25, 1874. Pp. 380. 18.7 x 13.5 cm.

A was an Angler who fished in a Stream.

B was a Builder and made a strong Beam.

E a poor Esquimaux lived on coarse Fare.

F was a Footman who powdered his Hair.

C was a Coachman who sat on a Box.

D was a Drover and drove a fat Ox.

G was a Gipsy who lived in a Tent.

H was a Hoppicker working in Kent.

I was an Idler and wasted his Time.

J was a Justice who punished all Crime.

M was a Milkmaid who carried a Pail.

N was a Navvy and worked on the Rail.

K was a Knight fully armed cap-a-pie.

L was a Lawyer and fond of his Fee.

O was an Ostler who cleaned a fine Hack.

P was a Pedlar and called with his Pack.

Q was a Quaker in Dress very plain.

R was a Reaper and cut down the Grain.

U was an Urchin loved Mischief and Sport

V was a Vintner who kept some old Port.

S was a Serjeant who drilled a Recruit.

T was a Tailor and made a fine Suit.

W was a Warder with a bunch of great Keys.

X like a Turnstile comes next if you please.

Y was a Yeoman who guarded the Stair.

Z was a Zany and played at a Fair.

The Picture Alphabet; or Child's A, B, C. Seventh Series No. 1. Concord: Published by Atwood & Brown, 1837. Pp. 16, paper cover. 9.5 x 6 cm.

A

Was an Angler, by whom I was told,
That he seldom caught ought save a very
bad cold.

B

Was a Birch rod, the terror of youth,
When they blotted their copies or told an
untruth

C

Was a cake, for twelfth-day a treat,
Made of currants and plums, most delicious
and sweet.

D

Was a Dandy, with waist scarce a span,
A frivolous insect, not half a man.

E

Was an Eagle, who flew in the skies,
And looked at the sun without winking his
eyes.

F

Was a Farmer, who rose before morn,
To shoot at the sparrows that plundered his
corn.

G

Was a Gipsy, a wandering cheat,
Who all kinds of nonsense can glibly repeat.

H

Was a Hawker, with all sorts of ware,
To entice you to buy, when you went to the
fair.

I J

Was an Idler, who thought it no crime,
To gamble his money, and squander his time.

K

Was a King, who is seen on his throne;
May Americans never have one of their own.

L

Was a Leopard, bright, spotted and grim,
I'd rather have sixpence than meddle with
him.

M

Was a Monkey, all frolick and glee,
And none are more happy in mischief than
he.

N

Was a Nag, ready saddled and still;
If you wish for a ride you may mount if you
will.

O

Was an Orphan, in want of relief;
I will give all my money to soften his grief.

P

Was a Piper, whose musick beat hollow,
The fabulous notes of your Pans, or Apollo.

Q

Was a Quill, late drawn from a goose;
When made in a pen, 'tis of excellent use.

R

Was a Rattle which made a great noise,
Like the clamorous chatter of rude girls and
boys.

S

Was a Scater, who practising grace,
Made a stumble and flattened his nose to his
face.

T

Was a Turk, of few words and sedate;
I wish flighty children would copy his gate

U V

Is my Uncle, how smiling he looks,
He has brought me a present of good new
books.

W

Was a Wrestler, stout hardy and tall;
If you grapple with him you'll be sure of a
fall.

X

Was a Xebec, a small Moorish ship,
In which their grandees take for pleasure, a
trip.

Y

Was a Youth, truly holy and wise,
Who studied bad actions to shun and despise.

Z

Was a Zechin, a Venetian coin,
I wish I'd ten thousand in some box of mine.

A was an Archer. (Illustrated by E. S. Hardy.) London: Ernest Nister; New York: E. P. Dutton & Co., [1895]. Pp. [14], including 4 pages of colored plates. 28 x 23 cm.

126

I WAS an Innkeeper,
who loved
to carouse;

J WAS a Joiner,
and built
up a house.

K WAS King William
once governed
this land;

L WAS a Lady, who
had a white hand.

M WAS a Miser,
and hoarded
up gold,

N WAS a Nobleman,
gallant
and bold.

O WAS an
Oyster-wench,
and went
about town;

P WAS a
Parson
and wore a
black gown.

Q WAS a Queen,
who was
fond of
good flip;

R WAS a Robber,
and wanted
a whip.

S WAS a Sailor,
and spent
all he got;

T WAS a Tinker,
and mended
a pot.

U WAS a Usurer,
a miserable
elf;

V WAS a Vintner,
who drank
all himself.

W WAS a Watchman,
and guarded
the door;

X WAS eXpensive,
and so became poor.

Y WAS a Youth,
that did not
love school;

Z WAS a Zany,
a poor,
harmless fool.

Tom Thumb's Alphabet, from Picture Baby Books, Aunt Mavor's Little Library [series]. Illustrated by W. McConnell. Engraved by the Brothers Dalziel. London: Routledge, Warne, and Routledge, [1860?]. Pp. [28]. 17.5 x 13.5 cm.

A was an Archer, who shot at a frog.

B was a Butcher, who had a great dog.

C was a Captain, all covered with lace.

D was a Drummer, who played with a grace.

E was an Esquire
with pride on his brow.

F was a Farmer,
who followed the plough.

G was a Gamester,
who had but ill-luck.

H was a Hunter,
who hunted a buck.

I was an Italian,
who had a white mouse.

J was a Joiner,
who built up a house.

K was a King,
so mighty and grand.

L was a Lady,
who had a white hand.

M was a Miser,
who hoarded up gold.

N was a Nobleman,
gallant and bold.

O was an Organ-Boy,
who played for his bread.

P a Policeman,
of bad boys the dread.

Q was a Quaker,
who would not bow down"

R was a Robber,
who prowled about town.

S was a Sailor,
who spent all he got.

T was a Tinker,
who mended a pot.

U was an Usher,
with dunces severe.

V was a Veteran,
who never knew fear.

W was a Waiter,
with dinners in store.

X was Expensive,
and so became poor.

Y was a Youth,
who did not like school.

Z was a Zany,
who looked a great fool.

"A was an Archer" (p. 28), from *Rhymes and Chimes for Little Folks.* New York:
Hurst & Company, Publishers. 24 x 18.5 cm.

A was an Archer, and shot at a frog,
B was a Butcher, and had a great dog.
C was a Captain, all covered with lace,
D was a Drunkard, and had a red face.
E was an Esquire, with pride on his brow,
F was a Farmer, and followed the plough.
G was a Gamester, who had but ill luck,
H was a Hunter, and hunted a buck.
I was an Innkeeper, who loved to bouse,
J was a Joiner, and built up a house.
K was King George, who once governed
　　this land,
L was a Lady, who had a white hand.
M was a Miser, and hoarded up gold,
N was a Nobleman, gallant and bold.
O was an Oysterman, who went about
　　town,

P was a Parson, and wore a black gown.
Q was a Queen, who was fond of good
　　flip,
R was a Robber, and wanted a whip.
S was a Sailor, and spent all he got,
T was a Tinker, and mended a pot.
U was an Usurer, a miserable elf,
V was a Vintner, who drank all himself.
W was a Watchman, and guarded the
　　door,
X was expensive, and so became poor.
Y was a Youth, that did not love school,
Z was a Zany, a poor harmless fool.

A was an Archer, or a New Amusing Alphabet for Children. Newark, N.J.: Printed and Published by Benjamin Olds, 1844. Pp. 16, paper cover. 10.5 x 7 cm.

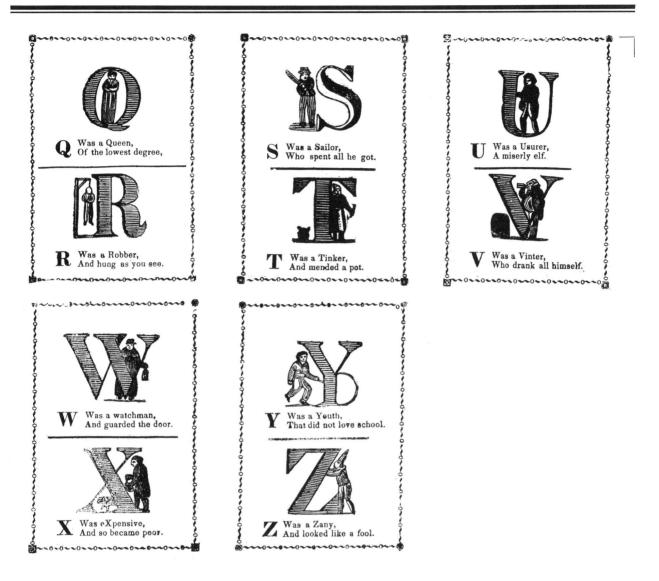

Q Was a Queen,
Of the lowest degree,

R Was a Robber,
And hung as you see.

S Was a Sailor,
Who spent all he got.

T Was a Tinker,
And mended a pot.

U Was a Usurer,
A miserly elf.

V Was a Vinter,
Who drank all himself.

W Was a watchman,
And guarded the door.

X Was eXpensive,
And so became poor.

Y Was a Youth,
That did not love school.

Z Was a Zany,
And looked like a fool.

"Nursery Rhyme Alphabet" (pp. 199–200, with colored plate), from *Mother Goose's Nursery Rhymes and Fairy Tales*. With Illustrations by Sir John Gilbert, John Tenniel, Harrison Weir, Walter Crane, W. McConnell, J. B. Zwecker, and Others. London, Glasgow, Manchester and New York: George Routledge and Sons, 1892. Pp. 320. 21.5 x 14.5 cm.

NURSERY RHYME ALPHABET.

A was the Archer who shot at a frog.

B was Bo-Peep, with her crook and her dog.

C was the Cow that jumped over the moon.

D was the Dish that ran off with the spoon.

E was Elizabeth, Betsey, and Bess.

F was the Forest where stood the bird's-net.

G Gaffer Longlegs; downstairs he'd a fall.

H Humpty Dumpty that sat on the wall.

I was the "I" who was going to St. Ives.

J Jacky Horner, on plum-pie he thrives.

K was King Cole with his fiddlers three.

L Little Gold-Hair, peeping, you see.

M Mother Hubbard who thought her dog dead.

N Little Netticoat, with a read head.

O the old Woman "upon market day;"

P was the "Pedlar" who passed by that way.

Q was the Queen of Hearts, tartlets she makes.

R was Red Riding Hood carrying the cakes.

S Simple Simon, the pieman beside.

T Tommy Tucker, for supper who cried.

U was the Unicorn, "beat around the town;"

V was Victoria—he fought for her crown.

W Whittington, who turned again,
Over great London as Lord Mayor to reign.

X is a letter that here we can spare.

Y "Yankee Doodle," that went to the fair;

Z is the Zany who laughed at him there.

Merry Alphabet. Alphabet Series. New York: McLoughlin Bro's., 1890. Pp. [14], including 6 pages of color plates. 21 x 16 cm.

A was an Archer who shot
at a frog
With an Arrow that might
have been shorter;
He shot at a frog, that sat on a log,
And made it jump into the water.

B was a Butcher who had a big dog,
Always on hand for a pow-wow;
It would bite, it would bark from
daylight to dark,
Oh, you should have heard it Bow-wow!

C was a Captain all
covered with lace,
With sword and with
trinkets to rattle;
He was fond of fine clothes, but you need not
suppose
That he ever took part in a battle.

D was a Doctor who rode
in a gig,
And many good people
attended;
And when they were ill he gave them a pill,
And soon their diseases were mended.

E is an Engineer firm at
his post,
To rules and to signals no
stranger;
Of his train he takes care, and
the passengers there,
And whistles "Down brakes!" when there's
danger.

F was a Farmer
who followed
the plough,
And planted his seeds in their season;
He could rake he could hoe, he could reap he
could mow,
And was proud of his farm with good reason.

G was a glutton who ate
like a pig,
With his nose quite into the
platter;
But though he would stuff he could not get enough,
And kept on growing fatter and fatter.

H was a Hunter who
went with his gun
Where rabbits and squir-
rels were plenty;
Much powder and shot he wasted, but not
One hit did he make in twenty.

I was an Indian ready for
war,
In boldness no white man
could match him;
And when on his steed he rode off with speed
'Twas no easy matter to catch him.

J was a Jockey who
rode a fine horse---
His colors were red
and yellow;
He rode at such pace that he won a great race,
And was voted a splendid fellow.

K was a King who sat up
on a throne
And thought he could live
in clover;
But so bad was he found that the people around
Were glad when his reign was over.

L was a Lady who had
a white hand
All covered with beau-
tiful rings;
She could knit, she could sew, she could play, and
I know
Do many more lady-like things.

M was a Miser who hoarded
up gold
Just for the love of such
treasure;
And never a cent for clothing he spent,
Or for anything else that gave pleasure.

N was a News-boy who
ran through the street,
Intent upon selling his
papers;
And when all were sold, as I have been told,
He cut up ridiculous capers.

O was the Organ that
stood in the church;
O the Organist played it
In such a fine way. it gave
joy every day
To the Organ-builder who made it.

P was a parson who wore
a black gown;
The Bible he kept ever
near him;
And so well did he preach, and such good lessons
teach,
That the young and the old went to hear him.

Q was a Quarrel 'twixt two
little boys,
And both were so greatly
offended,
That they fought and they fought, till one of them
thought
To cry "Quarter!" and then it was ended.

R was a Racket they
used as a bat---
Richard, and Robert and
Dennis---
When they met on the lawn where the net was
outdrawn
For their favorite game of Lawn Tennis.

S was a Sailor who followed
the Sea,
And none were so gay as his
lordship,
This jolly Jack tar, who knew every spar,
And was always at home when aboard ship.

T was a Tailor who mended
a coat,
Oh, but his fingers were
nimble!
The seams were all prest by a goose, and the rest
Was done with a needle and thimble.

U—an Umbrella
was borne o'er
the head
Of a dear little Urchin, named Billy,
When a sudden gust came, and oh, what a shame!
'Twas changed to a big water-lily!

V was the Vase in a mis-
sing valise;
W the Watchman who
found it;
X was the Ten dollar bill he had then,
With two or three Extra around it.

Y was a Yacht that bore a
blue flag,
And sailed off with speed
so amazing,
That she and her crew re-
ceived their just due,
And were worthy the prize and the praising.

Z was a Zany—a silly
young goose,
Who thought it would
be very. jolly
To stay out of school, and
to act like a fool;
But he lived to repent of his folly.

The Alphabet of Virtues. London: Darton & Co., inscribed June 20, 1856. Pp. [28].
16 x 16 cm.

141

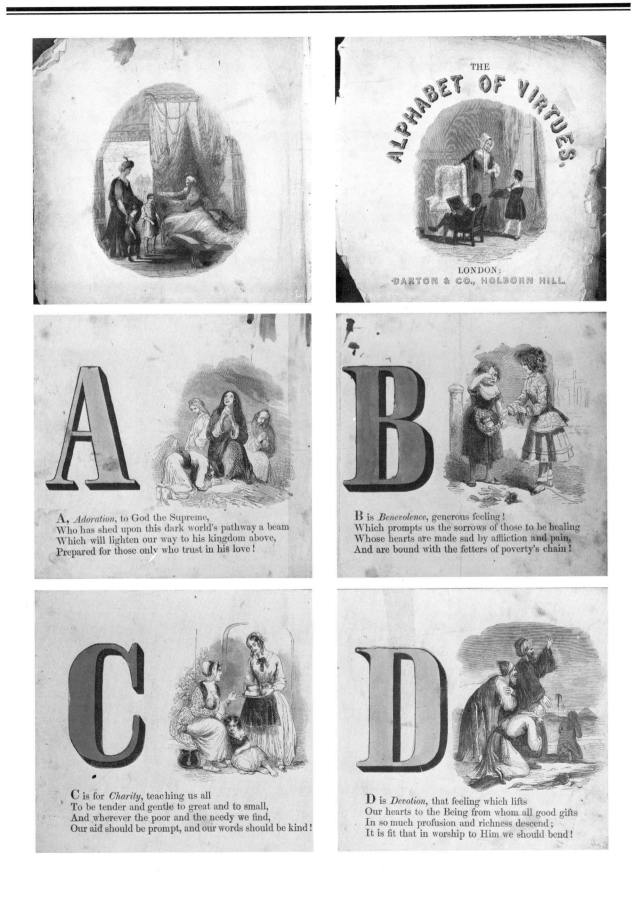

THE ALPHABET OF VIRTUES.

LONDON:
DARTON & CO., HOLBORN HILL.

A, *Adoration*, to God the Supreme,
Who has shed upon this dark world's pathway a beam
Which will lighten our way to his kingdom above,
Prepared for those only who trust in his love!

B is *Benevolence*, generous feeling!
Which prompts us the sorrows of those to be healing
Whose hearts are made sad by affliction and pain,
And are bound with the fetters of poverty's chain!

C is for *Charity*, teaching us all
To be tender and gentle to great and to small,
And wherever the poor and the needy we find,
Our aid should be prompt, and our words should be kind!

D is *Devotion*, that feeling which lifts
Our hearts to the Being from whom all good gifts
In so much profusion and richness descend;
It is fit that in worship to Him we should bend!

E is *Economy*—let us beware,
And of spending too much at a time have a care,
Lest some day or other we grieve to our cost
O'er the shillings and pence we have foolishly lost.

F is for *Faith*, which assists us to bear
Our losses and trials in this world of care,
By fixing the mind on that happier shore,
Where sorrow and trouble will vex us no more!

G is for *Gratitude*, which we should show
Towards all who assist us as onward we go
In this chequered way, which indeed would be drear,
Did we not meet with friends who are kind and sincere!

H is for *Hope*, may each one of us try
So to pass through this life that when called on to die,
With the terrors of death we may not fear to cope,
Sustained by a cheering and glorious Hope!

I is for *Industry;* let us work on,
While the idle and gay to their pleasure have gone;
The strength of our youth we should wisely engage
In providing a store for the wants of old age.

J is for *Justice*, protecting the right
Against the oppression of fraud and of might,
And enforcing that precept, so perfect and true,
"Do to men as you wish they should do unto you!"

K stands for *Kindness,*—our Saviour was kind,
And to imitate him should our hearts be inclined;
What a world this would be, if each one did his best
To relieve the afflicted and cheer the distressed!

L is for *Love ;* in the Bible we learn
That Jesus will never the little ones spurn,
His arms to receive them are always unclosed,
For of such is the kingdom of heaven composed!

M stands for *Modesty ;* we should all seek
To cast away pride, and be lowly and meek,
The merits of others should willingly own,
While confessing the faults to which *we* may be prone.

N, *Noble-mindedness,* steadfast and high,
Repelling dishonour and scorning a lie,
Preferring to riches, or splendour, or fame,
A conscience at ease, and a good, honest name!

O is *Obedience ;* let us obey
Our parents, who cherish us day after day,
As well as our teachers, by whom we are led
In the fair paths of learning and wisdom to tread.

P is *Politeness,* displaying a mind,
That is gentle and tender, good-natured, refined.
Little children should be with its graces embued,
And never be cross, or impatient, or rude.

Q is for *Quietness*, disliking fluster,
Avoiding all riot, and tumult, and bluster;
And shunning the ways of those bad girls and boys
Who vex other people by making a noise.

R is *Repentance;* if e'er we do wrong,
Our grief for the fault should be earnest and strong,
And whenever we chance to displease our kind friends,
We should do all we can to make hearty amends.

S is *Sobriety;* do not be thinking,
Like some folks, of nothing but eating and drinking;
Learn the maxim that cannot be too oft rehearst,
"Eat only when hungry, and drink when athirst!"

T is for *Truth*, which we all should observe,
And from which we should never be tempted to swerve;
Any sacrifice we may be called on to make,
Is better by far than a promise to break.

U is *Uprightness;* like this judge so grave,
Unflinching in duty, we ought to behave;
To the whispers of sin should our ears be denied,
When we're tempted to turn from strict duty aside!

V, *Veneration;* all those who act rightly,
Will never of serious matters speak lightly;
They who love God will treat Him with reverence and awe,
Nor dare to transgress His divine, holy law!

W is *Wisdom*, and oh, let us pray,
That from her sacred precincts we never may stray,
Our happiness then will for ever increase,
For her ways are all pleasant, her paths are all peace!

X is a letter that seldom is used,
But it's shape will remind us how sinners abused
Their Saviour and God, when, with brute, cruel force,
They compelled Him to bleed and to die on the *cross!*

Y is to teach us our bosoms should *Yearn*
With tender affection and love, in return
To our father and mother, and teachers and friends,
And we ought to thank God who such comforters sends!

Z stands for *Zeal*, which should fire our breasts,
When the cause we're engaged in on equity rests;
What our hands find to do must be done with good will,
In old age it will be time enough to stand still!

Thomas, Abel C. *The Alphabet Class.* Written for School Exhibitions. Boston: J. M. Usher, 1848. (Pp. 3–7, no illustration.) 16 x 10 cm.

A.

A was an Ant, that was prudent and wise
In laying up food for her winter supplies;
And seldom would any of comforts be scant,
If all were as prudent and wise as the Ant.

B.

B was a Bee, that looked well to his hive,
And only by industry labored to thrive.
A wholesome example for you and to me
May even be found in the neat busy Bee.

C.

C was a Crow, that was thievish and sly,
Who kept far away when the farmer was nigh.
Though corn was his living, alas for his lot!
The corn-stealing Crow by the farmer was shot.

D.

D was a Dove, that was gentle and mild,
A type of what *should* be the heart of a child.
When Christ was baptized of the Father above,
There settled upon him the form of a Dove.

E.

E was an Eagle, both valiant and free,
That ever the type of our country shall be.
O long may it be ere adversity mars
The Eagle-borne flag of the stripes and the stars.

F.

F was a Fox, that was cunning and fleet,
And ne'er asked for poultry when wishing to eat.
But once there befell him a woful mishap—
The crafty hen-*stealer* was caught in a trap.

G.

G was a Goose, that was silly enough,
And when we had cooked him we found he was tough.
We boiled him from morn till the kitchen was dark;
He must have been one of the two in the Ark.

H.

H was a Horse, that was free to submit
To carry or pull as his owner saw fit;
And since to hard labor his life he devotes,
O give him good treatment and plenty of oats.

I.

I was an Ibis, a bird, we've been told,
Long worshipped by millions in Egypt of old.
Redeemed would the *world* be from many a curse,
If none of mankind worshipped anything worse.

J.

J was a Jay-bird, that chattered all day,
And much we presume she had therefore to say.
Some *gossips* there are like this talkative bird,
Who tell rather more than their ears ever heard.

K.

K was a Katy-did, that chirped on a tree—
But like *other* ladies much trouble had she;
For while "*Katy* DID" was her positive cry,
"*Katy-*DID N'T," some neighbor was sure to reply.

L.

L was a Lamb, that, in freedom from sin,
An emblem of innocence always has been.
All cleaving to God, may it e'er be our lot
To be Lambs of His fold without blemish or spot.

M.

M was a Mouse, that would nibble the cheese,
And not say to pussy, "I'll eat, if you please."
But pussy looked well to the care of the house,
And asked not permission to eat up the Mouse.

N.

N was a Nightingale, that without fee
Sang sweetly to all who chose present to be.
Don't you wish he would come, with companions a
few,
And perch near the window and serenade *you?*

O.

O was an Owl, that was certainly wise,
For gravity sat in his solemn big eyes.
Some *people* in wisdom resemble this elf—
They both take it out in "Thinks I to myself."

P.

P was a Peacock, the dandy and fop
Of all sorts of creatures that flutter or hop.
Both Peacocks and dandies in *dressing* excel—
What *else* they are good for, no mortal can tell.

Q.

Q was a Quail, that in harvest went round,
To gather the grain as it fell on the ground.
The farmer-boy caught him when Christmas was nigh,
And ate the fat Quail in a holiday pie.

R.

R was a Rabbit, as timid and fleet
As anything ever man hunted to eat.
If I had *my* way, an escape I'd prepare,
And help the poor Rabbit away from the snare.

S.

S was a Snake; and I pray you take heed
Of the craft and the sting of the serpentine breed;
And let me remark, ere the letter I pass,
Be specially cautious of "Snakes in the grass."

T.

T was a Tiger, of as beautiful skin
As ever enwrapped a fierce spirit within.
How often for worth is mere beauty received!
How often, alas; we are sadly deceived!

V.

V was a Vulture, that built his nest high,
On the peak of a rock towering up to the sky.
Alas, that a bird with so lofty a nest
Should *not* be with mercy and tenderness blest!

W.

W was a Wren; and would any one spoil
The nest that she finished with patience and toil?
Not I, and not *you,* I am sure, would have part
In spoiling her nest or in breaking her heart.

X.

The X was so cross that all animals craved
From a name with an X to be evermore saved;
And so not an ear of you all will we vex
With an alphabet name that begins with an X.

Y.

Y was a Yellow-bird, happy and trim,
That built his nice nest on an apple-tree limb.
Much better for *him,* in his youth or old age,
To be his own master than shut in a cage.

Z.

Z was a Zebra, with stripes girded round,
Whose beauty and elegance far are renowned;
But *like* OTHER *beauties,* who shall not be named,
The Zebra is fickle, and hard to be tamed.

U.

(In unison—and courtesy together.)
The U we have passed, nor esteem it amiss;
And plainly and simply our reason is this:
The name of an animal would not be due,
And might give *offence* if we gave it to—U!

The Fireside Picture Alphabet. Of Humour and Droll Moral Tales or Words & Their Meanings. Illustrated. Boston: Mayhew & Baker, 1858. Pp. [26], printed in red and black. 19.4 x 12.8 cm.

A a.

ABLUTION,
The Act of Cleansing.

The little sweep has washed his face,
But not as we advise;
For black as soot he's made the soap,
And rubbed it in his eyes.

B b.

BARTER, *Exchange.*

Here's Master Mack presenting fruit,
Of which he makes display;
He knows he'll soon have Lucy's rope,
And with it skip away.

C c.

CATASTROPHE, *a Final Event,*
(generally unhappy.)

" O, here's a sad catastrophe ! "
Was Mrs. Blossom's cry;
Then — "Water! water! bring to me —
Or all my fish will die."

D d.

DELIGHTFUL,
Pleasant, Charming.

These boys are bathing in the stream
When they should be at school;
The master's coming round to see
Who disregards his rule.

E e.

ECCENTRICITY,
Irregularity, Strangeness.

We often see things seeming strange;
But scarce so strange as this : —
Here every thing is mis-applied,
Here every change amiss.

F f.

FRAUD,
Deceit, Trick, Artifice, Cheat.

Here is Pat Murphy, fast asleep,
And there is Neddy Bray;
The thief a watchful eye doth keep
Until he gets away.

G g.

GENIUS,
Mental Power, Faculty.

A little boy with little slate
May sometimes make more clear
The little thoughts that he would state
Than can by words appear.

H h.

HORROR,
Terror, Dread.

This little, harmless speckled frog
Seems Lady Townsend's dread;
I fear she'll run away and cry,
And hide her silly head.

I i. **J** j.

ICHABOD AT THE JAM.

ICHABOD, *a Christian Name.*
JAM, *a Conserve of Fruits.*

Enough is good, excess is bad;
Yet Ichabod, you see,
Will with the jam his stomach cram,
Until they disagree.

K k.

KNOWING,
Conscious, Intelligent.

Tho' horses know both beans and corn,
And snuff them in the wind,
They also all know Jemmy Small,
And what he holds behind.

L l.

LUCKY,
Fortunate, Happy by Chance.

We must admire, in Lovebook's case.
The prompt decision made,
As he could not have gained the wood
If time had been delayed.

M m.

MIMIC.
Imitative, Burlesque.

The Gentleman, who struts so fine,
Unconscious seems to be
Of imitation by the boy
Who has the street-door key.

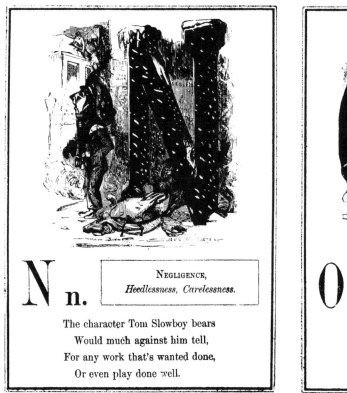

N n.

NEGLIGENCE,
Heedlessness, Carelessness.

The character Tom Slowboy bears
Would much against him tell,
For any work that's wanted done,
Or even play done well.

O o.

OBSTINACY,
Stubbornness, Waywardness.

The obstinacy of the pig
Is nature — as you see;
But boys and girls who have a mind
Should never stubborn be.

P p.

PETS,
Favorites, Spoilt Fondlings.

Some people say that Aunty Gray
To animals is kind;
We think, instead, they are over fed,
And kept too much confined.

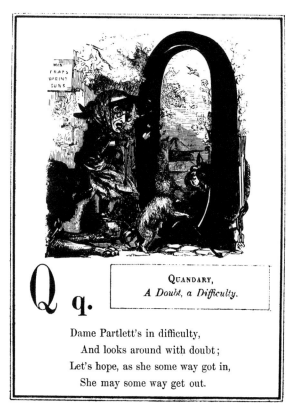

Q q.

QUANDARY,
A Doubt, a Difficulty.

Dame Partlett's in difficulty,
And looks around with doubt;
Let's hope, as she some way got in,
She may some way get out.

R r.

RIVALRY,
Competition, Emulation.

In every competition prize
This should be kept in view —
Whoever wins should be the one
Who does deserve it too.

S s.

SLUGGARD,
An Inactive, Lazy Fellow.

To lie so many hours in bed
You surely must be ill,
And need some physic, Master Ned,
As birch, or draught, or pill !

T t.

TOPSY-TURVY,
Upside Down, Bottom Top.

Here's Topsy-Turvy, upside down,
The ceiling seems the base ;
Reverse the ground and 'twill be found
The things are out of place.

U u. V v.

UNCOMMON VEGETATION.
UNCOMMON, *Rare, not Frequent.*
VEGETATION, *the Power of Growth.*

Th' uncommon vegetation, here,
With art has much to do ;
The trees are nature, but the fruit
Uncommon and untrue.

152

W w.

WONDER,
Admiration, Astonishment.

The wise may live and wonder still,
However much they know,
But simple Giles has wonder found
Within the penny show.

X x.

NO ENGLISH WORD BEGINS WITH THIS LETTER.

XANTIPPE,
A Greek Matron, Wife of Socrates.

Here's Socrates and Xantippe —
Philosopher and wife —
For gentleness renowned was he ;
She, better known for strife.

Y y.

YEARN,
To Grieve, to Vex.

Miss Cross has tried to reach the grapes,
She's tried and tried again —
And now she's vexed to think that all
Her efforts are in vain.

Z z.

ZANY,
A Buffoon, a Merry Andrew.

Here's Zany reading in a book,
With heels above his head ;
And, judging by his laughing look,
Finds fun in what he's read.

A a

An *Apple*, with its rosy cheek,
    We find a useful fruit.
An *Acorn*, planted in the ground,
    Will presently take root,
And, growing larger by degrees,
    Become a spreading tree ;
It is the very same with sin—
    How careful should we be !

B b

A *Boy* should gladly go to school,
    And learn to read and spell.
A *Bible* is the best of books,
    And he should read it well,
That he may know, with thankful heart,
    Forsaking sin and pride,
That Jesus Christ, the Son of God,
    For guilty sinners died.

C c

A useful creature is the *Cow*,
    Black, brindled, brown, or grey !
And *Corn*, the very staff of life,
    We feed on every day.
For every comfort we enjoy
    How grateful should we prove !
How gladly should we praise the Lord
    For all His care and love !

D d

How constant is the trusty *Dog* !
    How patient, brave, and good !
He guards the house, nor harms the *Duck*
    That comes to share his food.
Obedient still, with willing speed,
    He comes at every call ;
Oh, were *we* half as faithful found
    To Him who gives us all !

E e

The *Eels* that in the water swim,
    For food are very fine,
And new-laid *Eggs* are famous things
    To help a man to dine.
Whate'er we eat, whate'er we drink,
    To Him our praise should rise
Who spreads our table here below,
    And calls us to the skies.

F f

Let us be cheerful as the *Flower*,
    That sips the morning dew ;
But fearful as the timid *Fawn*,
    When sin appears in view.
And let us trust a Saviour's love,
    In trouble and in joy,
That we may find a lasting peace
    That nothing can destroy.

G g

The *Goat* climbs up the rocks and crags,
    And never is afraid.
Like *Grain*, before the reaper's hand,
    We all must droop and fade ;
Yet, if we trust a Saviour's love,
    No cause have we to fear,
For we shall mount to heaven above,
    And live for ever there.

H h

A *Helmet* is an iron hat,
    A *Hawk* a bird of prey ;
But God can safely guard my head,
    And drive my foes away ;
And He can pardon all my sins,
    And give me power to fly
Where angels wave their snowy wings,
    Above the starry sky.

I i

As black as *Ink* our sins abound,
    But God's almighty grace
Can soften hearts as cold as *Ice*
    With sunshine of His face :
Then let us pray the Lord of Life
    To melt our hearts of stone,
And write His law upon our minds,
    And mark us for His own.

J j

To well or spring we take the *Jug*
    For water every day,
And we may learn a lesson good
    From every chattering *Jay* ;
Cleanse thou, O Lord, my sinful heart,
    And keep my hand from wrong,
And lead me in Thy ways, and put
    A bridle on my tongue.

K k

The *Kite* flies high ! In purple robes
    The *King* and Queen are drest ;
But let me ever lowly live,
    With peace within my breast—
That peace which God alone can give—
    That, safe from sin and pride,
I may look up with joy, and trust
    In Jesus crucified.

L l

The *Lion* with the Lamb shall dwell,
    The *Leopard* with the kid,
And savage beasts no more shall do
    The deeds that once they did.
For why ? the Lord of life Himself
    Their fierceness shall destroy,
And reign through all the smiling earth
    In love, and peace, and joy.

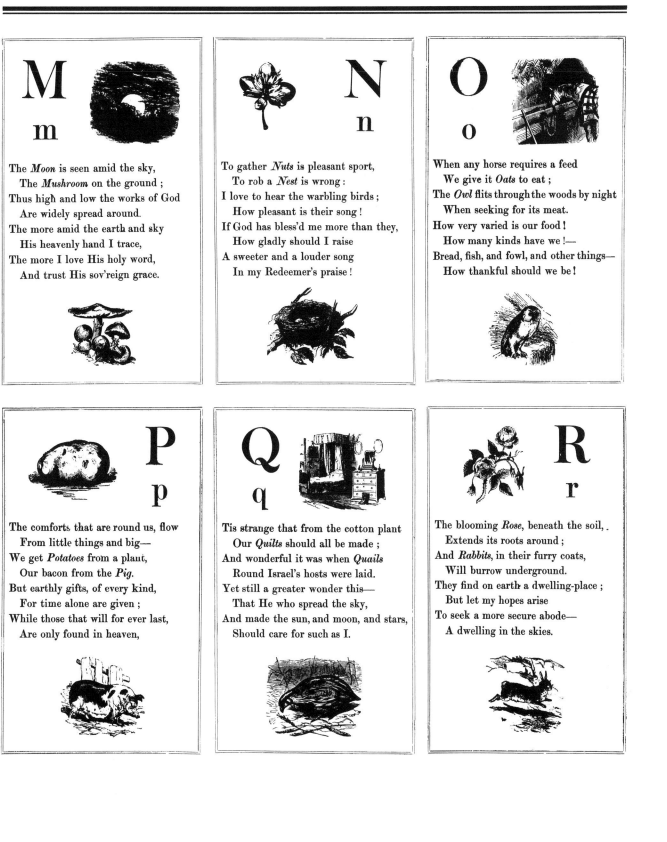

M m

The *Moon* is seen amid the sky,
　The *Mushroom* on the ground ;
Thus high and low the works of God
　Are widely spread around.
The more amid the earth and sky
　His heavenly hand I trace,
The more I love His holy word,
　And trust His sov'reign grace.

N n

To gather *Nuts* is pleasant sport,
　To rob a *Nest* is wrong :
I love to hear the warbling birds ;
　How pleasant is their song !
If God has bless'd me more than they,
　How gladly should I raise
A sweeter and a louder song
　In my Redeemer's praise !

O o

When any horse requires a feed
　We give it *Oats* to eat ;
The *Owl* flits through the woods by night
　When seeking for its meat.
How very varied is our food !
　How many kinds have we !—
Bread, fish, and fowl, and other things—
　How thankful should we be !

P p

The comforts that are round us, flow
　From little things and big—
We get *Potatoes* from a plant,
　Our bacon from the *Pig*.
But earthly gifts, of every kind,
　For time alone are given ;
While those that will for ever last,
　Are only found in heaven,

Q q

Tis strange that from the cotton plant
　Our *Quilts* should all be made ;
And wonderful it was when *Quails*
　Round Israel's hosts were laid.
Yet still a greater wonder this—
　That He who spread the sky,
And made the sun, and moon, and stars,
　Should care for such as I.

R r

The blooming *Rose*, beneath the soil,
　Extends its roots around ;
And *Rabbits*, in their furry coats,
　Will burrow underground.
They find on earth a dwelling-place ;
　But let my hopes arise
To seek a more secure abode—
　A dwelling in the skies.

S s

The *Ship* sails o'er the raging deep,
  Where *Shells* in beauty lie ;
And storms proclaim the mighty power
  Of Him who dwells on high.
The sea of life, by my frail bark,
  Alas! will soon be past ;
Oh, may we reach a happy port—
  A heavenly home—at last !

T t

The *Turk* within his *Tent*, bows down
  With face to Mecca's shrine ;
The Christian, with a humble heart,
  Turns to his Lord divine ;
And prays that all the world around
  May join in one accord
To know and fear, and love and serve,
  And magnify the Lord.

U u

Within the *Urn*, before the porch,
  The fair rose lifts its head ;
Umbrellas, when the storm comes on,
  Are o'er us widely spread.
Thus all the things on every side,
  That meet the roving eye,
Appear to be of use to man—
  Of what use, then, am I ?

V v

The *Vine's* rich clusters may be seen
  In many a pleasant spot ;
In *Villages* it twines its wreaths
  O'er many a lowly cot.
Oh, make me, Lord, a little branch !
  And, by Thy power divine,
Let me be grafted into Thee—
  The true and living Vine.

W w

The *Willows* o'er a *Waterfall*
  Are pleasant to the eye,
Their long green branches bending down
  Between us and the sky.
Oh, may I grow in Jesu's grace !
  And flourish here below
E'en like a goodly tree, that stands
  Where crystal waters flow.

X x

A *Xebeck* is a gallant ship
  That stems the ocean tide ;
And *Xerxes* was a mighty King
  That wept mid all his pride.
On land or ocean, rich or poor,
  Still humble let me be,
That every step I take, O Lord,
  May bring me nearer Thee.

Y y

The *Yew-tree* in the churchyard flings
  Its shadow o'er the grave ;
And with the *Yoke* the oxen till
  The fields where corn shall wave.
Prepare, O God, my stony heart,
  And make it, in Thy ways,
Yield fifty and a hundred-fold
  Of gratitude and praise.

Z z

Zaccheus climbed the Sycamore
  The Saviour's form to see ;
The *Zebra* o'er the desert flies—
  Swift, beautiful, and free ;
So let me fly, unfettered still
  By sin's deceitful snares,
And cast upon the Lord of life
  My sorrows and my cares.

The Beautiful A B C Book. Philadelphia: American Sunday School Union, in-scribed January 1, 1849. Pp. 27, including paper cover. 21 x 11.8 cm.

A stands for Ann and for anger too,
  That Ann's very angry is plain to the view.
In a fit of ill-temper she struck her young brother,
And grieved the fond heart of her kind gentle mother.

B stands for Ben Bounty, benevo-lent boy,
  To do good, is to Benny, his chief work and joy.
You here see him helping a poor, old, blind man,
For such he does always as much as he can.

C is for Clara who ne'er stops to look ;
  When she comes to a pond, or river, or brook,
Without waiting a minute, she dashes right in.
See ! she's now in the water quite up to her chin.

D is for Dicky, the dunce of the
    school,
    To have on the dunce cap, each
    day, seems his rule.
He never will study, likes better to play,
And his teacher now threatens to send him
    away.

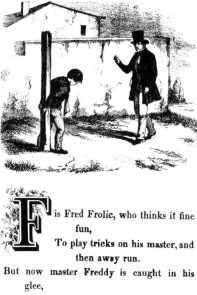

F is Fred Frolic, who thinks it fine
    fun,
    To play tricks on his master, and
    then away run.
But now master Freddy is caught in his
    glee,
And a trick has been played upon him, as you
    see.

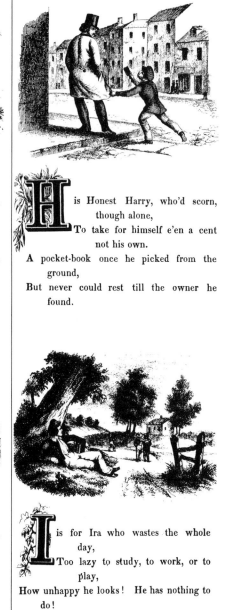

H is Honest Harry, who'd scorn,
    though alone,
    To take for himself e'en a cent
    not his own.
A pocket-book once he picked from the
    ground,
But never could rest till the owner he
    found.

E is Ellen Easy, good natured and
    mild,
    See how careless John Edwards her
    nice frock has spoiled.
"I'm sorry," said he, "that your clothes I
    have splashed."
"Never mind, John," said Ellen, "the frock
    can be washed."

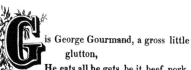

G is George Gourmand, a gross little
    glutton,
    He eats all he gets, be it beef, pork,
    or mutton;
He thinks of nought else by night, or by
    day.
He'll soon have a fit that will end him, folks
    say.

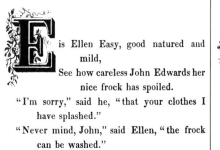

I is for Ira who wastes the whole
    day,
    Too lazy to study, to work, or to
    play,
How unhappy he looks! He has nothing to
    do!
I think that's the worst kind of business, don't
    you?

J is Jane Jealous, just see how she eyes
Little Julia, to whom has been given the prize!
Julia learned all her lessons, and sure I think 'twould be hard,
If such perseverance should lose its reward.

L is Laura who lies half the day
In bed, while her sisters at school are away.
Her mother declares when she rises so late,
No breakfast nor dinner, that day, will she get.

N is Nelly so neat, see how nicely she sews,
How neatly she mends her brother's torn clothes.
Little girls should learn early to hem, stitch, and fell,
And make themselves useful, like good little Nell.

K stands for Kit King, and stands also for kite,
To fly which, in the air, is Kit's greatest delight,
But see he's deserted by every school-mate,
For the school-bell has rung and Kit will be late.

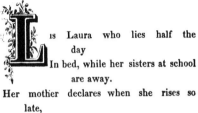

M is Miles Mann, and it is his delight,
To roam through the streets by day and by night,
But he's caught while he's breaking a pane with a stone,
And must spend all the night in the watch-house alone.

O stands for Orrin who quickly obeys,
And when sent of an errand, he never delays,
But goes to the place on a walk, jump, or run,
And hastens straight home when his errand is done.

P is Poll Prattle, whose tongue will
    not rest,
      And the neighbours all call her a
      talkative pest.
None can make her keep silent, or get in a
    word.
For shame Poll ! Such girls should be seen
    and not heard.

R is rude Richard, who made balls
    of snow,
      And pelted the girls as from
      school they did go.
And they all have declared that they'll leave
    school to-day,
Unless this rude boy is, at once, sent
    away.

T is Tom Takeit, who turned out a
    thief,
      He began it in childhood, ('tis my
      firm belief,)
By taking at school, a pen, pencil, or knife.
And now he is trying a prisoner's
    life.

Q is a queer boy, with many queer
    names,
      He quarrels at quoits and at all
      other games,
He is always disliked by the rest of the
    boys,
And wherever he is there is discord and
    noise.

S is Sue Selfish, the swing she has
    got,
      Though her friends wish to swing
      she will not move a jot,
And now they've determined to leave her
    alone ;
Pray who will then swing her when they
    are all gone?

U begins Useful, and useful you
    see
      Is this little Miss both at breakfast
      and tea,
No mother she has, yet she takes care of
    all,
Her father and brothers, and sisters so
    small.

V is Vain Jenny, with a new and gay hat,
And she thinks all the people are looking at that :
But indeed all the notice they take of her is,
To say, "what an ugly and vain little miss."

X stands for Xantippe for want of a better,
Her name's well begun with a very *cross* letter.
To her husband she proved a very bad wife,
And instead of a help, was the plague of his life.

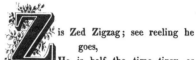Z is Zed Zigzag ; see reeling he goes,
He is half the time tipsy, as every one knows.
I've done when one word of advice I have said,
If you go with bad boys you may end like poor Zed.

W is Will Willful, who would have his own way,
And mounted the horse that was fast to the sleigh.
The horse started off with the boy on his back,
And poor master Will on his head came down, whack !

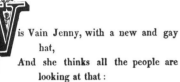Y is Young Yielding, who always says, Yes,
When tempted by those who warm friendship profess.
And now, with these boys, to the tavern he'll go.
It is wise, when thus tempted, to learn to say *No*.

162

My Pretty Verse Book. An Alphabet of Verses. London: The Religious Tract Society. Pp. 32 of text, and pp. 6 of colored plates. 18.2 x 13.8 cm.

MY PRETTY VERSE BOOK.

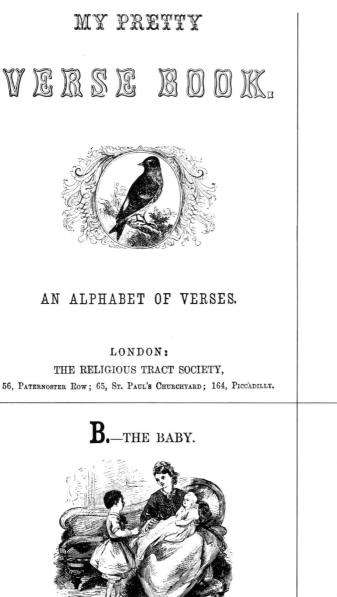

AN ALPHABET OF VERSES.

LONDON:

THE RELIGIOUS TRACT SOCIETY,

56, Paternoster Row; 65, St. Paul's Churchyard; 164, Piccadilly.

A.—THE ASS.

Poor Donkey! how I pity thee,
With burdens on thy back;
For whatsoe'er thy work may be,
Of woes thou hast no lack.

No lack of whip, no lack of stick,
Where'er poor donkey goes;
Thy skin, it should be very thick
To bear such heavy blows.

The dog may many a playmate find,
The cow in peace may be;
The horse may have a master kind,
But who is kind to thee?

Poor patient ass, thou art not fair,
Nor fleet of foot, nor wise,
Yet since thou didst my Saviour bear,
I will not thee despise.

B.—THE BABY.

Mamma, I wonder that you take
Such constant pains for baby's sake,
That you should feed and watch him so,
When all your love he cannot know.

And when I was a baby too,
Was I thus nurs'd and lov'd by you?
Mamma, I should remember still
How kind you were, and ever will.

Oh grant me, gracious God, I pray,
To be more dutiful each day,
To please mamma in all I do,
And keep her happiness in view.

C.—THE COW.

Come, children, listen to me now,
And you shall hear about the cow.
When Robert milks her morn and night,
She gives us *milk* so fresh and white;
And this, we little children think,
Is very nice for us to drink.

The curdled milk they press and squeeze,
And so they make it into *cheese*.
The cream they skim, and shake in churns,
And then it soon to *butter* turns.
When cow is dead, her flesh is good
For *beef*, which we may eat as food.

Then lime and bark the tanner takes,
And of her skin he *leather* makes;
And this we know they mostly use
To make us good strong boots and shoes;
And last of all, if cut with care,
Her horns make *combs* to comb our hair.
And so we learn, thanks to our teachers,
That cows are very useful creatures.

D.—THE DOG

I'll never hurt a little dog,
 But stroke and pat his head;
I like to see him wag his tail,
 I like to see him fed.

Then I will never whip my dog,
 Nor will I give him pain;
Poor fellow, I will give him food,
 And he'll love me again.

Dear little Tray, you're very good,
 And very useful too;
For do you know that he will mind
 What he is bid to do.

E.—THE EARTH.

Shaped like an orange or a ball,
 Our earth flies round the sun;
It does not turn aside at all,
 But ever onward runs.

Round the vast circle, once a year,
 It moves with rapid speed;
And thus the seasons all appear,
 And one by one recede.

These things, and many more as strange,
 We soon may better know,
Both in the lofty sky's wide range,
 And in the earth below.

Then since, in what God's hand has wrought,
 We can such wonders see,
How great and wise, beyond our thought,
 Must He who made them be!

F.—THE FOOLISH FISH.

"Dear mother," said a little fish,
 "Pray is not that a fly?
I'm very hungry, and I wish
 You'd let me go and try."

"Sweet innocent," the mother cried,
 And started from her nook,
"That horrid fly is meant to hide
 The sharpness of a hook."

Now, as I've heard, this little trout
 Was young and silly too,
And so he thought he'd venture out,
 To see what he could do.

And round about the fly he play'd,
 With many a longing look;
And often to himself he said,
 "I'm sure that's not a hook."

"I can but give one little pluck
 To try, and so I will."
So on he went, and lo, it stuck
 Quite through his little gill.

And as he faint and fainter grew,
 With hollow voice he cried,
"Dear mother, if I'd minded you,
 I should not thus have died."

G.—GREEN PASTURES.

I WALK'D in a field of fresh clover this morn,
Where lambs played so merrily under the trees,
Or rubb'd their soft coats on a naked old thorn,
Or nibbled the clover, or rested at ease.

And under the hedge ran a clear water-brook,
To drink from, when thirsty, or weary with play;
And so gay did the daisies and buttercups look,
That I thought little lambs must be happy all day.

And when I remember the beautiful psalm
That tells about Christ and his pastures so green;
I know he is willing to make me his lamb,
And happier far than the lambs I have seen.

If I drink of the waters, so peaceful and still,
That flow in his field, I for ever shall live;
If I love him, and seek his commands to fulfil,
A place in his sheepfold to me he will give.

The lambs are at peace in the fields when they play,
The long summer's day in contentment they spend;
But happier I, if in God's holy way
I try to walk always, with Christ for my Friend.

From "*Rhymes for My Children, by Mrs. Duncan.*" W. OLIPHANT and Co.,
Edinburgh.

H.—THE HEN.

THE hen, oh how fondly she cares for her brood!
She watches them always, provides them with
food,
Beneath her soft wings they are warm all the night,
To cherish and guard them is all her delight.

I love the kind bird who takes such great care,
And spreads out her wings to shelter them there,
And the dear little chicks that run there with
delight,
With cov'ring so downy, and soft eye so bright.

And this teaches a lesson I love too to learn,
For all that I see to instruction I turn;
The gracious Redeemer is watchful o'er me,
Though poor and quite young and unworthy
I be.

May He teach me to serve him, to trust him, and
love,
Then He still will protect me though reigning
above;
He'll guard me, and love me, and keep me from ill,
And though I'm unworthy, remember me still.

I.—WHAT AM I.

WHAT am I?—let me try to think:
The work of God am I;
Not merely born to eat and drink,
And, like the beasts, to die.

God made me for a higher end,
And wiser far than they;
To know and love him as my Friend,
And all his will obey.

For God his own dear Son once gave
To take my sins away;
And Jesus came to seek and save
The souls that went astray.

J.—JOHN DAY;

OR, "THOU, GOD, SEEST ME."

"No one will see me," said little John Day,
For his father and mother were out of the way,
And he was at home all alone.
"No one will see me," so he climb'd on a chair,
And peep'd in a cupboard to spy what was there,
Which of course he ought not to have done.

There stood in the cupboard, so sweet and so
nice,
A plate of plum cake, cut in many a slice,
"And apples so ripe and so fine.
Now no one will see me," said John to himself,
As he stretched out his arm to reach up to the
shelf—
"This apple, at least shall be mine."

John stopped, and put back the nice apple so red,
For he thought of the words his kind mother had
    said,
  When she left all these things in his care.
"And no one will see me," said he, "is not true,
For I've read that God sees us in all that we do,
  And is with us wherever we are."

Well done, John, your mother and father obey,
Try ever to please them and mind what they say,
  Even when they are absent from you;
And do not forget that though no one be nigh,
You never are out of the sight of God's eye,
  Who sees every thing that you do.

K.—THE KITE.

John White flew his kite one strong windy day,
A gale broke the tail, and it soon flew away.
And while he sat crying and sighing and sad,
Charley Gray came that way, a good-natured lad.
"Don't cry, wipe your eye," said he, "little Jack,
Stay here, never fear, and I'll soon bring it back.'
Up the tree climbed he, and brought the kite down;
"Many thanks, many thanks," said dear little
    John.

'Tis to sing a merry song
  To the pleasant morning light;
Why linger in my nest so long,
  When the sun is shining bright?
    Little infant this is why
    I sing so early in the sky.

To the little birds below,
  I do sing a merry tune;
And I let the ploughman know
  He must come to labour soon.
    Little infant this is why
    I am singing in the sky.

M.—THE MONTHS.

January brings the snow,
Makes our feet and fingers glow.
February brings the rain,
Thaws the frozen lake again.
March brings breezes loud and shrill,
Stirs the dancing daffodil.
April brings the primrose sweet;
Scatters daisies at our feet.
May brings flocks of pretty lambs,
Skipping by their fleecy dams.

L.—THE LITTLE LARK.

"I hear a pretty bird, but hark!
  I cannot see it any where;
Oh! it is a little lark,
  Singing in the morning air:
    Little lark, do tell me why
    You are singing in the sky?

June brings tulips, lilies, roses,
Fills the children's hands with posies.
Hot July brings cooling showers,
Apricots, and gilliflowers.
August brings the sheaves of corn,
Then the harvest home is borne.
Warm September brings the fruit,
Sportsmen then begin to shoot.
Fresh October brings the pheasant,
Then to gather nuts is pleasant.
Dull November brings the blast,
Then the leaves are whirling fast.
Chill December brings the sleet,
Blazing fire and Christmas treat.

N.—THE NEST.

WHO STOLE IT?

"To-whit! To-whit! To-whee!
Will you listen to me?
Who stole four eggs I laid,
And the nice nest I made?"

"Not I," said the cow. "Oh, no;
Such a thing I'd never do;
I gave you a wisp of hay,
But didn't take your nest away."

"Coo coo! said the dove,
I'll speak a word, my love;
Who stole that pretty nest
From a little red-breast?"

"Not I," said the sheep. "Oh no.
I wouldn't treat a poor bird so;
I gave wool the nest to line,
But the nest was none of mine."

"Caw! Caw!" cried the crow,
"I should like to know
What thief took away
A bird's nest to-day."

"Cluck! Cluck!" said the hen,
Don't ask me again!

Why I hav'n't a chick
Would do such a trick.
We all gave her a feather,
And she wove them together;
I'd scorn to intrude
On her and her brood."

"Chirr-a-whirr! Chirr-a-whirr!
We will make a great stir;
Let us find out his name,
And all cry, For shame!"

"I would not rob a bird,"
  Said little Mary Green;
"I think I never heard
  Of anything so mean."

" 'Tis very cruel, too,"
  Said little Alice Neal:
"I wonder if he knew
  How sad the bird would feel?"

A little boy hung down his head,
And hid his face so crimson red;
For HE stole that pretty nest
From little robin red-breast;
And he felt so full of shame,
I do not like to tell his name.

O.—THE ORANGE.

IN warmer climes than ours, we know,
God makes the oranges to grow,
And since not all are wanted there,
He kindly lets us have a share.

Go, now, sweet juicy orange, go
To yonder bed of pain and woe;
That poor sick child, in lowly cot,
The God of love has not forgot.

How good is God! how kind! how wise
Who all our wants each day supplies,
Sends good things to the rich man's door,
And to the dwellings of the poor.

P.—THE PET LAMB.

MY own pet lamb, I long to be
From envy, pride, and malice free;
Patient and mild and meek like thee,
      My own pet lamb.

I long to know my Shepherd's voice,
To make his pleasant ways my choice,
And in the fold like thee rejoice,
      My own pet lamb.

For me his tender care has spread
The word's pure milk, the living bread;
And there like thee I would be fed,
      My own pet lamb.

Q.—QUESTIONS AND AN ANSWER.

Who showed the little ant the way
    Her narrow hole to bore,
And spend the pleasant summer day
    In laying up her store?
The sparrow builds her clever nest
    Of wool and hay and moss;
Who told her how to weave it best,
    And lay the twigs across?
Who taught the busy bee to fly
    Among the sweetest flowers,
And lay his feast of honey by,
    To eat in winter hours?
'Twas God who showed them all the way,
    And gave their little skill;
And teaches children, if they pray,
    To do his holy will.

Faithful Robin Redbreast!
    With returning spring
Soon the birds will come again
    To glitter or to sing.
But, though some have gayer coats,
    Some a sweeter song,
You, friend Robin, stay with us
    All the winter long.

Come, then, Robin Redbreast,
    For you need not fear;
No rude boy is standing by,
    No sly pussy near.
Come nearer to the doorway, friend,
    For safely you may come:
There, eat your fill and take besides
    A tiny morsel home.

R.—ROBIN REDBREAST.

Pretty Robin Redbreast,
    Hopping in the snow,
Why are you so early here,
    I should like to know?
Did Mrs. Redbreast send you, pray,
    To get a dainty crumb,
And bid you bring your little ones
    A tiny morsel home?

S.—THE STARS.

What are those stars that shine on high,
    Which oft by night I view,
Like little holes bored in the sky,
    To let the glory through?
Those stars, though little in our sight,
    Are worlds which God has made;
He makes them shine so clear and bright
    In the dark evening shade.
I wonder much that eyes like mine
    Those starry worlds can see;
Great God! it was thy power Divine
    That made both them and me.

T.—TIT FOR TAT.

Children, as we sometimes see,
Don't agree, don't agree;
They fall out I grieve to say,
    In their hours of play.
One offends, and soon we learn,
He's offended in his turn;
And they say that tit for tat
    Is the rule for that.

Children, why such anger show?
Don't you know, don't you know,
You should not this rule obey?
　There's a better way.
If each should in turn offend,
Then would quarrels never end;
There's a better way than that,
　Or than tit for tat.

Though indeed it was unkind,
Never mind, never mind;
You should bear a little pain,
　So be friends again.
Those who in this world would live,
Must forget, and must forgive;
Bear these trifles like a man,
　That's the better plan.

U.—UP! UP!

Up! Up! little sister, the morning is bright,
And the birds are all singing to welcome the
　　light;
The buds are all opening; the dew's on the
　　flower;
If you shake but a branch, see there falls quite
　a shower.

The bee, I dare say, has been long on the wing,
Getting honey from every bright flower of Spring,
For the bee never idles, but labours all day,
And thinks, that it's better to work than to
　play.

The lark's singing gaily; it loves the bright sun,
And rejoices that now the gay Spring is begun;
For the Spring is so cheerful, I think 'twould be
　wrong
If we did not feel happy to hear the lark's song.

Get up; for when all things are merry and glad,
Good children should never be lazy and sad;
For God gives us daylight, dear sister, that we
May rejoice like the lark, and may work like the
　bee.

V.—THE VIOLET.

When April's warmth, unlocks the clod,
　Softened by gentle showers,
The violet pierces through the sod,
　And blossoms, first of flowers
So may I give my heart to God
　In childhood's early hours.

Some plants, in gardens only found,
　Are raised with pains and care;

God scatters violets all around,
　They blossom everywhere;
Thus may my love to *all* abound,
　And all my fragrance share.

Some scentless flowers stand straight and high,
　As signs of haughtiness;
But violets perfume land and sky,
　Although they promise less.
Let me, with all humility,
　Do more than I profess.

Sweet flower, be thou a type to me
　Of blameless joy and mirth,
Of widely scattered sympathy
　Embracing all God's earth,
Of early blooming piety,
　And unpretending worth.

W.—WORK AND PLAY.

Work while you work, and play while you play,
That is the way to be cheerful and gay.
All that you do, do with your might;
Things done by halves are never done right.

One thing at a time, and that one done well,
Is a very good rule, as many can tell.
Moments are useless if trifled away;
So work while you work, and play while you
    play.

X.—EXAMPLES OF EARLY PIETY.

What blest examples do I find
    Writ in the word of truth,
Of children that began to mind
    Religion in their youth!

Jesus, who reigns above the sky,
    And keeps the world in awe,
Was once a child as young as I,
    And kept his Father's law.

At twelve years old he talked with men,
    (The Jews all wondering stand;)
Yet he obeyed his mother then,
    And came at her command.

Samuel the child was weaned and brought
    To wait upon the Lord:
Young Timothy betimes was taught
    To know his holy word.

Then why should I so long delay
    What others learned so soon?
I would not pass another day
    Without this work begun.

Y.—YOUTHFUL PILGRIMS FROM HEATHEN LANDS.

Who are ye whose little feet,
    Pacing life's dark journey through,
Now have reach'd that heavenly seat,
    You had ever kept in view?
"I from Greenland's frozen land;"
    "I from India's sultry plain;"
"I from Afric's barren sand;"
    "I from islands of the main."

All their earthly journey past,
    Every tear and pain gone by,
Here together met at last,
    At the portal of the sky;
Each the welcome "come" awaits,
    Conquerors over death and sin.
Lift your heads, ye golden gates!
    Let the little travellers in.

Z.—ZION THE BEAUTIFUL.

Beautiful Zion, built above;
    Beautiful city that I love;
Beautiful trees for ever there;
    Beautiful fruits they always bear

Beautiful heaven where all is light;
    Beautiful angels clothed in white;
Beautiful robes the ransom'd wear;
    Beautiful all who enter there.

PRAYER FOR THE HOLY SPIRIT.

Come, Holy Spirit, come;
    O hear an infant's prayer;
Stoop down and make my heart thy home,
    And shed thy blessing there.

Thy light, thy love impart,
    And let it ever be
A holy, humble, happy heart,
    A dwelling place for thee.

LONDON: PRINTED BY WILLIAM CLOWES AND SONS, STAMFORD STREET, AND CHARING CROSS.

"Alphabet House" (13 pp., including 6 colored plates), from *The Toy Book Present*. Twenty-four Coloured Engravings. Plates by Kronheim. London: The Religious Tract Society, [1868]. 27 x 33 cm.

A-pply thine heart unto instruction. Prov. xxiii. 12.

C-reate in me a clean heart, O God. Psalm li. 10.

D-epart from evil, and do good. Psalm xxxiv. 14.

TWENTY-SIX little Letters, on pleasure intent,
At Alphabet House a holiday spent:
Observe now, and see in what order they went.

Their leader was A: then B C D E,
F G H and I J, K L M N O P:
Then Q, and then R, then S, and then T:

Next U V and W did their way wend,
And X Y and Z came up at the end:
Now learn to repeat them, my dear little friend.

S. H. O. U. T. with delight gave a SHOUT,
As, quick with permission dispersing about,
Amusement they sought within doors and out.

B-e not wise in thine own eyes. Prov. iii. 7.

E-nter ye in at the strait gate. Matt. vii. 13.

G-rieve not the Holy Spirit of God. Eph. iv. 3.

H-onour thy father and thy mother. Exodus xx. 12.

A in the garden a large Apple found,
Ripe, red, and rosy it lay on the ground;
A first divided, then handed it round.

B watched the Bees, all the summer day long
Busy the sweet honied flowers among,
Filling the air with their soft droning song.

C stroked the Cat as it slept in the sun,
C never sleeps till her lessons are done;
Puss is but Puss, and tasks she has none.

D called the Dog: in his kennel he lay,
But readily came at the summons to play;
Are *we* always willing and quick to obey?

F-ear God and keep his commandments. Ecc. xii. 13.

I love them that love Me. Prov. viii. 17.

E fetched the Eggs—three, two, five—making
ten;
One from the nest of a favourite hen
She begged, as a gift for sick little Ben.

F fed the Fowls : how eager they came
Clucking for food : it would fill me with shame
If children, forgetting themselves, did the same.

G heard a Goat bleat; and turning around,
Billy himself by the gateway he found :
Bill tossed his head and was off with a bound.

H saw the Horse, and he asked leave to ride;
Harry good-naturedly put him astride,
And round the wide meadow kept close to his side.

K-nock, and it shall be opened unto you. Matt. vii. 7.

L-ike as a father pitieth his children, so the Lord pitieth them that fear him. PSALM CIII. 13.

J-esus said, Suffer little children to come unto Me. LUKE XVIII. 16.

M-y son, give Me thine heart. Prov. xxiii. 26.

I pulled the Ivy which round the tree twined,
To make a green garland, whilst **J** sought to find
A Jackdaw which flew to the thicket behind.

K saw the Kine in the meadows, and learned
How the sweet milk to cheese could be turned,
Cream making butter if properly churned.

L loved the Lambs, how pretty their play !
Oh, to be gentle and harmless as they,
Happy and innocent all the long day !

M saw the Mole, with fur black as night :
It works under ground with scarce any sight,
Better than many who work in the light !

O-h, that thou wouldest bless me indeed ! 1 Chron. iv. 10.

P-raise the Lord; for the Lord is Good. Psalm cxxxv. 3.

N-ow is the day of salvation. 2 Cor. vi. 2.

S-eek ye the Lord while he may be found. Isaiah lv. 6.

T-hose that seek Me early shall find me. Prov. viii. 17.

N and **O** at dessert Nuts and Oranges sought;
When asked to take more, had enough as they
     thought,
And said "N O" with a "thank you," as little
     folks ought.

P heard the Parrot say, "How do you do?"
P said, "I'm wiser, Miss Polly, than you;
I know the words, and their *meaning* too!"

In the library **Q** saw a bust of the Queen:
"Hats off!" said Q. "If," said **R,** "we had seen
Her real in her Robes, how pleased we had been!"

S found the Scriptures; and happy was he
To read the sweet words from the book on his knee,
"Forbid not the children to come unto **ME**."

R-emember now thy Creator in the days of thy youth.
ECCLES XII. 1.

W-ash me, and I shall be whiter than snow. Psalm li. 7.

Z-ealous of good works. TITUS II. 14.

Y-e are bought with a price. 1 COR. VI. 20.

T asked the Time. Ah, soon home they must go;
Swiftly the pendulum moves to and fro,
Time waits for no one, as wise people know.

U, who was Useful, to help and to learn,
Ran to the kitchen, and bringing the Urn,
Tea and plum cake all partook of in turn.

V from the Vine gathered grapes for a treat;
W walked the large Waggon to meet;
And with full hands and hearts each took his seat.

X, Y, and **Z,** were sorry that they
Had found little to see, to hear, or to say;
But hoped to do better the next holiday.

*V-erily, verily, I say unto you, he that believeth on Me hath
everlasting life.* John vi. 47.

Grandmamma Easy's New Pictorial Bible Alphabet. London: Dean & Co. Pp. [8], hand-colored. 24 x 16.8 cm.

173

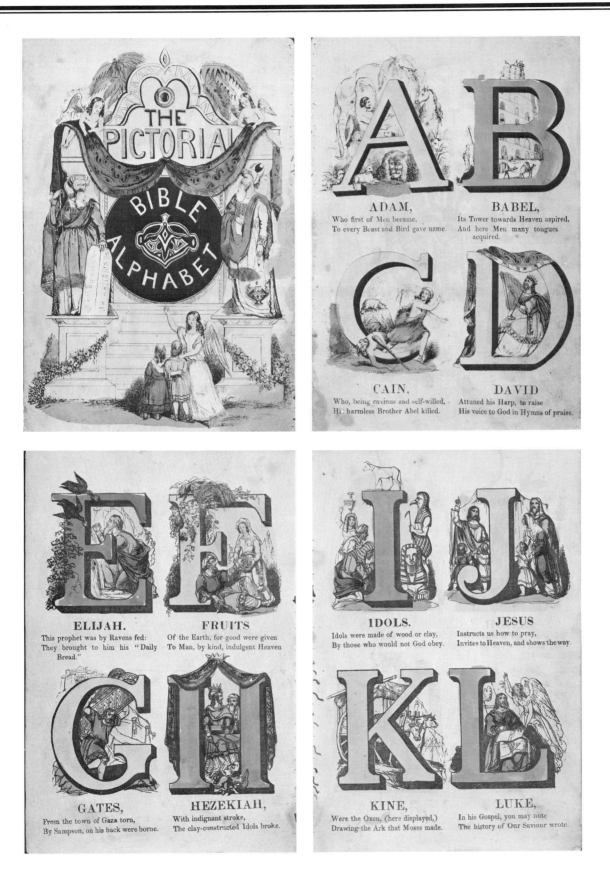

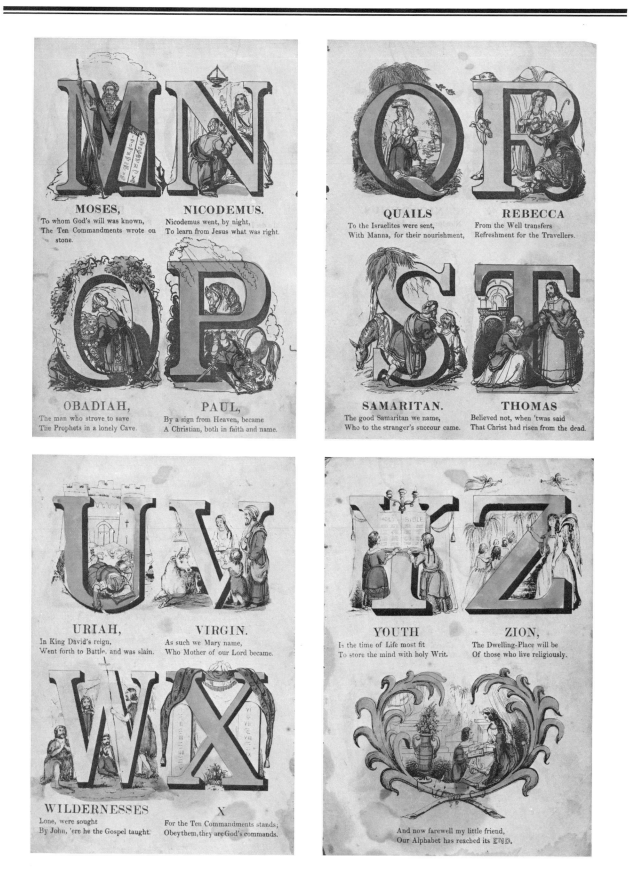

MOSES,
To whom God's will was known,
The Ten Commandments wrote on
stone.

NICODEMUS.
Nicodemus went, by night,
To learn from Jesus what was right.

OBADIAH,
The man who strove to save
The Prophets in a lonely Cave.

PAUL,
By a sign from Heaven, became
A Christian, both in faith and name.

QUAILS
To the Israelites were sent,
With Manna, for their nourishment,

REBECCA
From the Well transfers
Refreshment for the Travellers.

SAMARITAN.
The good Samaritan we name,
Who to the stranger's succour came.

THOMAS
Believed not, when 'twas said
That Christ had risen from the dead.

URIAH,
In King David's reign,
Went forth to Battle, and was slain.

VIRGIN.
As such we Mary name,
Who Mother of our Lord became.

WILDERNESSES
Lone, were sought
By John, 'ere he the Gospel taught.

X
For the Ten Commandments stands;
Obey them, they are God's commands.

YOUTH
Is the time of Life most fit
To store the mind with holy Writ.

ZION,
The Dwelling-Place will be
Of those who live religiously.

And now farewell my little friend,
Our Alphabet has reached its END.

''The Alphabet'' (52 pp.), from *Our Baby's Bible Alphabet.* Charmingly Written by Aunt Charlotte. With Original Drawings by George Spiel. Juvenile Publishing Co., Copyright 1899 by K. E. Boland. 24.5 x 17 cm.

OUR BABY'S

BIBLE ALPHABET

CHARMINGLY WRITTEN
BY
AUNT CHARLOTTE

"Train up a child in the way he should go; and when he is old, he will not depart from it."
—PROVERBS xxii, 6.

WITH ORIGINAL DRAWINGS
BY
GEORGE SPIEL

COPYRIGHT 1899, BY K. E. BOLAND

JUVENILE PUBLISHING CO.

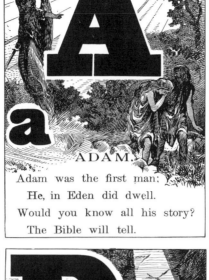

ADAM.

Adam was the first man;
  He, in Eden did dwell.
Would you know all his story?
  The Bible will tell.

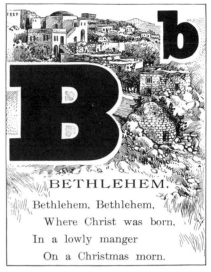

BETHLEHEM.

Bethlehem, Bethlehem,
  Where Christ was born,
In a lowly manger
  On a Christmas morn.

CHRIST.

Christ, the loving Savior,
  Who died that we might live;
To all the little children,
  His blessing he did give.

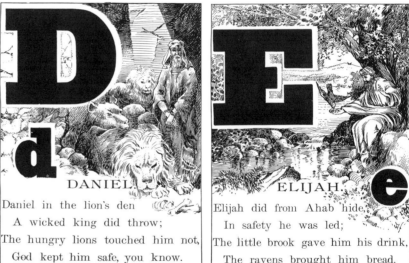

DANIEL.

Daniel in the lion's den
  A wicked king did throw;
The hungry lions touched him not,
  God kept him safe, you know.

ELIJAH.

Elijah did from Ahab hide,
  In safety he was led;
The little brook gave him his drink,
  The ravens brought him bread.

FELIX.

Felix heard the words of Paul,
  And he was badly scared;
For he had been a wicked man,
  God's teachings he had dared.

GOLIATH.

Goliath said to great King Saul,
  "I'll meet your troops alone."
But David took his trusty sling
  And slew him with a stone.

HEROD.

Herod was a wicked king
  Who told his soldier's bold,
That Christ must die and they must kill
  All baby boys not two years old.

ISAAC.

Isaac was on the altar placed,
  Abraham's love of God to test,
When an angel came from heaven above
  Made Isaac free, his father blest.

JOSEPH.

Joseph to some merchantmen
  Was by his brothers sold;
They dipped his coat in blood of goat
  And there a lie they told.

KEZIAH.

Keziah was a lovely maid,
  Fairest of all to see
In all the land both far and near;
  Daughter of Job was she.

LOT.

Lot's wife from Sodom driven out,
  Her God she disobeyed;
She looked back once upon her home
  And into salt was made.

MOSES.

Moses in the rushes hidden
  And found there by a maid,
Wrote ten great laws on slabs of stone,
  That God might be obeyed.

NOAH.

Noah built an ark of wood,
  And when the waters came,
Kept safe all creatures God had made
  Until the flood had gone.

OBEDIENCE.

Obedience, a word that God
  Would have his children guard;
In life it makes our pathway bright,
  In death it brings reward.

PETER.

Peter lay bound in prison walls,
  "Rise up and follow me,"
An angel from the Lord did cry,
  "Come forth! I'll set you free."

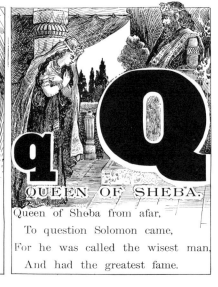

QUEEN OF SHEBA.

Queen of Sheba from afar,
  To question Solomon came,
For he was called the wisest man,
  And had the greatest fame.

RUTH.

Ruth, sweet maid in Moab dwelt,
And gleaned the fields of wheat.
Blessed was she by Boaz rich
While kneeling at his feet.

SAMSON.

Samson was the strongest man,
The lion fierce he fought;
He tore the mighty pillars loose,
And great destruction wrought.

THOMAS.

Thomas doubted the power of Christ,
His love could not perceive;
But Jesus spoke of faith in God,
And Thomas did believe.

URIAH.

Uriah was a soldier bold,
In war was very brave;
To serve his king in war for right
His life he freely gave.

VIRGIN MARY.

The Virgin in a manger low,
Gave birth to Christ the King;
"Peace on earth, good will to men,"
The angels loud did sing.

WANDERER.

Wanderer and prodigal
Who far away did roam;
His father did a feast prepare
When he at last came home.

XODUS.

'Xodus tells the story well,
As you can plainly see,
How God did lead the Israelites
All safely through the sea.

YOUNG CHILDREN.

Young children dear, to whom Christ
"Suffer them all to come,   said,
Of such the kingdom of heaven is,"
Let will of God be done.

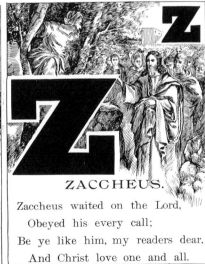

ZACCHEUS.

Zaccheus waited on the Lord,
Obeyed his every call;
Be ye like him, my readers dear,
And Christ love one and all.

The Christian Alphabet, Illustrating the Leading Facts Recorded in the New Testament. Baltimore: Fielding Lucas, Jr.; Philadelphia: Ash & Mason, Juvenile Emporium. Pp. [13], hand-colored. 17 x 11 cm.

Matt. Ch. 2 V. 13.

An angel thus to Joseph said,
To Egypt flee, till Herods' dead.

Matt. Ch. 27 V. 19.

Dreams from above made Pilates wife,
Petition for the Saviour's life.

John Ch. 5 V. 4.

Bethesda's bath still failed to save,
Unless an angel blessd the wave.

Luke Ch. 9 V. 13.

Emanuel with the Apostles talk'd,
As they towards Emmaus walk'd.

Matt. Ch. 4 V. 3.

Christ thrice was tempted but in vain,
Satan o'er him, no power could gain.

Matt. Ch. 26 V. 39.

Father, this cup pass from thy son,
Yet not my will, but thine be done.

Gold when misused will surely lead,
The prodigal with swine to feed

Herod, the children killed in vain,
In hopes to have the Saviour slain.

Judas Iscariot, as we're told,
Betray'd his Lord for sums of Gold.

King of the Jews, in scorn they cried,
When on the cross our **SAVIOUR** died.

Lazarus was rescued from the grave,
And shewed Christ's mighty power to save.

Millstones were cast into the sea,
To shew what bad mens fate would be.

New hopes in all the nation's smil'd,
When Christ appeared, a little child.

Luke. Ch. 2 V 27.

Quickly the leper who beleives,
And asks; from Christ new health receives.

Mark. Ch. 1 V 41.

Ocean could smooth its stormiest wave,
When Christ, his servants came to save.

Matt. Ch. 14 V 31.

Riches a curse are, misapplied,
So Dives found them when he died.

Luke Ch. 16 V 23.

Poor penitents who humbly pray,
The Lord will never send away.

Luke. Ch. 18 V 13.

Samaritan! thou good and kind,
In thee the wounded, comfort find.

Luke Ch. 10 V. 33.

Matt. Ch. 27 V. 29.

Thorns on his precious head they place,
And mock their Saviour to his face.

Rom. Ch. 1 V. 22.

Xenophon wise in the heathen school,
Was in true wisdom but a fool.

John Ch. 14 V. 27.

Union, said Christ, and peace I have,
I give not as the world doth give.

Matt. Ch. 19 V. 21.

"**Y**oung man" said Christ if thou wouldst be
Sav'd, now sell all and follow me.

John Ch. 4 V. 7.

Wonders strange our Lord did tell,
This Woman at Samarias well.

Luke Ch. 1 V. 40.

Zacharia's house was told,
What all the world should soon behold.

"Alphabet of the New Testament" (12 pp., including 6 colored plates), from *Routledge's Scripture Gift Book,* Containing Alphabet of the Old Testament, Alphabet of the New Testament, History of Joseph, History of Moses. With Ninety-Six Illustrations, Printed in Colours by Leighton. London and New York: George Routledge and Sons, [1866]. 27.5 x 23 cm.

Agabus took Paul's girdle, and bound both his hands and feet,

And said, " Thus will the Jews the owner of this girdle treat,

If to Jerusalem he goes, the brethren to meet."

Blind Bartimæus sat and begged, beside the great highway ;

But when he heard that Christ was come, he cried aloud to say,

" Thou Son of David hear me!" The Lord gave him sight that day.

Cornelius, the Centurion, was in a vision told

To send for Peter, who would all the truth of God unfold.

Dorcas spent time in charity, the poor and hungry fed,

Made clothing for the orphans, and gave the widows bread.

Elymas, who with wicked words the Apostles would withstand,

Was struck with blindness, and ask'd who would lead him by the hand.

Felix, the Roman Governor, before whom Paul was brought,

Trembled to hear the holy truth that the Apostle taught.

Good Samaritan indeed was he, who stopped upon his way,

To help the wounded traveller, who bruised and senseless lay ;

Then gently took him to an inn, and his account would pay.

Herodias, whose DAUGHTER danced before that evil King,

Herod the Tetrarch, who had sworn to grant her anything,

Demanded that John Baptist's head they in a dish should bring.

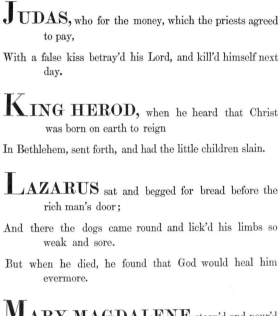

JUDAS, who for the money, which the priests agreed to pay,

With a false kiss betray'd his Lord, and kill'd himself next day.

KING HEROD, when he heard that Christ was born on earth to reign

In Bethlehem, sent forth, and had the little children slain.

LAZARUS sat and begged for bread before the rich man's door;

And there the dogs came round and lick'd his limbs so weak and sore.

But when he died, he found that God would heal him evermore.

MARY MAGDALENE stoop'd and pour'd upon the Saviour's feet,

From a box of alabaster, precious ointment fresh and sweet.

NICODEMUS, Ruler of the Jews, to Jesus came by night,

To listen to the blessed words that fill'd his soul with light.

ONESIMUS was he who came from Paul to Philemon;

The great Apostle wrote to say he' loved him as a son.

PAUL, wreck'd upon a foreign coast and in a savage land,

Lighted a fire, when suddenly there fasten'd on his hand

A viper; yet the people there unhurt did see him stand.

QUEEN BERNICE with King Agrippa came to Cæsarea,

And there, within the judgment hall, they sent for Paul, to hear

The things which that Apostle taught without a sign of fear.

RHODA, who stood and listen'd to the knocking at the gate,

Knew the Apostle Peter's voice; but left him there to wait,

While joyfully she told, that he'd escaped from Herod's hate.

SIMEON, a holy man, who pray'd and waited for God's grace,

Was told that he should live to see the Saviour of his race:

How joyfully he look'd upon the infant Jesus' face.

TERTULLUS was the orator, who before Felix sought

The life of Paul, and urged that he should be to judgment brought.

VIRGIN most pure and holy was the mother of our Lord,

And in that manger lowly Kings and Wise Men adored

The Christ, who came that sinful man to God should be restored.

WOMAN OF SAMARIA was she who at the well

Listen'd with wonder to the things that Jesus had to tell.

X is a cross, and by the cross our blessed Saviour died.

That we might come to God and live, our life He sanctified.

YOUNG, good, and wealthy, was a man who came the Lord to see,

And asked, "What shall I do that I in Heaven may live with Thee?"

Then Christ, who loved him, said:—"Leave all, and come and follow me."

ZACCHÆUS was the publican who, running on before

That he might look on Jesus, climb'd up a sycamore.

The Illustrated Alphabet of Scripture History, with Morning and Evening Prayers and Hymns for Children. Boston: Published by J. H. Abbott, [ca. 1852]. Pp. [26], partially poorly colored. 18 x 13.5 cm. [illustrated alphabet]

The Illuminated Scriptural Alphabet. Baltimore: J. B. Keller; Philadelphia: R. Magee. Pp. [26], hand-colored accordion pages. 13.8 x 8.8 cm. [text of alphabet]

ADAM, from the dust did God create,
To dwell in Eden's bowers, in blissful state;
But Sin—a serpent we should ever shun,—
Poisoned a life so happily begun.

BENJAMIN'S cup was found, it is true,
In the mouth of his sack, and the gold with it, too;
But poor little Ben, though in very great grief,
Had this joy to sustain him—he wans't a thief.

CAIN was a man of wild passions, 'tis said;
Abel was gentle as the lambs that he led:
They were brothers; but Cain very envious grew
Of his dear gentle brother, whom he wickedly
slew.

A. A dan the first man, full plainly we vie,

Praying to Gd, as good men ought to do.

B. Was young Benjamin, happy and free,

Till the cup was discovered, as thus we may see.

C, Is for Cain, who his brother did kill, Who bore him the kindest of brotherly will.

DANIEL refused to obey the decree
Of a king, who commanded that God should not be
In worship bowed down to. The king threw him, then,
All defenceless, he thought, in the wild lion's den.
But the God whom he worshipped was with him to save
From the wrath of *two* kings,—king beast and king knave.

EVE of the fruit of all trees might make food
In the garden, save one, that of *Evil* and *Good*.
And the snake that we read of is the very same
devil
That tempted poor Eve, and that tempts us to evil.

A FROG is a very small, mean-looking thing;
But here are some frogs that once frightened a
king!
So despise not God's creatures however lowly
their fate,—
Fer an army of frogs conquered Egypt the great.

D. Gives us Daniel, most holy of men, Whom God saved from death in the wild Lion's den.

E. Is for Eve, as the picture we give, Created, we're told, from Adam's own rib.

F, For the Frogs that got frisking about,

A plague to all Egypt there can't be a doubt.

GOLIAH, a giant of terrible size,
Clad in armor, all up from the feet to the eyes,
Met in battle young David, who was afterwards
    King,
With no armor but Faith—yet a very good thing,
For by this, David slew him with a stone from a
    sling.

G. For Goliah, on Israel's plain,
    By David the valiant, was certain-
ly slain.

HAGAR—poor Hagar, in agony wild,
Prays for some water to give her dear child ;
And God, who is ever a hearer of prayer,
Sends his angel to save in the hour of despair.

H. Is poor Hagar in agony wild,
    Who prays for the water to save
her poor child.

ISAAC, no murmur escaping him, laid,
At the word of his father, his neck 'neath the blade ;
And that father, the Father of life to obey,
Raised his arm his dearly beloved to slay.
Thus a lesson of two-fold   obedience was taught,
Ere the ram that we see in the thicket was caught.

I. Is for Isaac, the meek little boy,
    Who Abraham in faith, was about to
destroy.

JACOB, journeying, prayerful, friendless. lone,
Pillows, to sleep, his head upon a stone.
God sends, to comfort him, in dream of even,
Angels on ladder, reaching down from heaven.

J. Is for Jacob, whose wonderous
    dream,
Saw Angels ascending to Heaven, 'twould
seem.

KING !—The people of Israel asked for a king :
God told them they asked for a very bad thing.
But they still sought a king, to be "like other
    nations ;"
So the Lord let them follow this silliest of fashions.

K, Is King Saul, first king of the land,
    To whom David played at his
royal command.

'LOT, from Sodom escape ! with your family, fly !
Ere the judgment of God pours down from the
    sky.
Escape for your lives ! neither look back nor halt !'
Mrs. Lot did look back, and was turned into salt.

L, May be Lot, whose wife looking
    behind,
Turn'd all into salt, in scripture we find.

MOSES, early saved from death by water,
By God's kind care thro' Pharaoh's daughter,
By strange coincidence, from water saves
The hosts whom Pharaoh drove into the waves;
And when again he led them as a flock,
Their lives he saved by water from the rock.

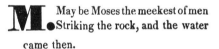

M. May be Moses the meekest of men
Striking the rock, and the water
came then.

NOAH, who by faith saw the fierce deluge pour,
Was 40 years building his ark for that hour
Tho' oftentimes mocked, yet his faith stood the
shock,
As his ark stood the waves. 'Tis sinful to mock.

N. Was old Noah, whose ark carried
him
O'er the wide waters deep, where no other
could swim.

OG, King of Bashan, a proud remnant—the last,
Of those wonderful giants whose deeds fill the
past,
Slept on bedstead of iron, full nine cubits long,
And four cubits wide, which, like him, was made
strong.
But, said Israel, "O giant! thy strength we defy!"
And they conquered King Og at the field
Ed-re-i.

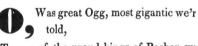

O, Was great Ogg, most gigantic we'r
told,
To one of the proud kings of Bashan w:
sold.

PHAROAH God's people to the sea pursued,
With armed bands, in proud and vengeful mood;
The sea, obedient to the prophet's rod,
Received and bore them thro' a path, dry shod.
Onward rushed Pharoah, with his raging host,—
The waves enveloped them, and all were lost.

 P. Was King Pharaoh, whose host as
we see,
Were every one drowned in the ruffled
Red Sea.

QUEEN ESTHER grieves—in Shushan's palace
mourns:
At Haman's plot her indignation burns.
Heroic virtue pleads against despair,
And wins the day—as heaven is won—by prayer.

Q. Was Queen Esther, who pleaded
so well,
She gained all her wish, as the scripture
will tell.

RUTH loved Naomi—would not leave her lone—
But Orpa, like the world, wept—kissed—was
gone!
The Lord a recompense in full bestowed:
She reaps (not gleans) what her kind heart hath
sowed.

R. Begins Ruth, whose good fortune
it was,
to glean in the field, and be succoured by
Boaz.

SAMSON swerves not from his path
To avoid a lion's wrath.
Nor from duties e'er should we,—
Though beset by lions!—flee.

TRUMPETS no uncertain strain
E'er should sound on battle plain.
Not such blast as that, I trow,
Crushed the walls of Jericho.
Nor uncertain shall that be—
The last that sounds—to thee and me.

URIAH'S murder such sad wrongs portray,
As mark sin's progress to our later day.
As oaks from acorns, from small errors grow,
Theft, intrigue, murder—all the train of woe.

S May be Samson, of power and skill,
Who parted the jaws, and the lion did kill.

T Is the Trumpet, to battle that calls,
And threw into fragments great Jericho's walls.

U Is Uriah, in hard battle slain,
He fought, but his courage and skill were in vain.

VASHTI, fearless, yet afraid, kept the law, yet disobeyed;
For, by law the Persian claims strangers shall not see his dames.
But this law the king, besotted deep in wine, most like forgot it;
So he sent his little eunuch, in white pants and yellow tunic,
To command his royal spouse to attend the night's carouse.
Vashti disobeyed most queenly—and was banished—oh, how
    meanly!

WIZARD or witch, of Endor as of Eld,
Have from society been long expelled;
But Endor's witch prophetic visions read,
And Samuel prophesied when he was dead.
From the dead prophet's lips the ears of Saul
Received death's summons, and obeyed the call.

XERXES, Persia's King, on slaughter
Bent,—as kings, we know, were wont,
Bridges built, to cross the water
Of the far-famed Helespont.
In barbaric pomp and splendor,
Poured his legions into Greece:
Greece had heroes to defend her—
Witness thou, O Salamis!

V Vashti, a Queen of Persia so bright,
Was driven away from her robes of light.

W The old Witch of Endor, is this, as we find,
Raising Samuel to Saul, and disclosing mankind.

X Is for Xerxes, the Scriptures you search,
Honour thy parents, and reverence the Church.

YOUTH should present reverence show
To the youth of long ago !
For yon form in life's decline
Once was young and bright as thine.

The children mocked : the prophet's prayer
Consigned them to the hungry bear.

ZACHARIAH, a prophet of old,
Talks with an angel at night ; and behold,
Riding upon a red horse, in his sight,
A man, and behind, horses speckled and white.
Of visions, and omens, and angels the day
Has passed ; and a brighter, a holier way
Of communion is open'd ;—a Saviour hath risen,
To win us from earth and from sin up to Heaven.

 Were the youths by the bears all
destroyed,—
Because the great prophet they sorely
annoyed.

Zachariah in a vision saw, nor was
he at a loss,
To tell the vision that he saw, prophetic of
the Horse.

Clarke, F., *A New Pictorial Scripture Alphabet,* for the Assistance and Amusement of Very Young Learners. New York: Turner & Hayden; Cincinnati: W. H. Moore & Co.; New Orleans: D. Baker, 1845. Pp. [27]. 11 x 8.8 cm.

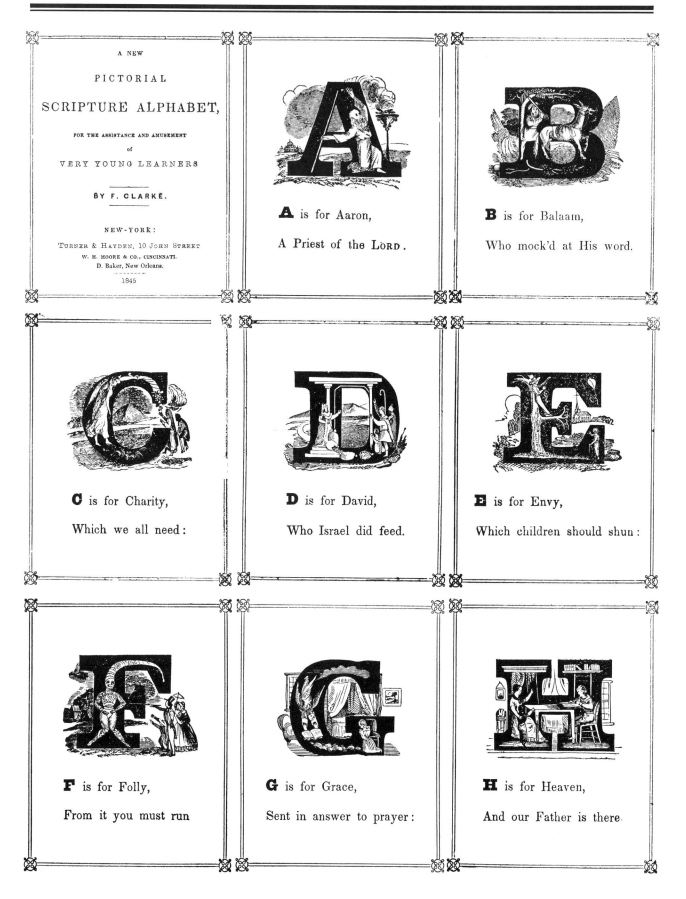

A NEW

PICTORIAL

SCRIPTURE ALPHABET,

FOR THE ASSISTANCE AND AMUSEMENT

of

VERY YOUNG LEARNERS

BY F. CLARKÉ.

NEW-YORK:

TURNER & HAYDEN, 10 JOHN STREET
W. H. MOORE & CO., CINCINNATI.
D. Baker, New Orleans.

1845

A is for Aaron,

A Priest of the LORD.

B is for Balaam,

Who mock'd at His word.

C is for Charity,

Which we all need:

D is for David,

Who Israel did feed.

E is for Envy,

Which children should shun:

F is for Folly,

From it you must run

G is for Grace,

Sent in answer to prayer:

H is for Heaven,

And our Father is there.

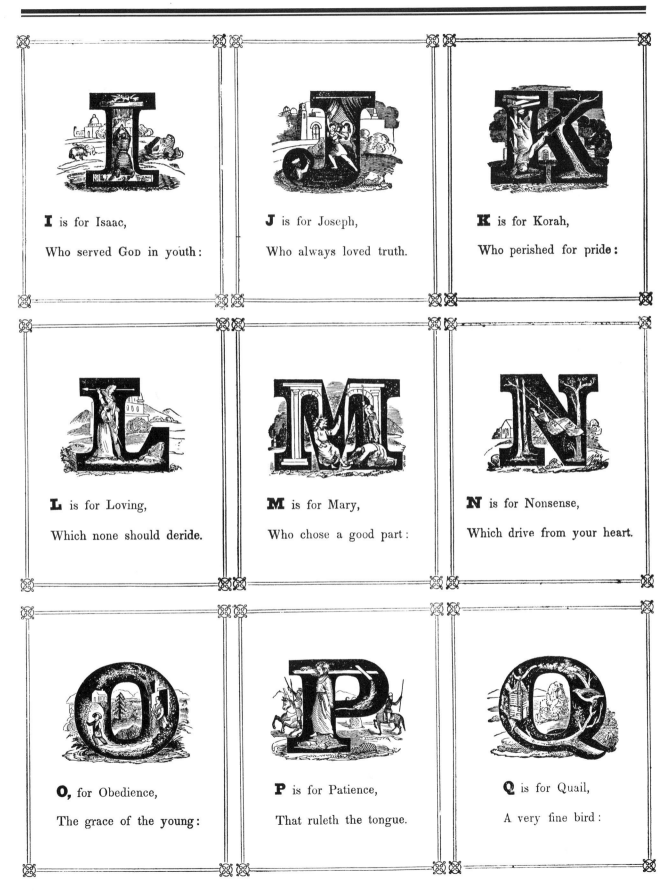

I is for Isaac,

Who served GOD in youth:

J is for Joseph,

Who always loved truth.

K is for Korah,

Who perished for pride:

L is for Loving,

Which none should deride.

M is for Mary,

Who chose a good part:

N is for Nonsense,

Which drive from your heart.

O, for Obedience,

The grace of the young:

P is for Patience,

That ruleth the tongue.

Q is for Quail,

A very fine bird:

R is for Robin,

Whose song you have heard.

S is for Samuel,.

A prophet of old :

T is for Temperance,

More valued than gold.

U is for Union,

The wise must approve :

V is for Virtue,

That good men will love.

W, for Wisdom,

More precious than fame :

X is for Xerxes,

Whom Greece overcame.

Y is for Youth,

Who should never be vain :

Z is for Zebra,

That flies from the rein.

"The Railway A.B.C." (12 pp., including 6 colored plates), from *Aunt Louisa's London Picture Book*. Comprising A. Apple Pie. Nursery Rhymes. The Railway A.B.C. Childhood's Happy Hours. With Twenty-Four Pages of Illustrations, Printed in Colors by Kronheim. London: Frederick Warne and Co.; New York: Scribner and Co., 1868. 26.8 x 22.8 cm.

A is the Arch; underneath are the rails,

To carry the passengers, baggage, and mails.

B is the Bell, which rings loudly and clear,

And tells that the train which we wait for is near.

C is the Carriage, where William must stand

With your coat on his arm and your bag in his hand.

D is the Driver, just starting the train,

He cares not for cold, nor for wind, nor for rain.

E is the Engine, that wondrous machine

So prettily painted with scarlet and green.

F is the Fire; just look at the stoker,

He is stirring the coals with a long iron poker.

G is the Guard, all in silver and blue,

Telling his mate that the next train is due.

H is the Horse-box, a neat little room,

Where the pony may travel with Harry his groom.

I is the Iron of which rails are made,

And J is the Junction where two lines are laid.

K is the Key, which fastens the door

When the carriage is full, and will not hold one more.

L is the Lamp, which the porter will light,

If we pass through a tunnel or travel at night.

M are the Mails from all parts of the land,

To the General Post in St. Martin's-le-Grand.

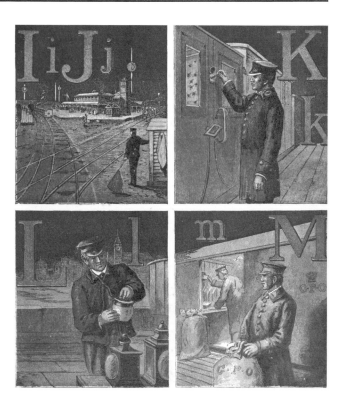

N is the News-boy, who cries "Here you are!

"*Punch*, *Times*, *Daily Telegraph*, *Standard*, and *Star*."

O are Officials, in uniform coats,

With pencils, and paper on which they take notes.

P is the Platform at Charing Cross station,

Which has gained for the Builder a great reputation.

Q is the Queen, just come out of the train,

And her carriage will take her to Windsor again.

R are the Rails which the workmen are laying;

They labour all day, and have no time for playing.

S is the Steam which comes out of the funnel,

And gets into our eyes when we go through a tunnel.

T is the Tunnel which runs through the hill,

And is hollowed and built with most wonderful skill.

U is the Uproar the boys like to make,

When they hear the trains rattle, and see the arch shake.

V is the Viaduct, built with great pains,

To carry the Railway which carries the trains.

W is the Watchman, with flags in his hand,

Who ten times a day at the crossing must stand.

X is the Excursion, from Brighton which comes,

With passengers, soldiers, and rifles, and drums.

Y is the Yeoman, just come up from Kent,

He farms his own land, and he never pays rent.

"The Wandering A B C" (p. 319), from *Little Folks.* A Magazine for the Young. Vol. 3, no. 72. London, Paris & New York: Cassell, Petter & Calpin, [1872]. 21.1 x 16.2 cm.

ONE day all the letters determined to roam,

And sought a conveyance to take them from home.

A mounted an Ass with an air of great pride;

And *B* in a Boat down the river did glide;

C ran for a Cab and drove off full of glee;

Whilst *D* on a Donkey rode after slowlie;

E borrowed an Elephant, heavy and strong;

And *F* on a Fox cantered gaily along;

G on a Giraffe seem'd quite up in the sky;

And *H* on his Horse gave them all the go-by;

I on an Ibis passed fleet as the wind,

Leaving *J's* old Jackass a long way behind;

K said, "I'm so light and so delicate too,

A Kitten will carry me all the world through;"

L bought a Lion from the gardens in town;

And *M* a fine Monkey had also sent down;

N on a Nanny-goat managed quite well,

Though he said her rough coat had not quite a nice smell;

O in an Omnibus seem'd most at his ease;

And *P* had a Pony with two broken knees;

Q had not a nag, so astride on a Quail,

He flew a long way with his face to its tail;

R on a Railway enjoyed a nice trip;

Whilst *S* went for a sail in Her Majesty's Ship;

T rode on a Tiger striped brown and white;

And *U* on a Unicorn looked a fine sight;

V a Velocipede worked rapidly;

And *W* on a Walrus back went to sea;

X said, "It's *ex*pensive to go far away,

So at home *Y* and I together will stay;"

Said *Z*, "You'll be dull if you do not go out,

Look at me how I ride on my Zebra about."

Father Tuck's Express A B C. Father Tuck's "Holiday" Series. London, Paris, New
York: Raphael Tuck & Sons, [1890]. Pp. [14], in color. 24 x 33 cm.

197

C for the Comfort of folk in the train,

C for the Carriage which drives down the lane.

D for the Danger of mending the line,

E for Excursion on holiday fine.

F for the Foot-warmer for the small feet Of Flora and Frank so rosy and neat.

G for the Goods-train that here you can see,

H for the Hurry of one, two, and three.

I for the In-coming train drawing nigh,

J for the Journey—they now say good-bye,

K for the Kiss, with a tear in the eye.

L for the Lancers who come from the wars,

M for the Milk which is left at our doors.

N for the News and the Newspaper stall,

O for the Omnibus— room for us all.

P for the Platform from which we depart
Away to the country when the trains start.

Q for the Queen's train, the best on the line,

R for Refreshment-room where we can dine.

S for the Signal and T for the Train,
It waits till the sheep are safe once again.

U for the Upset of baggage and cage,

V for the Viaduct shown on this page.

W for Waiting-room where we must wait,
Sleepy we get if the train's very late.

X, Y and Z are here on a truck shown
        Where all the other big letters are thrown,

They've journeyed from Lessonland to tell you and me
        How delightful the hours in that country can be.
                                Father Tuck.

The New Historical Alphabet. Dean & Son's New Coloured Two Penny Books, Nurse Rockbaby's Pretty Story Books. London: Dean & Son, [1852]. Pp. [11], including paper cover. 16 x 10.8 cm.

204

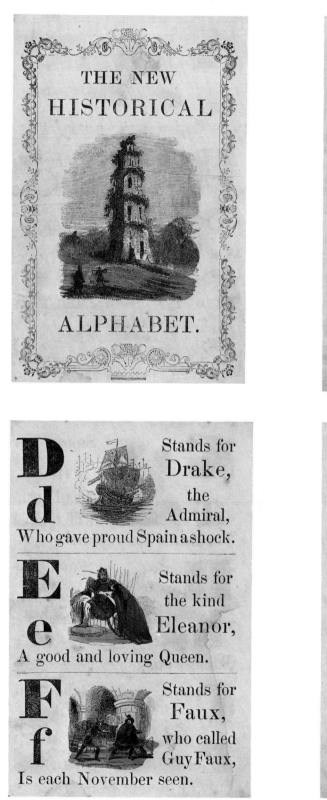

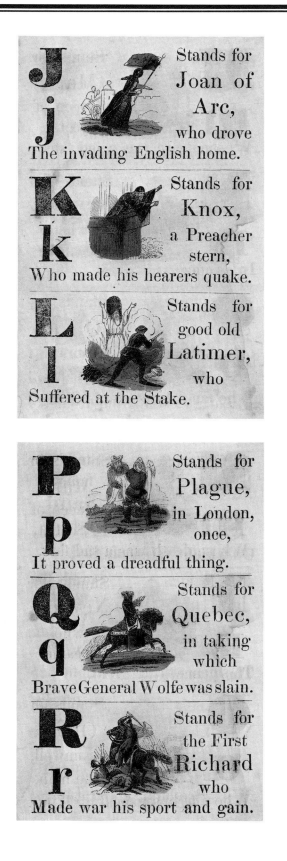

J j Stands for **Joan of Arc,** who drove
The invading English home.

K k Stands for **Knox,** a Preacher stern,
Who made his hearers quake.

L l Stands for good old **Latimer,** who
Suffered at the Stake.

P p Stands for **Plague,** in London, once,
It proved a dreadful thing.

Q q Stands for **Quebec,** in taking which
Brave General Wolfe was slain.

R r Stands for the First **Richard** who
Made war his sport and gain.

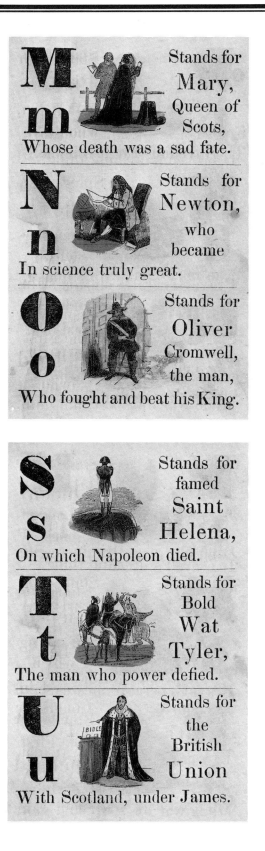

M m Stands for **Mary,** Queen of Scots,
Whose death was a sad fate.

N n Stands for **Newton,** who became
In science truly great.

O o Stands for **Oliver Cromwell,** the man,
Who fought and beat his King.

S s Stands for famed **Saint Helena,**
On which Napoleon died.

T t Stands for Bold **Wat Tyler,**
The man who power defied.

U u Stands for the British **Union**
With Scotland, under James.

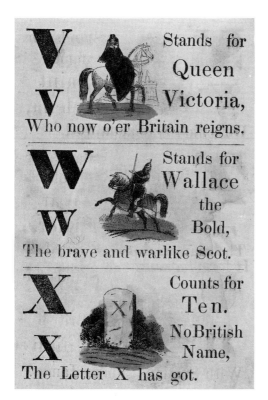

V Stands for Queen Victoria,
Who now o'er Britain reigns.

W Stands for Wallace the Bold,
The brave and warlike Scot.

X Counts for Ten. No British Name,
The Letter X has got.

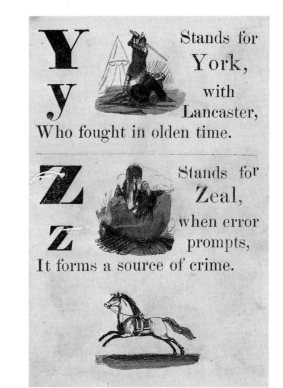

Y Stands for York, with Lancaster,
Who fought in olden time.

Z Stands for Zeal, when error prompts,
It forms a source of crime.

The Union A B C. Boston: Degen, Estes & Company, [1864]. Pp. [14], in red and blue. 21.6 x 16 cm.

207

A is America,

land of the free.

B is a Battle,

our soldiers did see.

C is a Captain,

who led on his men.

D is a Drummer

Boy, called little Ben.

E is the Eagle,

that proudly did soar.

F is our Flag,

that shall wave evermore.

G is a Gun,

that is used in the war.

H is for Hard-

tack, you scarcely can gnaw.

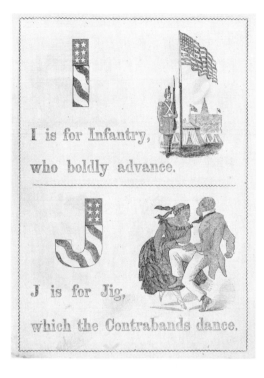

I is for Infantry,

who boldly advance.

J is for Jig,

which the Contrabands dance.

K is for Knapsack,

they carry along.

L is for Lancer,

bold, fearless, and strong.

M is for Monument,

to honor the brave.

N is for Negro,

no longer a slave.

O is an Officer,

proud of his station.

P is the President,

who ruled the great nation.

Q is for Quarters,

guarded with care.

R is Retreat,

may you never be there.

S is a Sailor,

who respected will be.

T is a Traitor,

that was hung on a tree.

U is the Union,

our Soldiers did save.

V is for Volunteer,

noble and brave.

W is for War,

which we all of us rue.

X is a Letter

which you must learn too.

Y is a Youth,

who a soldier would go.

Z is Zouave,

who charged on the foe.

The Child's Illustrated Alphabet. Philadelphia: John S. Cotton and Co. Pp. [8].
25.3 x 17.1 cm.

211

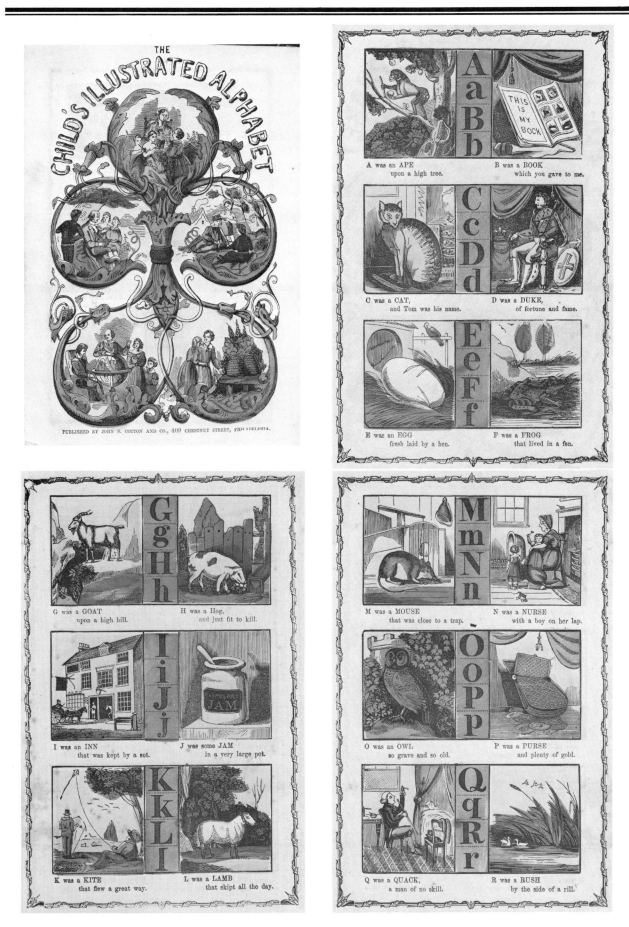

Alphabet on pp. 5–6, from *Mother Goose's Melodies for Children,* or Songs for the Nursery with Notes, Music and an Account of the Goose or Vergoose Family and With Illustrations by Henry L. Stephens and Gaston Fay. New York: Hurd and Houghton, 1869. Pp. xxii, 186. 23.8 x 17.4 cm.

A for the ape, that we saw at the fair;
B for a blockhead, who ne'er shall go there;

C for a cauliflower, white as a curd;
D for a duck, a very good bird;
E for an egg, good in pudding or pies;
F for a farmer, rich, honest, and wise;
G for a gentleman, void of all care;
H for the hound, that ran down the hare;

I for an Indian, sooty and dark;
K for the keeper, that looked to the park;

L for a lark, that soared in the air;
M for a mole that ne'er could get there;

N for Sir Nobody, ever in fault;
O for an otter, that ne'er could be caught;

P for a pudding, stuck full of plums;
Q was for quartering it, see here he comes;

R for a rook, that croaked in the trees;
S for a sailor, that ploughed the deep seas;

T for a top, that doth prettily spin;
V for a virgin of delicate mien;
W for wealth, in gold, silver, and pence;
X for old Xenophon, noted for sense;
Y for a yew, which forever is green;
Z for the zebra, that belongs to the Queen.

''A Was an Ape'' (pp. 88–100), from Lear, Edward, *Nonsense Botany, and Nonsense Alphabets,* Etc. Etc. Fifth Edition. London and New York: Frederick Warne & Co., 1889. Pp. 142. 22 x 17 cm.

A

A was an Ape,
Who stole some white Tape,
And tied up his Toes
In four beautiful Bows.

a!

Funny old Ape!

B

B was a Bat,
Who slept all the Day,
And fluttered about,
When the Sun went ·away.

b!

Brown little Bat!

C

C was a Camel,
You rode on his Hump,
And if you fell off,
You come down such a Bump!

c!

What a high Camel!

D

D was a Dove
Who lived in a Wood,
With such pretty soft Wings.
And so gentle and good.

d!

Dear little Dove!

E

E was an Eagle
Who sate on the Rocks,
And looked down on the Fields
And the far-away Flocks.

e!

Beautiful Eagle!

F

F was a Fan
Made of beautiful Stuff,
And when it was used
It went—Puffy-puff-puff!

f!

Nice little Fan.

G

G was a Gooseberry,
Perfectly Red ;
To be made into Jam
And eaten with Bread.

g!

Gooseberry Red !

H

H was a Heron
Who stood in a Stream,
The length of his Neck
And his Legs was extreme!

h!

Long-legged Heron!

I

I was an Inkstand
Which stood on a Table
With a nice Pen to write with,
When we are able!

i!

Neat little Inkstand!

J

J was a Jug,
So pretty and white,
With fresh Water in it
At Morning and Night.

j!

Nice little Jug!

K

K was a Kingfisher,
Quickly he flew,
So bright and so pretty
Green, Purple, and Blue.

k!

Kingfisher, Blue!

L

L was a Lily
So white and so sweet,
To see it and smell it
Was quite a nice treat!

l!

Beautiful Lily!

M

M was a Man
Who walked round and round,
And he wore a long Coat
That came down to the Ground.

m!

Funny old Man!

N

N was a Nut
So smooth and so brown,
And when it was ripe
It fell tumble-dum-down.

n!

Nice little Nut!

O

O was an Oyster
Who lived in his Shell,
If you let him alone
He felt perfectly well.

o!

Open-mouth'd Oyster!

P

P was a Polly
All red, blue, and green,
The most beautiful Polly
That ever was seen.

p!

Poor little Polly!

Q

Q was a Quill
Made into a Pen,
But I do not know where
And I cannot say when.

q!

Nice little Quill!

R

R was a Rattlesnake
Rolled up so tight,
Those who saw him ran quickly
For fear he should bite.

r!

Rattlesnake bite!

S

S was a Screw
To screw down a box,
And then it was fastened
Without any locks.

s !

Valuable Screw !

T

T was a Thimble
Of silver so bright,
When placed on the finger
It fitted so tight !

t !

Nice little Thimble !

U

U was an Upper-coat
Woolly and warm,
To wear over all
In the snow or the storm.

u !

What a nice Upper-coat !

V

V was a Veil
With a border upon it,
And a riband to tie it
All round a pink bonnet.

v !

Pretty green Veil !

W

W was a Watch,
Where in letters of gold
The hour of the day
You might always behold.

w !

Beautiful Watch !

X

X was King Xerxes,
Who wore on his head
A mighty large Turban,
Green, yellow, and red.

x !

Look at King Xerxes !

Y

Y was a Yak
From the land of Thibet,
Except his white Tail
He was all black as jet.

y !

Look at the Yak !

Z

Z was a Zebra
All striped white and black,
And if he were tame
You might ride on his back.

z !

Pretty striped Zebra !

The Tiny Picture Book. Charlestown, Mass.: George W. Hobbs. Pp. [29]. 8.6 x 6.8 cm.

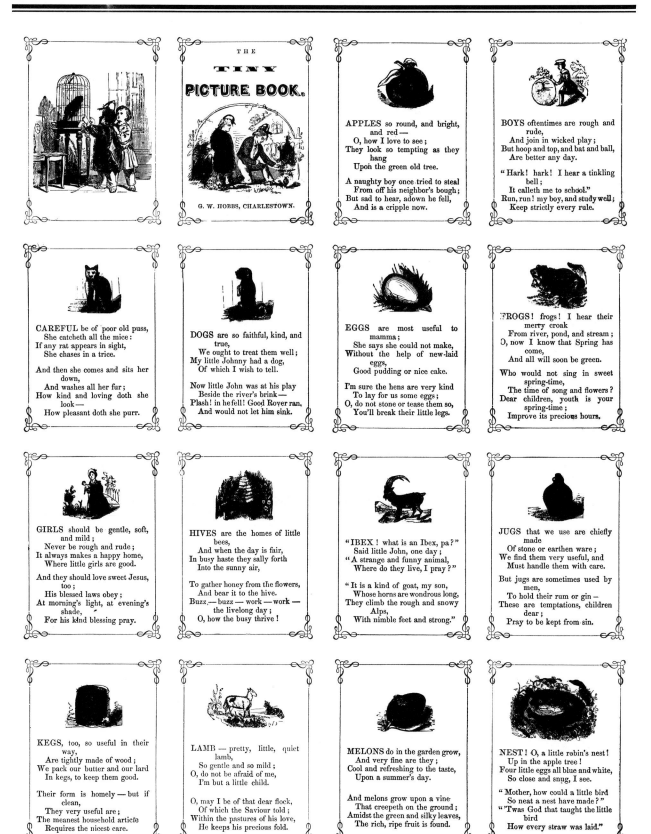

THE

TINY

PICTURE BOOK.

G. W. HOBBS, CHARLESTOWN.

APPLES so round, and bright,
    and red —
  O, how I love to see;
They look so tempting as they
    hang
  Upon the green old tree.

A naughty boy once tried to steal
  From off his neighbor's bough;
But sad to hear, adown he fell,
  And is a cripple now.

BOYS oftentimes are rough and
    rude,
  And join in wicked play;
But hoop and top, and bat and ball,
  Are better any day.

"Hark! hark! I hear a tinkling
    bell;
  It calleth me to school."
Run, run! my boy, and study well;
  Keep strictly every rule.

CAREFUL be of poor old puss,
  She catcheth all the mice:
If any rat appears in sight,
  She chases in a trice.

And then she comes and sits her
    down,
  And washes all her fur;
How kind and loving doth she
    look —
  How pleasant doth she purr.

DOGS are so faithful, kind, and
    true,
  We ought to treat them well;
My little Johnny had a dog,
  Of which I wish to tell.

Now little John was at his play
  Beside the river's brink —
Plash! in he fell! Good Rover ran,
  And would not let him sink.

EGGS are most useful to
    mamma;
  She says she could not make,
Without the help of new-laid
    eggs,
  Good pudding or nice cake.

I'm sure the hens are very kind
  To lay for us some eggs;
O, do not stone or tease them so,
  You'll break their little legs.

FROGS! frogs! I hear their
    merry croak
  From river, pond, and stream;
O, now I know that Spring has
    come,
  And all will soon be green.

Who would not sing in sweet
    spring-time,
  The time of song and flowers?
Dear children, youth is your
    spring-time;
  Improve its precious hours.

GIRLS should be gentle, soft,
    and mild;
  Never be rough and rude;
It always makes a happy home,
  Where little girls are good.

And they should love sweet Jesus,
    too;
  His blessed laws obey;
At morning's light, at evening's
    shade,
  For his kind blessing pray.

HIVES are the homes of little
    bees,
  And when the day is fair,
In busy haste they sally forth
  Into the sunny air,

To gather honey from the flowers,
  And bear it to the hive.
Buzz.— buzz — work — work —
  the livelong day;
  O, how the busy thrive!

"IBEX! what is an Ibex, pa?"
  Said little John, one day;
"A strange and funny animal,
  Where do they live, I pray?"

"It is a kind of goat, my son,
  Whose horns are wondrous long,
They climb the rough and snowy
    Alps,
  With nimble feet and strong."

JUGS that we use are chiefly
    made
  Of stone or earthen ware;
We find them very useful, and
  Must handle them with care.

But jugs are sometimes used by
    men,
  To hold their rum or gin —
These are temptations, children
    dear;
  Pray to be kept from sin.

KEGS, too, so useful in their
    way,
  Are tightly made of wood;
We pack our butter and our lard
  In kegs, to keep them good.

Their form is homely — but if
    clean,
  They very useful are;
The meanest household article
  Requires the nicest care.

LAMB — pretty, little, quiet
    lamb,
  So gentle and so mild;
O, do not be afraid of me,
  I'm but a little child.

O, may I be of that dear flock,
  Of which the Saviour told;
Within the pastures of his love,
  He keeps his precious fold.

MELONS do in the garden grow,
  And very fine are they;
Cool and refreshing to the taste,
  Upon a summer's day.

And melons grow upon a vine
  That creepeth on the ground;
Amidst the green and silky leaves,
  The rich, ripe fruit is found.

NEST! O, a little robin's nest!
  Up in the apple tree!
Four little eggs all blue and white,
  So close and snug, I see.

"Mother, how could a little bird
  So neat a nest have made?"
"'Twas God that taught the little
    bird
  How every straw was laid."

"O, how I hate an ugly owl!"
Cried little Johnny Lee;
This is a very silly hate,
In Johnny's heart to be.

Our God did make the hooting
owl,
For purpose good and wise;
O, there is nothing we should hate,
But sin's unholy guise.

PIGS we are apt to treat with
scorn,
But this is hardly fair,
For very useful is poor pig,
You surely will declare.

He helps to form our sausages,
And they are very good;
His bristles make our brushes, and
His pork we love for food.

QUAILS fill my mind with holy
thoughts;
For when the chosen tribe
Were wandering in the wilderness
Jehovah was their guide.

When hungry, to the Lord they
cried;
He sent them quails for food.
God will send us, in hour of need,
Whatever is for good.

ROSES are very fair to see,
And fragrant is their breath;
Their soft perfume doth scent the
air
The sweetest after death.

O, let us die in holy peace;
And may our deeds of love
Bear witness of a holy life,
A pledge of rest above.

SWANS float upon the waters
blue;
How beautiful the sight!
Their snowy plumage, graceful
form,
And neck so arched and light!

Old poets say, the swan doth sing
One song with dying breath;
How sweet the thought — with
holy song
To welcome coming death!

TIGERS are handsome, noble
beasts,
But O, most fierce are they!
With mighty strength and bloody
grasp,
They pounce upon their prey.

So beauty is of little worth,
Without a gentle mind;
Though few are handsome, yet
we all
Can gentle be, and kind.

URNS were much used in olden
time;
The bodies of the dead
Were burnt to ashes, and the dust
In urns deposited.

And often, on the tombstones now,
We see carved out an urn,
To tell us all we are but dust,
To which we must return.

VINES form a cool, refreshing
shade,
And grapes are fine and fair,
Hanging in purple clusters — O
They look so rich and rare!

Our Saviour saith, "I am a vine,
My branches shall ye be;
I will abide with you in love,
If ye abide in me."

WOLVES are both fierce and
cruel beasts,
And feed on little lambs,
If they perchance do stray away
From the kind shepherd's hands.

We are the lambs of Jesus' fold;
O, may we never stray
From our good Shepherd, lest
we lose
The straight and narrow way.

XEBECS are ships with three
small masts,
And light and fast they sail,
But cannot stand a boisterous
storm,
Or weather a rude gale.

This life is like a wide-spread sea;
And, guided by the hand
Of Him who made us, we sail on
To reach a heavenly land.

YACHTS are small pleasure
boats, both light
And airy in their form;
They float upon a summer sea,
But anchor in a storm.

Our anchor is the hope of heaven;
When storms of sorrow lower,
Secure and firm, we will not fear,
Even in the darkest hour.

ZEBRAS in form are like our
horse,
Though not so tall and slim;
Striped and glossy, smooth and
bright,
And beautiful their skin.

They are not docile, like the horse,
They treat man with disdain;
They spurn the rider and his whip,
His bridle, bit and rein.

"The Baby's Own A B C," from *The Old Corner Annual: A Collection of Stories and Pictures for the Little Ones Arranged by Uncle Charlie*. London and Sydney: Griffith, Farran, Okeden & Welsh (Successors to Newbery and Harris), [1889]. Pp. [16]. 24.4 x 18.4 cm.

A, was an Apple,
And put in a pie,
With ten or twelve others
All piled up so high.

B, was tall Biddy,
Who made the puff paste
And put sugar and lemon-peel
Quite to my taste.

C, is a Cheese,
But don't ask for a slice,
For it serves to maintain
A whole nation of mice.

D, was Dick Dump,
Who did nothing but eat,
And would leave book and play
For a nice bit of meat.

E, is an Egg,
In a basket with more,
Which Jenny will sell
For a shilling a score.

F, was a Forester,
Dress'd all in green,
With a Cap of fine fur,
Like a King or a Queen.

G, was a Greyhound,
As swift as the wind;
In the race or the course
Left all others behind.

H, was a Hoyden,
Not like you, nor like me,
For she tumbled about
Like the waves of the sea.

I, was the Ice,
On which William would skate;
So up went his heels,
And down went his pate.

J, was Joe Jenkins,
Who play'd on the fiddle,
And began twenty tunes,
But left off in the middle.

K, was a Kitten,
Who jumped at a cork,
And learn'd to eat mice
Without plate, knife, or
fork.

And **L**, was a Lady,
Who made him so wise;
But he tore her long train,
And she cried out her eyes.

M, was Miss Mira,
Who turn'd in her toes,
And poked down her head
Till her knees met her nose.

And **N**, Mr. Nobody,
Just come from France;
Said he'd set her upright,
And teach her to dance.

O, a grave Owl:
To look like him Tom tried;
So he put on a mask,
And sat down by his side.

P, was a Pilgrim,
With a staff in his hand,
Return'd weary and faint
From a far distant land.

Q, was the Queen
Of Spades, I've heard say,
In her black velvet girdle,
Just dress'd for the play.

Here's Ralph with his Raree-
show,
Calling so loud;
But I'd rather give two-pence
To look at the crowd.

S s

S, was a Soldier,
　　Ready to fly
To kill all our foes,
　　Or to eat a mince pie.

U u

And **U,** an Umbrella,
　　Saved Bell t'other day
From a shower that fell,
　　While she turn'd the new
　　hay.

W w

W, was a Witch,
　　Who set off at noon
To visit her Cousin,
　　The Man in the Moon.

S s
T t
U u
V v
W w
X x

T, was a Traveller,
　　Hast'ning on while 'twas light,
In the hope of a cottage
　　To rest in at night.

V, was a Village,
　　Where lived near the brook
The renown'd Uncle Charlie,
　　Who made you this Book.

X, was Xantippe,
　　A woman so cross,
That when she was dead,
　　The world said 'twas no
　　loss.

Y, was a Youth,
　　Who walked in the Park,
And play'd on the Flute,
　　Till he made the Dogs
　　bark.

Y y
Z z

Z, was a Zealander,
　　Whose name was Van Bley :
So here ends my song,
　　And I wish you Good-day.

Fisher's Edition, Young America's Library A B C Book. Philadelphia, New York, Baltimore, and Boston: Fisher & Brother, Publishers. Pp. [17], including paper cover. 27 x 19.3 cm.

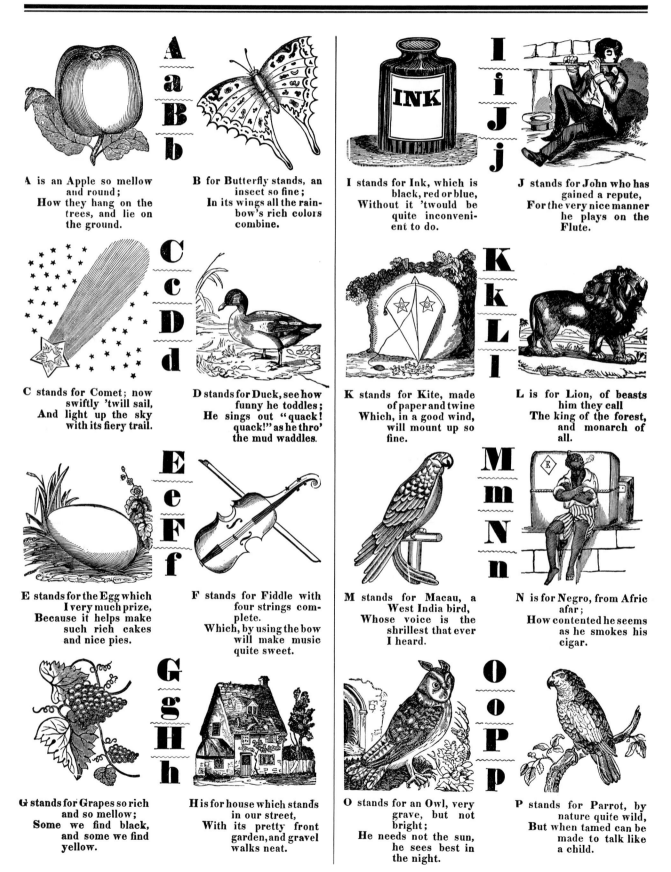

A is an Apple so mellow and round;
How they hang on the trees, and lie on the ground.

B for Butterfly stands, an insect so fine;
In its wings all the rainbow's rich colors combine.

I stands for Ink, which is black, red or blue,
Without it 'twould be quite inconvenient to do.

J stands for John who has gained a repute,
For the very nice manner he plays on the Flute.

C stands for Comet; now swiftly 'twill sail,
And light up the sky with its fiery trail.

D stands for Duck, see how funny he toddles;
He sings out "quack! quack!" as he thro' the mud waddles.

K stands for Kite, made of paper and twine
Which, in a good wind, will mount up so fine.

L is for Lion, of beasts him they call
The king of the forest, and monarch of all.

E stands for the Egg which I very much prize,
Because it helps make such rich cakes and nice pies.

F stands for Fiddle with four strings complete.
Which, by using the bow will make music quite sweet.

M stands for Macau, a West India bird,
Whose voice is the shrillest that ever I heard.

N is for Negro, from Afric afar;
How contented he seems as he smokes his cigar.

G stands for Grapes so rich and so mellow;
Some we find black, and some we find yellow.

H is for house which stands in our street,
With its pretty front garden, and gravel walks neat.

O stands for an Owl, very grave, but not bright;
He needs not the sun, he sees best in the night.

P stands for Parrot, by nature quite wild,
But when tamed can be made to talk like a child.

Q is a letter that looks
like an O,
But it's not, as the quirl
at the bottom will
show.

R is a Rose which is red,
or is white;
And its beautiful scent
is the ladies de-
light.

Y stands for Yellow-Bird,
happy and free,
Who warbles his songs
from the branch
of a tree.

Z stands for Zebu; just
look at him now·
Tho' a hump on his
back, yet he's
horns like a cow.

LESSONS OF FEW LETTERS.

arch	grit	nose		aunt	good	nine
beat	hare	oats		bite	home	tail
cash	jilt	pear		clay	jail	pole
door	king	quay		dark	kind	quit
east	life	rake		each	link	rest
fair	stop	make		once	fowl	zeal
house		goose		roach		plate
mouse		loose		coach		slate
nurse		blest		brawl		drown
purse		drest		crawl		frown
grate	drain	bench	blank	fleet	shine	drink	chest
prate	grain	tench	thank	greet	thine	think	beast
urge	vain					
when	yarn					
maid	shop					
time	lime					
rude	mute					
line	pine					
leap	heap					
load	coat					

S stands for Sloop which
floats on the seas
And sails very fast urged
on by the breeze.

T stands for Trumpet
which sounds the
alarms,
And in battle it calls the
soldier to arms.

U stands for Uncle, who
often I've seen
Busily occupied rolling
the Green.

V is a Volunteer, brave,
true, and bold,
Who is in the cause of
his country en-
roll'd.

W is Wind-Mill that stands
on the lawn;
You can get your meal
there when they've
ground up the corn.

X stands for a plant re-
sembling this;
Its botanical name is
the X-imensis.

Little Lily's Alphabet. With Rhymes by S. M. P. and Pictures by Oscar Pletsch. London: Frederick Warne & Co., [1865]. Pp. [27]. 26.9 x 18.2 cm.

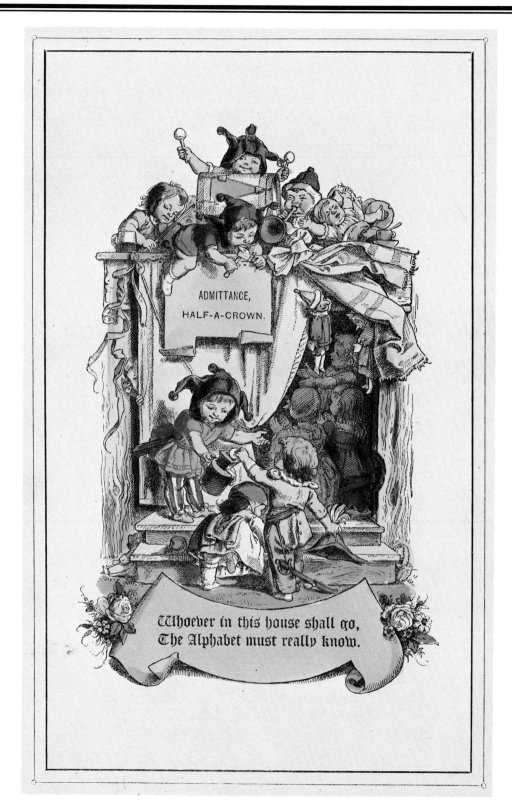

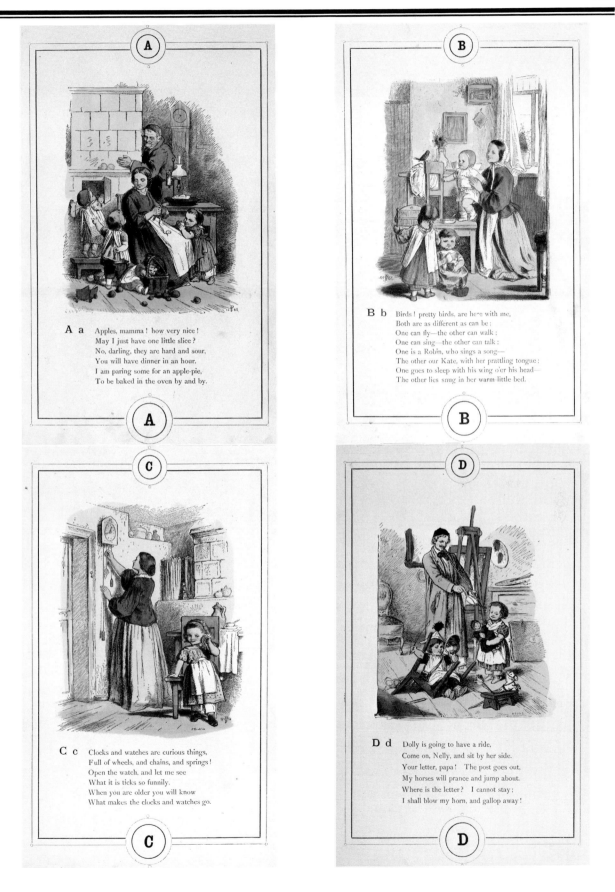

A a Apples, mamma! how very nice!
May I just have one little slice?
No, darling, they are hard and sour,
You will have dinner in an hour.
I am paring some for an apple-pie,
To be baked in the oven by and by.

B b Birds! pretty birds, are here with me,
Both are as different as can be;
One can fly—the other can walk;
One can sing—the other can talk:
One is a Robin, who sings a song—
The other our Kate, with her prattling tongue;
One goes to sleep with his wing o'er his head—
The other lies snug in her warm little bed.

C c Clocks and watches are curious things,
Full of wheels, and chains, and springs!
Open the watch, and let me see
What it is ticks so funnily.
When you are older you will know
What makes the clocks and watches go.

D d Dolly is going to have a ride,
Come on, Nelly, and sit by her side.
Your letter, papa! The post goes out,
My horses will prance and jump about.
Where is the letter? I cannot stay;
I shall blow my horn, and gallop away!

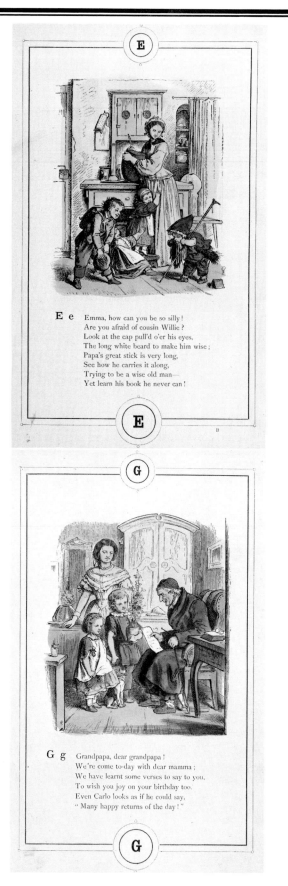

E e   Emma, how can you be so silly!
Are you afraid of cousin Willie?
Look at the cap pull'd o'er his eyes,
The long white beard to make him wise;
Papa's great stick is very long,
See how he carries it along,
Trying to be a wise old man—
Yet learn his book he never can!

F f   Fishes, fishes, out of the sea,
Springing and jumping about with glee.
You 've splash'd the water over the floor,
And wetted my clean white pinafore!
Suppose I should put my finger in—
Would you bite it, I wonder, you little thing?
Stay where you are, poor foolish fish,
Or else you 'll be fried and put in a dish!

G g   Grandpapa, dear grandpapa!
We're come to-day with dear mamma;
We have learnt some verses to say to you,
To wish you joy on your birthday too.
Even Carlo looks as if he could say,
"Many happy returns of the day!"

H h   Hens and chickens, come along!
I have something here for you;
Here they come, oh, what a throng!
Cocks and hens and puppies too!
Dash, the house-dog looks quite grave,
Poor old doggy, you must wait;
Don't you know I always save
Bones for you upon my plate.

I

I i I for a soldier would like to go,
To fight and shoot with a gun, you know.
Alas! my boy, I once felt the same,
And fought for glory and love of fame;
Now I am lame, and a cripple, you see,
That is all fighting has done for me.

J

K

K k Katie is two years old to-day,
Her new white frock is very gay;
Her birthday presents are all quite new,
A rabbit, a cake, and a doll's house too.
Katie will give mamma a kiss,
For such pretty toys and a cake like this.

K

L

L l Lucy, won't you come in and play?
No, I should like to listen all day;
Here's a man with an organ, who plays a tune,
I am very glad I came out so soon.
I have a penny to spend to-day,
I shall give it to him when he goes away.

L

M

M m Madam, any milk to-day?
Come, I have no time to stay.
Knock! knock! does no one hear?
You lazy thing, you do not care.
Knock! knock! Oh, I cannot stay!
Oh, there's a mouse! how it runs away!
Ah! now I can hear a noise and see
A light, which is a pleasure to me.

M

N n Nelly! I can the lock undo!
Do let me in to play with you.
No, no, Sir! no ; you are not good ;
You are always naughty, and so rude!
Stay where you are, outside the door,
We'll play by ourselves, as we did before.

O o Oh, Freddy! look at that little boy,
He has a sword—such a pretty toy!
And now he is buying some fruit, you see,
Should you not like some for you and me?
No, Polly, not I—if we spend it all,
We shall have no money to buy a ball.

P p Pancakes, mamma!   Oh, may I try
To mix the eggs, and milk, and flour?
Then you can fry them by and by,
They will be ready in an hour.
Well, stir it quickly, Isabel,
You must work hard to do it well.

Q q Quiet and still dear Annie stands,
While I brush her hair in glossy bands ;
Sometimes I pull, and she always tries
To bear it well, and she never cries.
I can plait her hair very quickly now,
And tie the ends with a pretty bow.

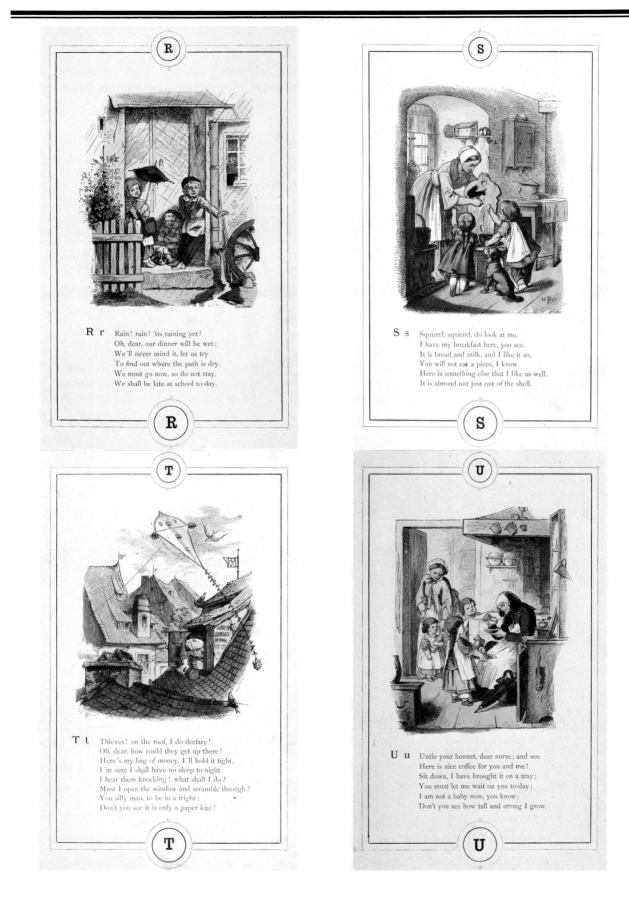

R r   Rain! rain! 'tis raining yet!
   Oh, dear, our dinner will be wet;
   We'll never mind it, let us try
   To find out where the path is dry.
   We must go now, so do not stay,
   We shall be late at school to-day.

S s   Squirrel, squirrel, do look at me,
   I have my breakfast here, you see.
   It is bread and milk, and I like it so,
   You will not eat a piece, I know.
   Here is something else that I like as well,
   It is almond nut just out of the shell.

T t   Thieves! on the roof, I do declare!
   Oh, dear, how could they get up there!
   Here's my bag of money, I'll hold it tight,
   I'm sure I shall have no sleep to-night.
   I hear them knocking! what shall I do?
   Must I open the window and scramble through?
   You silly man, to be in a fright;
   Don't you see it is only a paper kite!

U u   Untie your bonnet, dear nurse; and see.
   Here is nice coffee for you and me!
   Sit down, I have brought it on a tray;
   You must let me wait on you to-day;
   I am not a baby now, you know;
   Don't you see how tall and strong I grow.

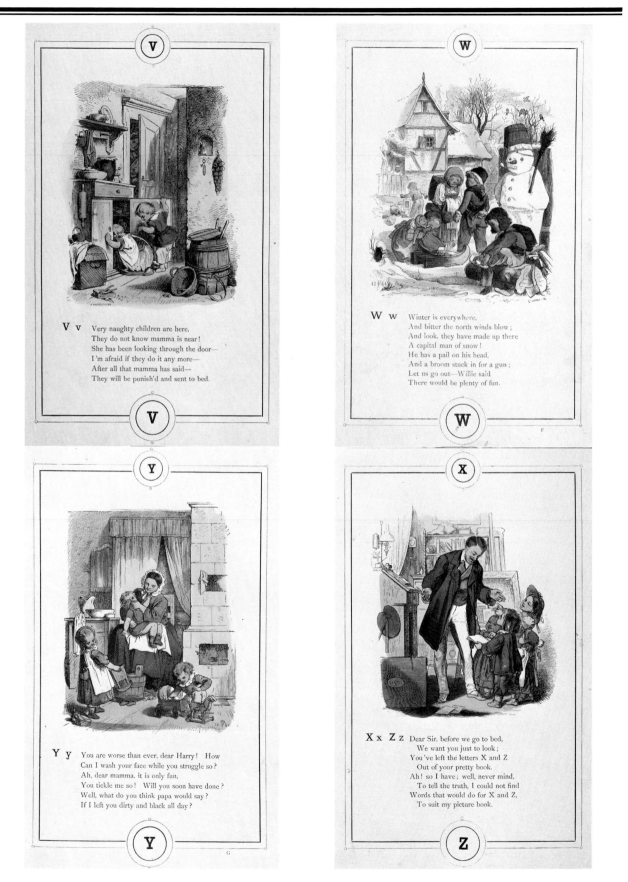

V v Very naughty children are here,
They do not know mamma is near!
She has been looking through the door—
I'm afraid if they do it any more—
After all that mamma has said—
They will be punish'd and sent to bed.

W w Winter is everywhere,
And bitter the north winds blow;
And look, they have made up there
A capital man of snow!
He has a pail on his head,
And a broom stuck in for a gun;
Let us go out—Willie said
There would be plenty of fun.

Y y You are worse than ever, dear Harry! How
Can I wash your face while you struggle so?
Ah, dear mamma, it is only fun,
You tickle me so! Will you soon have done?
Well, what do you think papa would say?
If I left you dirty and black all day?

X x Z z Dear Sir, before we go to bed,
We want you just to look;
You've left the letters X and Z
Out of your pretty book.
Ah! so I have; well, never mind,
To tell the truth, I could not find
Words that would do for X and Z,
To suit my picture book.

ABC. An Alphabet Written and Pictured by Mrs. Arthur Gaskin. London: Elkin Mathews; Chicago: A. C. McClurg & Co., 1895. Pp. [56]. 18.8 x 12.5 cm.

I FOR THE INK I'M
WRITING TO FATHER
I MUST TAKE GREAT
PAINS FOR IT'S DIFFICULT
RATHER

J FOR JENNIE AND J
FOR JOHN. OH
WHAT QUEER HATS
THEY BOTH HAVE ON

K FOR MY KITE WHICH
FLIES IN THE SKY
OVER THE FIELDS AND
EVER SO HIGH

L FOR THE LILY YOU
ARE REALLY VERY
TALL. I OFTEN TRY TO
REACH YOU BUT I AM
FAR TOO SMALL

M FOR THE MOON
WITH HER SOFT
SILVERY LIGHT OH HOW
KIND SHE IS TO LIGHT
THE WORLD AT NIGHT

N FOR NED, HE THROWS
HIS BALL SO HIGH
I REALLY THINK SOME
TIMES HE TRIES TO
TOUCH THE SKY

O FOR THE OCEAN SO
DEEP AND SO BLUE
SEE THE BOATS SAIL-
ING I WONDER
WHERE TO

P FOR THE PIGEONS
LITTLE POLLY EACH
DAY FEEDS THEM WITH
CORN SHE HAS ·20
THEY SAY

Q FOR OUR DEAR LIT-
TLE QUEEN OF THE
MAY THIS IS HER
THRONE WE HAVE
CROWNED HER TO DAY

R FOR THE RABBITS THEY ARE EVER SO BONNY, THEY WILL PLAY WITH RUTH & HER BROTHER JOHNNIE

S FOR THE SNOW SO VERY COLD & WHITE POOR LITTLE BIRDS WHERE WILL YOU SLEEP TO NIGHT?

T HIS IS THE LETTER WHICH WE CALL 'T' AND HERE'S A CUP FOR DOLLIE AND ME

U FOR UMBRELLA IT IS VERY PLAIN I REALLY MUST HURRY I THINK IT WILL RAIN

V FOR THE VINE WHICH GROWS ON OUR WALL TAKE CARE WILLIE MIND YOU DON'T FALL

W FOR WINNIE SHE LOVES TO SWING ALL DAY. SEE THE NAUGHTY WIND HAS BLOWN HER HAT AWAY

X IS SO SIMPLE YOU WILL KNOW IT AT ONCE AND NEVER FORGET IT UNLESS YOU'RE A DUNCE

Y FOR THE YARD WHERE LIVE THE FOWLS AND DUCKS I SEE A HEN AND CHICKENS JUST LISTEN HOW SHE CLUCKS

Z 26 LETTERS YOU SEE WE HAVE READ BEGINNING WITH A & ENDING WITH Z

"The Picture Alphabet, in Rhyme." (Pp. 59–70), from *Stories and Rhymes for Children.* Boston: W. J. Reynolds & Co. Pp. 70. 17.4 x 10.6 cm.

A a ARK

A is an Ark,
  With a window and door
It was built long ago,
  For the safety of Noah.

B b BOY.

B is a Boy,
  With hoop and stick;
He beats the hoop
  And follows quick.

C c COW.

C is a Cow.
  She feeds on grass and hay,
And gives you milk
  For supper every day.

D d DOG.

This Dog from a dish
  His dinner would steal,
But the cook on his head
  A smart blow makes him feel.

E e EAGLE.

E is an Eagle,
  A bird who soars high,
And can look at the Sun
  Without winking his eye.

F f FOX.

F is a Fox,
  Famed as a cunning elf;
So full of tricks,
  He oft outwits himself.

G g GIRL.

G is a Girl,
  With a quiet look;
She sits in a chair,
  And reads in a book.

H h HARP.

H is a Harp,
  Which, beaten, flings
Sweet music from
  Its wiry strings.

I i J j JOHNNY.

J is Master Johnny,
  From school just let loose;
He looks quite afraid
  To say Bo to this goose.

K k KITE.

K is a Kite,
  In which school-boys delight;
It mounts in the air
  To a very great height.

L l LION.

L is a Lion,
  With long shaggy mane;
He can scarcely be held
  By a strong iron chain.

M m MILL.

M is a Mill,
  Which stands on a hill;
But when the wind blows
  It never stands still.

N n NAG.

N is a Nag,
  With saddle and stirrup;
He sets out on a trot
  Whenever you chirp.

O o OWL.

O is an Owl,
  Which sleeps by day,
And through the night
  Seeks for its prey.

P p PEACOCK.

P is a Peacock;
  His tail makes him proud,
But his voice, I am told,
  Is ugly and loud.

Q q QUAIL.

Q is a Quail,
  A quarrelsome bird;
It bites its own brothers,
  I often have heard.

R r RABBIT.

R is a Rabbit;
  He trembles and fears;
His legs are quite short,
  And quite long are his ears.

S s SWAN.

S is a Swan,
  With arched neck and long wings,
All her life she keeps still,
  But when dying she sings.

T t TOP.

T is a Top;
  When whipped it spins round,
But when you stop whipping
  It falls to the ground.

U u V v VINE.

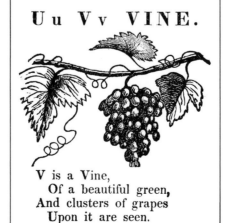

V is a Vine,
  Of a beautiful green,
And clusters of grapes
  Upon it are seen.

W w WATCH.

A Watch tells the time,
  Both the hour and the minute·
The spring makes it go,
  And is shut up within it.

X x.

X is a cross letter;
  It stands for a cross;
But to fit it a picture
  I am at a loss.

Y y YOUNG SOLDIER.

Y is a Young Soldier;
  He stands for a guard,
And must keep himself waking,
  Which sometimes is hard.

Z z ZEBRA.

Z is a Zebra,
  All covered with stripes;
It comes in for a place
  With the last of the types.

The Spring of Knowledge or the Alphabet Illustrated. Marks' Edition. London: J. L. Marks, [1850]. Pp. [8], hand-colored. 17.7 x 11.7 cm.

THE
SPRING OF KNOWLEDGE,
OR THE
ALPHABET
ILLUSTRATED.

A a
Stands for acorn that grows on a tree,

B b
Stands for Butterfly, lovely to see.

F f
Is a Fox a leaping the fence,

G g
Is a Goose by the Fox made a prey.

H h
Is a Hay maker turning the hay,

C c
For a Castle, most grand to behold,

D d
For a Dutchess, bedizen'd with gold,

E e
Is an Elephant, endow'd with great

I i
Is an Idler, wont go to school,

J j
Is a Jester playing the fool,

K k
Is a Kitten with marks down her face.

L l.
A young lady making thread lace,

M m
Is the Mill, where ripe corn is ground,

N n
A black Negro tilling the ground.

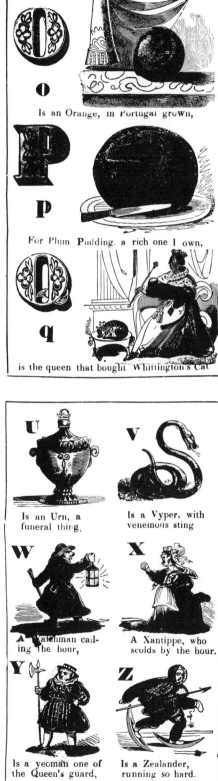

O o
Is an Orange, in Portugal grown,

P p
For Plum Pudding, a rich one I own,

Q q
is the queen that bought Whittington's Cat

R r
Master Richard with his ball and bat,

S s
A white Swan, upon the clear lake,

T t
Is a Tiger, who lurks in the brake.

U
Is an Urn, a funeral thing.

V
Is a Vyper, with venemous sting

W
A Watchman calling the hour,

X
A Xantippe, who scolds by the hour.

Y
Is a yeoman one of the Queen's guard,

Z
Is a Zealander, running so hard.

"A Was an Ant" (pp. 101–13), from Lear, Edward, *Nonsense Botany, and Nonsense Alphabets,* Etc., Etc. Fifth Edition. London and New York: Frederick Warne & Co., 1889. Pp. 142. 22 x 17 cm.

A

A was an Ant
Who seldom stood still,
And who made a nice house
In the side of a hill.

a!

Nice little Ant!

B

B was a Book
With a binding of blue,
And pictures and stories
For me and for you.

b!

Nice little Book!

C

C was a Cat
Who ran after a Rat,
But his courage did fail
When she seized on his tail.

c!

Crafty old Cat!

D

D was a Duck
With spots on his back,
Who lived in the Water,
And always said, Quack!

d!

Dear little Duck!

E

E was an Elephant,
Stately and wise;
He had Tusks and a Trunk,
And two queer little Eyes.

e!

O what funny small Eyes!

F

F was a Fish
Who was caught in a net,
But he got out again,
And is quite alive yet.

f!

Lively young Fish!

G

G was a Goat
Who was spotted with brown:
When he did not lie still,
He walked up and down.

g!

Good little Goat!

H

H was a Hat
Which was all on one side,
Its crown was too high
And its brim was too wide.

h!

O! what a Hat!

I

I was some Ice
So white and so nice,
But which nobody tasted,
And so it was wasted.

i!

All that good Ice!

J

J was a Jack-daw
Who hopped up and down
In the principal street
Of a neighbouring town.

j!

All through the town!

K

K was a Kite,
Which flew out of sight
Above houses so high
Quite into the sky.

k!

Fly away, Kite!

L

L was a Light
Which burned all the Night,
And lighted the gloom
Of a very dark room.

l!

Useful nice Light!

M

M was a Mill
Which stood on a Hill,
And turned round and round
With a loud hummy sound.

m!

Useful old Mill!

N

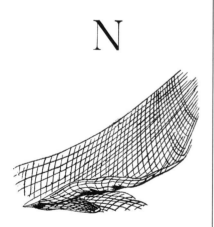

N was a Net
Which was thrown in the sea,
To catch fish for dinner
For you and for me.

n!

Nice little Net!

O

O was an Orange
So yellow and round;
When it fell off the tree,
It fell down to the ground.

o!

Down to the ground!

P

P was a Pig
Who was not very big,
But his tail was too curly,
And that made him surly.

p!

Cross little Pig!

Q

Q was a Quail
With a very short Tail,
And he fed upon corn
In the evening and morn.

q!

Quaint little Quail!

R

R was a Rabbit,
Who had a bad habit
Of eating the flowers
In gardens and bowers.

r!

Naughty fat Rabbit!

S

S was the Sugar-tongs
Nippity-nee,
To take up the Sugar
To put in our tea.

S!

Nippity-nee!

T

T was a Tortoise
All yellow and black;
He walked slowly away,
And he never came back.

t!

Torty never came back!

U

U was an Urn
All polished and bright,
And full of hot water
At noon and at night.

u!

Useful old Urn!

V

V was a Villa,
Which stood on a hill
By the side of a river
And close to a mill.

v!

Nice little Villa!

W

W was a Whale
With a very long Tail,
Whose movements were frantic
Across the Atlantic.

w!

Monstrous old Whale!

X

X was King Xerxes,
Who more than all Turks is
Renown'd for his fashion
Of fury and passion.

x!

Angry old Xerxes!

Little Pet's Picture Alphabet. New York: McLoughlin Bros. Pp. [15], including paper cover. 16 x 13 cm.

Y

Y was a Yew,
Which flourished and grew
By a quiet abode
Near the side of a road.

y!

Dark little Yew!

Z

Z was some Zinc
So shiny and bright,
Which caused you to wink
In the Sun's merry light.

z!

Beautiful Zinc!

A was an ARAB, and had a dark skin,

B was a BEGGAR, both ragged and thin.

C was a CANDY MAN, and sold
lots of sweets,

D was a DRUNKARD, and slept
in the street.

G · was a GERMAN, and drank
lager beer,

H was a HUNTER, who had
just killed a deer.

E was an ELF, who danced with
a FAIRY,

F was a FOX, both cunning and
wary.

I was an INDIAN, and shot with
his bow,

J was a JUGGLER, and made a
great show.

K was a KNIGHT, and carried a lance.

M was a MUSIC man and played a nice tune,

L was a LADY, learning to dance.

N was a NEGRO, chasing a Coon.

O was an OSTRICH, and is said to eat stones,

Q was a QUAKER, and wore a broad brim,

P was a PANTHER, and gnawed up the bones.

R was REBECCA his wife, and was thin.

S was a STAG, a species of deer,

U was a UNION-Boy, and had a large flag,

T was a TURK, and born without fear.

V was a VETERAN, and had but one leg.

W was WINTER, the season of snow,

Y was the YOUTH, who smoked a cigar,

X was an EXQUISITE, and fond of a show.

Z was a ZOUAVE, who had been to the war

Childs Own Picture Alphabet or Step by Step to Learning. Philadelphia & Baltimore: Fisher & Brother, Publishers. Pp. [15], including paper cover. Hand colored. 27.4 x 20 cm.

A Stands for Artillery-men,
whose guns we abhor,
Though they do but their duty
when a nation's at war.

D Stands for Donkey, at which
all the dogs bark,
Though his burden he carries from
morn until dark.

B Stands for Boatman, who is
plying the oar,
Taking his passengers safe to the
shore.

E Is an Eagle, whose eye is so
bright,
It fears not to gaze on the eastern
sun's light.

C Stands for Charger with his
rider is prancing,
To the front rank of battle is
boldly advancing.

F Stand for Fowls, the turkey,
hen, and their brood,
Which near the barn door are
picking up food.

G Stands for Gas-light, that
brightens the street,
Guiding at night the wayfarer's
feet.

K Stands for Kettle, you see
through the door,
While Kate, in the Kitchen, is
sweeping the floor.

H Stands for Hawk, which
soars very high,
To seize on the heron that skims
through the sky.

L Is a pet Lamb that lies on
the grass,
And is fed by a lady that chances
to pass.

I Stands for Indian, whose king
is here decked:
J Are the Jewels his javelins
protect.

M Is a Man, who is mending
his mat,
Whilst his cat, a good mouser, is
catching a rat.

N Stands for Nightingale, that all the night long
Pours merrily forth her sweet, plaintive song.

Q Is a Quarry of marble so white,
And near it some Quails are about taking flight.

O Is the Ourang Outang, an odd creature, see,
Who sits, with his club, on the stump of a tree.

R Is a Ram, who to graze leads the sheep,
And round him young rabbits most playfully leap.

P Stands for Ploughman, breaking the ground,
And near him are little Pigs running around.

S Stands for Shepherd, who sits on the rock,
Attentively watching his own little flock.

T Stands for Tiger, a ferocious wild beast,
That roams in the woods of the far distant East.

W Stands for Windmill, that turns round and round,
And makes into meal the corn which is ground.

U Stands for Urchin, who tells falsehoods and swears,
And now he is caught stealing apples and pears.

X Stands for Xerxes, the great Persian king.

Y Is for Youth, of lifetime the Spring.

V Is the Vineyard where purple grapes shine,
And near it the vessel that presses out wine.

Z Stands for Zones, many thousand miles' girth,
Which divide heat and cold throughout the wide earth.

The Alphabet Ladder, or a Gift for the Nursery. New York: S. King, inscribed December 25, 1822. Pp. 16, hand colored. 15.8 x 10.3 cm.

G g

G_ Is a nice Goose
For Michaelmas day.

H h

H_ Is a Horse
To gallop away.

I i

I_ Stands for Ivy
That grows on the wall.

J j

J_ For a Jackdaw
That loudly can call.

K k

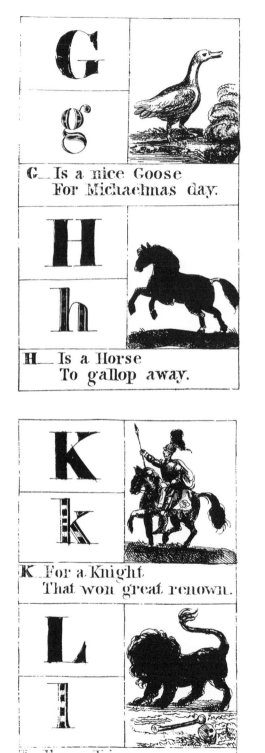

K_ For a Knight
That won great renown.

L l

L_ For a Lion
That fought for the crown.

M m

M_ Is a Miller
That grinds down the Corn.

N n

N_ Is a Naughty Boy
That cries every morn.

O — Is an Orange
So round and so sweet

P — Is a Pedlar
That stands in the street

Q — Is a Quince
That grows on a tree.

R — Is a Rosebud
Most lovely to see.

S — Is a Ship
That sails on the Ocean.

T — Is a top
That is often in motion.

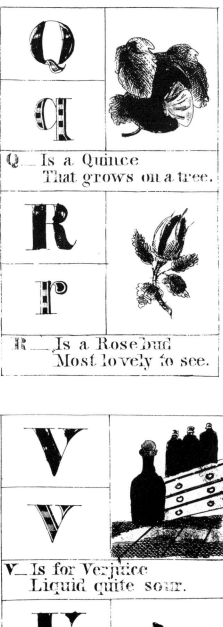

V — Is for Verjuice
Liquid quite sour.

U — Is an Usurer
Pofsefs'd of great power

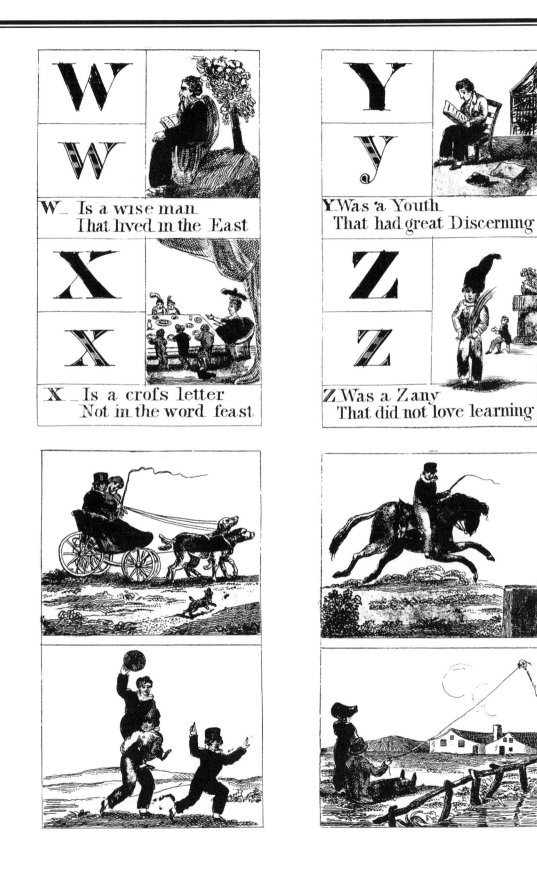

W_ Is a wise man
That lived in the East

Y Was a Youth
That had great Discerning

X _ Is a crofs letter
Not in the word feast

Z Was a Zany
That did not love learning

"The Child's Alphabet" (pp. 5–10), from *The Picture Book for Little Children.*
London: The Book Society, [1864]. Pp. 60. 31.5 x 24.5 cm.

THE CHILD'S ALPHABET.

A

is in A-rbour, and
in w-a-iting for te-a,
in be-a-utiful we-a-ther,
and a s-a-il on the se-a;

a

in d-a-rkness and sh-a-de,
in a cle-a-r ple-a-s-a-nt d-a-y,
in w-a-lk for a l-a-dy, and
a se-a-t by the w-a-y.

B b

b-egins B-oat, and is in har-b-our and B-ay,
in B-at and in B-all, in B-attle and B-ray,
in B-owl and in B-ut, in B-oiler and tu-b,
in B-u-bb-le and B-urst, in B-rush and in scru-b.

C c

is in C-ow, in C-row, and in C-all,
in C-hicken and C-alf, in C-rab and in C-rawl;
in bis-c-uit and C-ake, in C-at and in mi-c-e,
in C-ream and in C-heese, in C-o-c-oa and ri-c-e.

D d

begins D-onkey, is in goo-d and in ba-d,
in D-ove, D-uck, and D-rake, in D-og and in la-d,
in D-oll and in D-arting, in D-uster and mai-d,
in roa-d and in ri-d-e, in gar-d-en and spa-d-e.

E e

is in E-l-e-phant, in E-agl-e and Ee-l,
in E-y-e and in E-ar, in br-e-ad and in m-e-al;
in butt-e-r and E-ggs, in coff-ee and t-e-a,
in p-e-pp-e-r and spic-e, and in busy-b-ee.

F f

begins F-ather, is in F-ish and in f-ry,
in F-lag and in F-eather, in F-owl and in F-ly;

F f

in F-ig and in F-lax, in wol-f and in F-lock,
in F-ruit and in F-lavour, in F-ringe and in F-rock.

G g

is in G-oose, in G-reen, and in G-rass,
in G-rove and in G-lobe, in G-as and in G-lass;
in G-ate and in G-ig, in G-allop and G-o,
in somethin-g and nothin-g, in plou-g-h and in G-row.

H h

begins H-orse, is in H-ouse and in H-ive,
in H-og and in H-oof, in t-h-ras-h and in t-h-rive,
in H-at and in H-oop, in H-ook and in H-oe,
in coac-h and in H-earse, in s-h-un and in s-h-ow.

I i

is in I-nsect, in I-ce and in I-nk,
in I-nn and in I-vy, in v-i-olet and p-i-nk,
in h-i-nge and in jo-i-nt, in eng-i-ne and tra-i-n,
in p-i-cture and pa-i-nt, in ra-i-l and in cha-i-n.

J j

begins J-ay, is in J-oke and J-ackdaw,
in J-elly and J-am, in J-ug and in J-ay,
in j-ust and in J-udge, in j-ump and in j-oin,
in J-uice and in J-ar, in J-ew and re-j-oin.

K k

begins K-itten, is in K-id and in
    K-ite,
in lar-k and in spar-k, in K-ing
    and in K-night,

K k

in coo-k and in ba-k-er, watch-
    ma-k-er and cloc-k,
in K-iss and in k-ind, in as-k and
    in K-noc-k.

L l

is in L-ighthouse, in L-amp and in L-ink,
in L-ion and L-amb, in l-ook and in b-l-ink,
in L-ightning and L-urid, in L-aurel and l-ove,
in b-l-ack and in b-l-ue, in vei-l and in g-l-ove.

M m

begins M-ouse, is in M-ilk and in ho-m-e,
in M-et and in M-eat, in M-arch and in roa-m,
in M-oon and in M-ay, in M-op and in broo-m,
in M-oth and in M-onth, in M-usic and roo-m.

N n

is in N-est, in N-ight and in N-oon,
in cotto-n and cor-n, in ma-n and balloo-n,
in curra-n-ts and N-uts, in N-eedle and pi-n,
in stocki-n-gs and fla-nn-el, in iro-n and ti-n.

O o

begins O-wl, is in O-range and t-o-p,
in b-o-x and in b-o-y, in h-o-use and in sh-o-p,
in b-oo-t and in sh-o-e, in h-o-t and in c-o-ld,
in o-n-e and in tw-o, in y-o-ung and in o-ld.

P

is in P-igeon, in P-udding, and
  P-ie,
in P-alace and P-ark, in p-ee-p and
  in p-ry,

p

in P-leasure and P-ain, in la-p and
  in ga-p,
in soa-p and in P-an, in stra-p and
  in ca-p.

Q q

begins Q-uail, is in Q-uince and in q-uire,
in Q-uilt and in Q-uill, in Q-ueen and es-q-uire,
in Q-uestion and q-uote, in q-uench and re-q-uite,
in Q-uick and re-q-uest, in Q-uake and in q-uite.

R r

is in R-abbit, in R-ive-r, and R-ill,
in R-aisins and R-ibbons, in colla-r and f-r-ill,
in wa-rr-en and wa-r-e, in pape-r and st-r-ing,
in fi-r-e and in g-r-ate, in R-obe and in R-ing.

S s

begins S-quirrel, is in S-hells and in S-and,
in S-atin and S-ilk, in s-it and in s-tand;
in S-ugar and S-alt, in ci-s-tern and S-ea-s,
in fro-s-t and in S-now, in leave-s and in tree-s.

T t

is in T-hrush, in T-rumpe-t and T-oy,
in ra-tt-le and ca-tt-le, in T-urkey and T-roy;
in T-able and T-ray, in ba-t and in gna-t,
in T-eapo-t and T-reacle, in ca-t and in ra-t.

U u

begins U-ncle, is in U-mbrella and
   c-u-t,
in a-u-nt and in co-u-sin, in sh-u-te
   and in sl-u-t,

U u

in U-sher and U-mpire, in m-u-mble
   and m-u-tter,
in u-se and ab-u-se, in f-u-mble and
   spl-u-tter.

V v

is in V-iper, in v-ulgar and cle-v-er,
in V-iew and in V-ice, in clea-v-e and in se-v-er,
in V-ictuals and V-espers, in sie-v-e and in wea-v-e,
in se-v-en and hea-v-en, in lea-v-e and in slee-v-e.

W w

begins W-orm, is in W-ind, and W-indmill,
in W-asp and in flo-w-ers, in W-ater and W-ill;
in W-ell and in W-et, in W-ant and in W-oe,
in w-arm and in Watch, in w-ear and in se-w.

X x

is in e-x-press, is in X-er-x-es, and wa-x,
in e-x-port and e-x-pect, in X-aviers and fla-x;
in e-x-act and e-x-tinct, in se-x and in fi-x,
in fo-x and in bo-x, in ve-x and in mi-x.

Y y

is in Yellow-hammer, in y-outh and in y-ou,
in stra-y and in sta-y, in y-ear and in Y-ew;
in jo-y-ful and merr-y, in bu-y and in pla-y,
in wa-y and in monke-y, in y-east and in ha-y.

Z z

begins Z-ebra, is in free-z-e and in mai-z-e,
in Z-ephyr and bree-z-e, in snee-z-e and in bla-z-e,
in z-eal and in z-est, in bai-z-e and in qui-z,
in si-z-e and in fur-z-e, in bu-z and in fi-z.

, ; : .

This , is a comma, and this ; semicolon,
One dot for full stop, and two : for a colon.

To these, dear children, we hope you'll attend,
And our Alphabet with them we bring to an end.

The Mother's Picture Alphabet. London: S. W. Partridge & Co., [1887]. Pp. 59.
21 x 16.5 cm.

A—my dear child—the
first letter—is here:
One that in many a word
does appear.

B begins Bible, the Book
we so prize;
That teaches us all to be
holy and wise.

A begins Arch, under which, in the rain,
We sheltered awhile till the sun shone again.
A begins Apple, so juicy and sweet,
That, when ripe in Autumn, we all like to eat.
A begins Acorn—the oak's seed, you know:
How strange that from it such a big tree should grow!
Anchor, made strong, the deep sea-bed to grip;
That stops in a moment the mightiest ship.

B begins Boy, in a studious mood,
While others blow Bubbles, or stray in the wood.
Also Balloon, that soars up in the sky:
I should not much like to be mounting so high.
Bramble, on which, when the autumn comes round,
The Blackberry cluster is sure to be found.
B begins Butterfly, coloured so gay;
Also the Bee, out at work all the day.
B begins Boat, lying there in the sun;
Also the Beach, a nice spot for a run.
Bellows, that helps us to kindle the fire.
Brush, that to keep our hair smooth we require.
Bell, that bright, pretty, and tinkling thing,
That, when little Susan is wanted, we ring.
Bandbox—we all know what that is, no doubt;
And Basket—a thing we could scarce do without.
Bag, that dear Robert to school with him takes;
And Broom, for the litter the fading rose makes.

C begins Cobbler, at work in his stall, Shaping out soles for the wax-end and awl.

D stands for Dora, so thoughtful and dear, And D for a Drink from the spring cool and clear.

C for the Chair, too, in which his wife sits,
And C for the Cotton she busily knits.
C begins Cow, that such sweet milk doth yield,
And also the Cowslip that grows in the field ;
Also Carnation—how sweet its perfume !—
And Crocus, that in the cold spring-time doth bloom.
Church, where we all love on Sunday to go. ,
Castle, that towers o'er the country below.
Cherry, a nice fruit, so shining and sweet.
Cascade, where the waters rush down swift and fleet.

D begins Dove, too, a fond, gentle bird,
Of whose loving nature we often have heard.
And Damson, a fruit very nice in a pie ;
And Deer—in the green glade how graceful they lie !
The Dahlia, one of our handsomest flowers ;
And Daisy, that dear little favourite of ours.
D begins Dog, but I hope he won't tease
Those pretty young Ducks sailing under the trees ;
And Drover, who, with his stick under his arm,
Drives back, every evening, the herd to the farm.

DO YOU KNOW YOUR ALPHABET?

If you do, find out the twenty-six letters in these four lines :—

God gives the grazing ox his meat,
    And quickly hears the sheep's low cry ;
But man who tastes His finest wheat
    Should joy to lift His praises high.

E begins Egg, in the bird's pretty nest;
Oh may no rude hand its dear treasures molest.

F begins Fanny, whose dear brother, Fred,
Has got a large basket of Fruit on his head.

Also a large one, just boiled, in a cup:
I daresay our Edward would soon eat it up.
Ewe, how she fondles the lamb at her side!
Eagle, that soars to the clouds in his pride.
Elder, with berries all purple and brown.
Earthquake, that tumbles the houses all down.
Easel, where, sketching, the young artist sat:
I wish I could draw such an Engine as that.
Elm, that in summer spreads out its green boughs;
A shelter and shade for the sheep and the cows.
Elk, a wild beast, with long horns like a deer,
That bounds o'er the rocks without danger or fear.
And E for an Elephant, big, tall, and strong,
That carries or drags heavy burdens along.

How pleased she appears, with her armful of Flowers,
So Fragrant and Fresh after yesterday's showers.
F begins Football—what capital Fun!—
Again it flies up, and how fast the lads run!
Ford, where in shallowest water they wade.
Ferns, like green Feathers, adorning the glade.
Fir, a dark tree that towers up in the sky.
Fox, a strange animal, cunning and sly.
Fawn, a young deer, very timid and mild,
That loves best to roam where the heath-bells grow
    wild.
Feather, like what baby wears in his hat:
The dear little fellow—so Fair and so Fat.

ELEPHANT MARKET IN INDIA.

G begins Grandpa: how
baby does stare
At the pretty Gold watch he
is showing him there.

H begins Hen—fond, affec-
tionate thing—
Observe how she hides her
chicks under her wing.

Greyhound, a dog very nimble and slim—
The fastest of runners would never catch *him*.
Goat, that can clamber up hills steep and high.
Gooseberries—nice in a tart or a pie.
Grasshopper, too, that sings loud in the Grass.
Grapes, growing ripe in the Greenhouse of Glass.
Gig, with the swift horse that Gallops along ;
Also Guitar, very sweet with a song.
Gleaner, the Girl with her big sheaf of corn,
Who leans on the Gate she passed through at
    morn.
Globe, like a map on a very large ball,
Marked with the lands, and the oceans, and all.
Gardener, with hoe turning up the hard Ground,
Else in the Garden rank weeds
    would abound.
G for a Girl, Gaping wide, as you
    see ;
A sign that in bed she now ought
    to be.

Hovel, where nightly they shelter and sleep.
Hive, the bees' Home, where their Honey they keep.
H begins Henry, with Hand on his Hoop :
Young Herbert's Hat, too, who by him does stoop.
Hay, that the Haymakers heap on the wain
Bearing the load to the farm down the lane.
Hook, often used to hang anything on.
Horse, when I'm bigger I'll ride behind John.
Horn— on the river it sounds very sweet.
Hamper, a basket for things nice to eat.
Hoe, by whose help we root weeds up with ease.
Hatchet, so useful in cutting down trees.
Hyacinths wild, that in shady woods grow ;
Hollyhocks, too, what a beautiful show !
Harrow, for breaking the clods—a spiked frame ;
Also an English town named just the same.
House—why, 'tis dear grandpapa's, I declare ;
He's opened the Hothouse to give his plants air.

I begins Infant, with fat cheeks and hands: Dressed in his pinafore, ribbons, and bands.

J begins Judge : he looks rather severe, But they who act rightly have nothing to fear.

Ibex, a creature with horns like a goat.
Inkstand—John writes such a beautiful note!
Ivy, that covers, as though with a screen,
Papa's garden wall with its leafage so green.
Island, a place circled round by the sea.
Image-boy—few look so cheerful as he.
Ibis, a bird that, in Egypt, I've read,
Was worshipped while living, and honoured when
    dead.
Ice, spread like glass right across the long pond ;
Of gliding upon it the skaters are fond.
When cold winds have caused all this water to
    freeze,
Then see how the Icicles hang from the trees !

Jaguar, a tiger, that haunts wooded rocks.
Jackal, an animal much like a fox.
Jet—how it sparkles against the tall trees !
Junk, a strange vessel, used by the Chinese.
Jug, that each morning Jane fills at the spring,
Fresh water for breakfast her mother to bring.
Jam—very nice, as most children will own—
In the picture two pots of the finest are shown.
Jay, the harsh singer, most country lads know.
Jars—in the pantry they stand in a row.
Jonquil, a flower that in spring loves to bloom.
Jasmine, that breathes all around its perfume.

JAY.

K begins Kettle, that sings on the fire.
Keys, that to open our locks we require.

Kittens, that frisk by their old mother's side,
Who watches their gambols with fondness and pride.
Kangaroo, roaming through lands far away.
Kestrel, that, perched on high, watches its prey.
Kit for the butter, a vessel of wood.
Kitchen, where Ann cooks our dinner so good.
Kilns, for lime burning, that smoke day and night ;
Kingfisher, too, with its plumage so bright.
Kid—'tis a name for the young of the goat.
Kerchief—in winter, to wrap round the throat.
Knit, as mamma does when evening comes on.
Knife, such as uncle brought dear brother John.
Kate, our dear auntie, who asked us to tea,
And gave a kind Kiss to my brother and me.
Kent, a fine county, with much orchard-land.
And King, a great ruler, mighty and grand.

L begins Lighthouse, that shows a bright Light,
To guide the poor sailor at sea in the night.

Lightning, that darts from the black, angry sky.
Ladder, that helps us to reach very high.
Lemon, a yellow fruit, juicy and sour.
Lily, a lovely and sweet-scented flower.
Lupins, so blue, in the garden that grow.
Larkspur ; and Lilac—a beautiful show.
Leopard ; and Lion, well known for his roar.
Loaf, that the baker's man brings to the door.
Lane, where in summer the roses we find.
Lamp, that we use when for reading inclined.
Lavender, prized for its perfume so sweet.
Lantern, that lights, in the darkness, our feet.
Ladle ; and Letter, for post by-and-by.
Lamb ; also Lime-tree, that blooms in July.
Leaves of the tree in the dark forest-bower ;
Leaves of the green grass, and Leaves of the flower.
Love, Learning, Lollipops, Luncheon as well,
And other nice things, begin with an L.

M begins Moorland, so
barren and still,
Where the path winds along
beside the old Mill.

N begins News-boy, with
papers to sell:
What a good thing it is to
learn to read well!

Mountain, that towers up aloft to the sky—
'Twould take us a long time to clamber so high.
Mist, that, in autumn, rolls up the hill-side.
Mouse, that so loves in the pantry to hide.
Melon, a large fruit, with rough, barky rind.
Mushroom, that oft in the Morning we find.
Moon, that at evening, so calm and so bright,
On all things around sheds her pale silver light.
Music—we all like to play and to sing.
May-bloom, that covers the hedge in the spring.
Mower, who stands in the Meadow so blithe,
And cuts down the grass with his well-sharpened
scythe.
Milkmaid, who sits there, with round, rosy cheek:
The cow standing by her, so patient and meek.
Monkey—a mischievous creature is he.
Milk-can, that holds the nice Milk for our tea.
Macaw, much admired for his gay-coloured wings;
And Magpie, who loves to hoard glittering things.

At Nine, he leaves one at each customer's door;
And by Noon he will sell all he carries, and more.
Nuts, such as Neddy, our Nephew so good,
Brought in a bag from the thick hazel-wood.
Nest, that we spied in the coppice to-day
(We never take one of the bird's eggs away).
Nettle, a weed that is found everywhere;
It painfully stings if you do not take care.
Nurse, who so gently soothes baby to sleep;
Night, when the stars from the firmament peep;
Newcastle, famous of old for its coals;
Northampton, for boots with strong uppers and soles;
Noah, whom God in the great ark shut in,
Before He would drown the bad world for its sin.
Good Nehemiah, whose heart was so pained
To see how his country the Sabbath profaned.

O begins Organ; the tune is so gay,
The children could' stand there and listen all day.

P begins Princess, now Queen, loved and dear;
Gladly we welcome her Jubilee year.

Here, give the man this, and let dear baby see ;
How he stares at the figures in wonder and glee !
O begins Orange, a fruit you well know.
Oak-tree, so sturdy, on which acorns grow.
Ostrich, a bird whose fine feathers we prize.
Onions, that Jane of the greengrocer buys.
Owl, a strange bird, that at night loves to hoot.
Opossum, an animal ; Olive, a fruit.
Omnibus—how I should like a long ride,
If dear Uncle Oscar would sit by my side !
Oyster, whose shells are collected by boys,
And made into grottos, 'mid shouting and noise.
Oats, that the Ostler gives Jack every day.
Otter, that loves in the water to play.
Obelisk, too, a tall pillar of stone,
Inscribed with the deeds that great people have done.

OTTER.

P begins Prayer, such as dear little Ned
Beside mamma prayed, before going to bed.
P begins Primrose, a pretty spring flower.
Parasol, useful in sunshine and shower.
Plum, a nice fruit, very good in a pie.
Pear, such as often at market we buy.
Plough, that in spring o'er the rough field is drawn.
Peacock, a fine bird that struts on the lawn.
Poplar, a tree very slender and tall.
Pie, and Plum-Pudding, that pleases us all.
Pen, that we write with ; and Postman, who calls,
With letters and Packets, at hovels and halls.
Also Policeman, with bull's-eye so bright,
Who goes round to see all is safe in the night.
Pail, that Poll carries about when she cleans.
Palm-tree, so common in all Eastern scenes.
Padlock, with which Papa fastens the gate.
Pole, a long tree-stem, so tall and so straight.
Pelican, Parrot—birds very well known.
Pickaxe ; and Pillar, a column of stone.

Q begins Queen, dear to you and to me,
And honoured by all in her grand Jubilee;
For fifty long years our loved ruler she's been,
And the prayer of us all is, "God bless our good Queen!"

R begins Rosa; how pleased she appears
To watch those plump Rabbits, with long, silky ears!

Q begins Quarrel—one angry word,
And oh, what a host of bad passions is stirred!
Quill, that papa can make into a pen,
And with it write letters to dear brother Ben.
Quince, a nice fruit, like a large yellow pear,
That grows on a tree now become very rare.
Quagga, an animal; Quail, a plump bird,
Whose cry in the springtime we sometimes have heard.
Quarry, a pit where they dig out the stone,
Just down by the hill-side, so barren and lone
Q for a Quack who pretends to great skill,
And boasts of his wonderful potion or pill.
Quilt, the warm cover, so carefully spread,
By nurse's kind hands, on my snug little bed.
Question, the word of inquiry we ask
When difficult subjects occur in our task.
Quiet, the silence mamma bids us keep
While trying to hush the dear baby to sleep.

Rose, the fair flower with so sweet a perfume,
The queen of the garden, the joy of the room.
Rainbow, a many-hued arch in the sky.
Rocks, that rise up in the ocean so high.
Rower, whose sturdy hands ply the stout oar,
Driving the boat through the surf of the shore.
Rake, that is used to turn over the hay;
Rick, the tall pile when they store it away.
River, where James goes to bathe every morn.
Reaper, the man who cuts down the ripe corn.
Raft, built of logs, or of stout trunks of trees,
Bearing men safely o'er rivers and seas.
Raspberries—see how they hang in the sun.
Rover, with Robert, just out for a run.
Rush, that bends gracefully over the Rill.
Ravine, a deep hollow pass in the hill.
Ruth, the good maiden of whom you may read
In the Book of all books—a sweet story indeed.

S begins slave. Who can look without pain
On that agonised face, and that whip, and that chain?

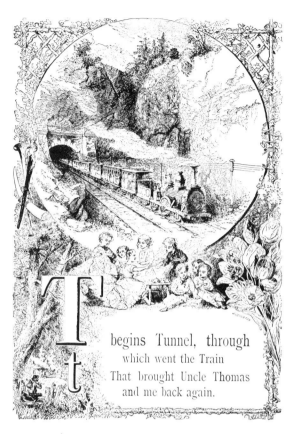

T begins Tunnel, through which went the Train
That brought Uncle Thomas and me back again.

Squirrel, that acorns and nuts loves to hide.
String, with which Susan's great bandbox was tied.
Shell—on the beach what a number we found !
Spade—papa used it to turn up the ground.
Swan, that so gracefully floats on the Stream.
Sun, that arises with bright ruddy beam.
Strawberry, too, a soft fruit, very sweet.
Shoes, papa buys me to wear on my feet.
Sleep, for dear baby ; and Shed, for the Sheep.
Sickle, a curved knife, with which the men reap.
Spectacles, grandmamma wears on her nose.
Snowdrop, the earliest Spring flower that blows.
Ship, a large vessel that sails on the Sea.
Slate—mamma says she will buy one for me.
Scissors, we cut with ; a Sieve, Stool, and Shower ;
And Sceptre, well known as the emblem of power.

Ticket—the guard did not ask me for mine ;
Telegraph, too, by the side of the line ;
Trellis—the cross-wood up which the plants grow ;
Tulips, full blown, what a beautiful show !
Tea-party, given as Teacher's kind Treat,
With Table, Tray, Teapot, and Teacups so neat.
Trunk of the Tree that the woodmen cut down
For Timber to build the Tall Tower in the Town.
Turnpike, or Toll-gate, across the high road ;
Throne, for the monarch ; Tusk, Tiger, and Toad ;
Thistle, a weed very prickly and rank ;
Thyme, the sweet plant that we found on the bank.
Trumpet, well known for its loud-sounding blare ;
Torch, that to light them at night the men bear ;
Traveller—see how he sits on the stile :
Perhaps he's been walking for many a mile.
Top—when you're older I'll buy one for you.
Tongue—it should speak what is loving and true.

U
u begins Urn, that at
tea-time Jane brings,
When we all love to hear
how it hisses and sings.

V
v begins Van, such as, last
Whitsuntide,
Took out our school-class for
a holiday ride.

Also Umbrella, that keeps us so dry,
When the heavy rain pours from the black angry
sky.
Union—in the picture its power we see,
Where five men united pull down that great tree.
Union-jack, the famed flag of our land.
Usher, the second at school in command.
Underwood—bushes that grow beneath trees.
Uncle—a fine romp I had on his knees,
Up, a good word in our memory to keep,
When we wake in the morning, refreshed, from our
sleep.

Viaduct, too, the arched road, high and strong,
On which our good horses went trotting along.
Village, the cluster of houses we passed :
And so we arrived at the common at last.
Vine, whose ripe grapes we all think such a treat.
Vessel, that holds our spring-water so sweet.
Violin, Vincent is learning to play,
(He finds it not easy, I venture to say).
Volcano, a mountain that bursts into flame ;
The picture contains one—Vesuvius by name.
Violet, too, a most sweet-scented thing,
That often we meet with in woods, in the spring.
Vase, a large pot used for holding our flowers.
Verandah, that shelters from sunshine and showers.
Vagrant, who strays without home in the land.
Volume, a book, such as this in your hand.

W many a Word does begin;
As Water-wheel, Walnut, Wheat, Wheelbarrow, Win.

X stands for ten, 'tis a number we know, Recalling Mount Sinai in ages ago,

Wind, that blows over the common so strong :
It drives, as you see, the poor children along.
Ah, Walter, my boy, for your cap you must run ;
Though William, behind, calls it capital fun.
Windmill, whose great sails but rarely stand still.
Waggon—the team has just come up the hill.
Well, that supplies us with Water to drink.
Willow, that droops by the cool river's brink.
Wasp, very fond of a ripe plum or peach.
Wreck—a sad sight, lying there on the beach.
Wall-flower ; and Weeds, by the roadside so rank.
Wren—you should see her neat nest in the bank.
Wall, in our garden, where sweet roses climb.
Watch, like papa has, to show
 him the time.
Winter, that scatters the leaves
 in the Wood ;
And Wheat, that will give us
 such very good food.

When Moses ascended and took from God's hands,
Writ on tables of stone, these ten great Commands.
I.
Worship the Lord God, thy Maker, alone ;
II.
And bow not to idols of wood or of stone.
III.
Speak not God's name without reverence and awe,
Or He will reprove thee for breaking this law.
IV.
Remember the Sabbath, of all days the best :
Work six, keep the seventh for worship and rest.
V.
Honour thy parents, if thou wouldst live long.
VI.
Thou shalt not kill, with the sword or the tongue.
VII.
Avoid thoughts and actions unclean or impure.
VIII.
Beware that thou steal not, although thou be poor.
IX.
Thou no false witness 'gainst any shalt bear,
X.
Nor covet thy neighbour's more bountiful share.

Y begins Yule-log, that blazes so bright,
Round which You sit on a cold Christmas night.

Z the last letter, which seldom we need,
As you will discover, when books you can read.

Yew, a long-lived, and dark shadowy tree,
That often in old country churchyards we see.
Yacht, a small vessel, so nice for a sail ;
That skims like a bird, in a favouring gale.
Gay Yellow-hammer, a sweet lively bird.
York Minster, of this fine cathedral you've heard.
Yoke, that connects those two oxen, so strong,
The lad in the picture is leading along.
Yeoman (or Beef-eater) well known at court.
Yarmouth, a favourite seaside resort.
Yawl, a ship's boat, that we saw on the shore,
The day that papa took us all to the Nore.

Ż begins Zenith, the sky overhead,
Where shines the pale moon, as we lie in our bed.
Also Zaccheus, who climbed up a tree,
That, as he was short, he the Saviour might see.
Also Zoological Gardens, where Ned
One day went to see the wild animals fed ;
Among them the Zebra, Zibet and Zebu,
The Zuna and Zerda—all there in the Zoo.

ZEBU.

Footsteps on the Road to Learning; or The Alphabet in Rhyme. New Haven: S. Babcock, 1850. Pp. 16. 10.7 x 7.2 cm.

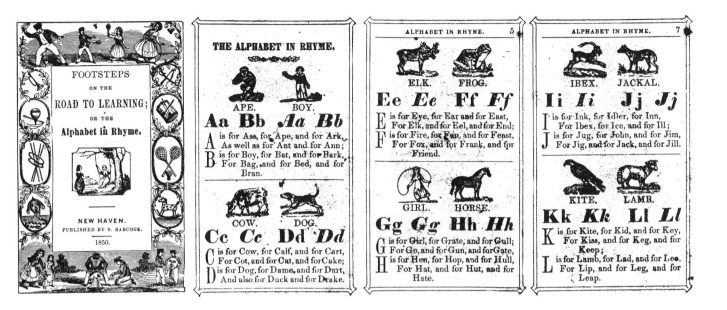

THE ALPHABET IN RHYME.

APE.   BOY.

Aa Bb *Aa Bb*

A is for Ass, for Ape, and for Ark,
  As well as for Ant and for Ann;
B is for Boy, for Bat, and for Bark,
  For Bag, and for Bed, and for Bran.

COW.   DOG.

Cc *Cc* **Dd** *Dd*

C is for Cow, for Calf, and for Cart,
  For Cot, and for Cat, and for Cake;
D is for Dog, for Dame, and for Dart,
  And also for Duck and for Drake.

ALPHABET IN RHYME.   5

ELK.   FROG.

Ee *Ee* **Ff** *Ff*

E is for Eye, for Ear and for East,
  For Elk, and for Eel, and for End;
F is for Fire, for Fan, and for Feast,
  For Fox, and for Frank, and for Friend.

GIRL.   HORSE.

Gg *Gg* **Hh** *Hh*

G is for Girl, for Grate, and for Gull;
  For Go, and for Gun, and for Gate,
H is for Hen, for Hop, and for Hull,
  For Hat, and for Hut, and for Hate.

ALPHABET IN RHYME.   7

IBEX.   JACKAL.

Ii *Ii* **Jj** *Jj*

I is for Ink, for Idler, for Inn,
  For Ibex, for Ice, and for Ill;
J is for Jug, for John, and for Jim,
  For Jig, and for Jack, and for Jill.

KITE.   LAMB.

Kk *Kk* **Ll** *Ll*

K is for Kite, for Kid, and for Key,
  For Kiss, and for Keg, and for Keep;
L is for Lamb, for Lad, and for Lee,
  For Lip, and for Leg, and for Leap.

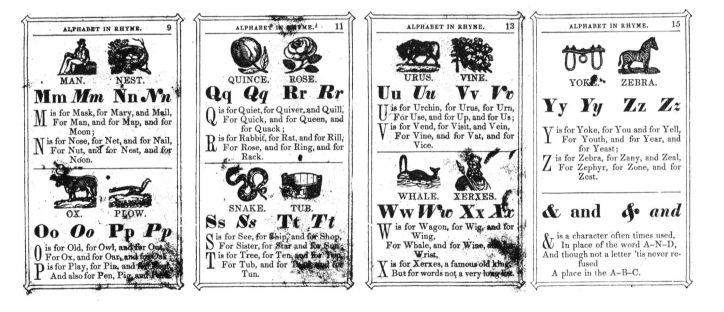

ALPHABET IN RHYME.   9

MAN.   NEST.

Mm *Mm* **Nn** *Nn*

M is for Mask, for Mary, and Mail,
  For Man, and for Map, and for Moon;
N is for Nose, for Net, and for Nail,
  For Nut, and for Nest, and for Noon.

OX.   PLOW.

Oo *Oo* **Pp** *Pp*

O is for Old, for Owl, and for Oat,
  For Ox, and for Oar, and for Oak;
P is for Play, for Pin, and for Pout,
  And also for Pen, Pig, and Poke.

ALPHABET IN RHYME.   11

QUINCE.   ROSE.

Qq *Qq* **Rr** *Rr*

Q is for Quiet, for Quiver, and Quill,
  For Quick, and for Queen, and for Quack;
R is for Rabbit, for Rat, and for Rill,
  For Rose, and for Ring, and for Rack.

SNAKE.   TUB.

Ss *Ss* **Tt** *Tt*

S is for See, for Ship, and for Shop,
  For Sister, for Star and for Sun;
T is for Tree, for Ten, and for Top,
  For Tub, and for Toad, and for Tun.

ALPHABET IN RHYME.   13

URUS.   VINE.

Uu *Uu* **Vv** *Vv*

U is for Urchin, for Urus, for Urn,
  For Use, and for Up, and for Us;
V is for Vend, for Visit, and Vein,
  For Vine, and for Vat, and for Vice.

WHALE.   XERXES.

Ww *Ww* **Xx** *Xx*

W is for Wagon, for Wig, and for Wing,
  For Whale, and for Wine, and Wrist,
X is for Xerxes, a famous old king,
  But for words not a very long list.

ALPHABET IN RHYME.   15

YOKE.   ZEBRA.

Yy *Yy* **Zz** *Zz*

Y is for Yoke, for You and for Yell,
  For Youth, and for Year, and for Yeast;
Z is for Zebra, for Zany, and Zeal,
  For Zephyr, for Zone, and for Zest.

& and *& and*

& is a character often times used,
  In place of the word A–N–D,
And though not a letter 'tis never refused
  A place in the A–B–C.

Child's Treasury of Knowledge. Boston: Wier & White. Pp. [27], including paper cover. 17 x 14.5 cm. [left]

The Pretty Picture A. B. C. With Rhymes to Please My Friends and Me. London, Edinburgh, and New York: T. Nelson and Sons. Pp. 30. 22.7 x 16.6 cm. [right, text only]

270

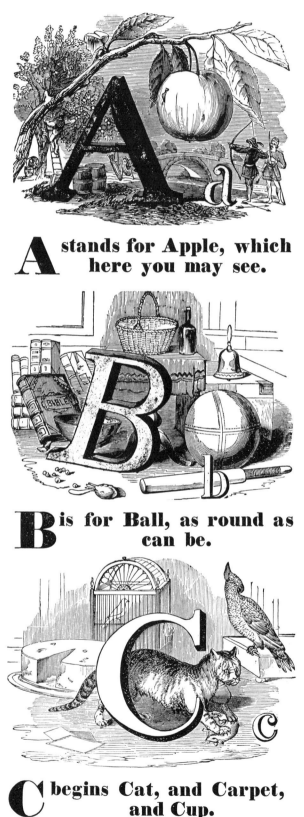

A stands for Apple, which here you may see.

A begins Apple, Aunt, Annie, and Aim;
A is in master, and A is in dame.
A begins Archer, Ape, Arrow, and Arch;
A is in sugar, soap, treacle, and starch.
A begins Arthur, Ant, Andrew, and Axe;
A is in hammer, in nails, and in tacks.
A begins Alfred, Ann, Agnes, and Arm;
A is in meadow, lane, cottage, and farm.
A begins Anger, and Ankle, and Ache;
A is in custard, and mustard, and cake.
A begins Amy, and Ada, and Ass;
A is never in school, but is always in class.

B is for Ball, as round as can be.

B begins Bible, Ball, Basket, and Boy;
B is always in trouble, but never in joy.
B begins Bottle, Ball, Bertha, and Bess;
B is always in robes, but is never in dress.
B begins Baby, Baize, Box, Bag, and Bowl;
B is always in cabbage, but never in cole.
B begins Baker, Bread, Bun, Beef, and Bat;
B is always in lobster, but never in sprat.
B begins Bonnet, and Basin, and Bees;
B is always in shrub, but is never in trees.
B begins Business, finishes job;
B begins, and B finishes, Barb, Bib, and Bob.

C begins Cat, and Carpet, and Cup.

C begins Carpet, Cat, Claw, Cage, and Cheese;
C is always in ice-house, but never in freeze.
C begins Cockatoo, Charlotte, and Cows;
C is always in branches, but never in boughs.
C begins Cards, Canary, and Crowns;
C is always in frocks, but is never in gowns.
C begins Clara, Charles, Cherries, and Cook;
C is always in pictures, but never in book.
C begins Coffee, Cup, Cocoa, and Cream;
C is always in stitches, but never in seam.
C begins Candy, Cock, Currants, and Cake;
C is always in pickle, but never in bake.

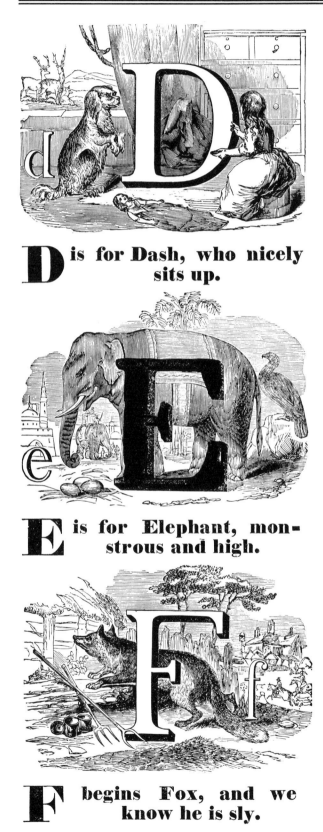

D is for Dash, who nicely sits up.

E is for Elephant, monstrous and high.

F begins Fox, and we know he is sly.

D begins Daughter, Doll, Dog, Deer, and Doe;
D is always in sadness, but never in woe.
D begins Deborah, Dora, and Dan;
D is always in childhood, but never in man.
D begins Dumpling, and Damson, and Dick;
D is always in cudgel, but never in stick.
D begins David, and Daisy, and Date;
D is in handle, and chest-of-drawers great.
D begins Donkey, Duke, Duck, Drake, and Drum;
D is always in candy, but never in plum.
D begins Dresser, Desk, Darling, and Door;
D is always in thousands, but never in more.

E begins Elephant, Eagle, and Eye;
E is never in pudding, but always in pie:
E begins Edward, Eliza, and Earth;
E is always in laughter, but never in mirth.
E begins Eva, and Elbow, and Eggs;
E is never in arms, but is always in legs.
E is in river, in lake, and in sea;
E is in breakfast, and dinner, and tea;
E is in red, green, yellow, and blue;
E is always in me, but is never in you.
E begins Emma, Earl, Esther, and Ear;
E is never in month, but is always in year.

F begins Farmhouse, Fox, Fir-tree, and Fence;
F is always in halfpence, but never in pence.
F begins Flowers, Forks, Frolic, and Fun;
F is always in rifle, but never in gun.
F begins Fire, Field, Flora, and Fred;
F is always in muffin, but never in bread.
F begins Francis, and Frances, and Flight;
F is always in left, but is never in right.
F begins Fender, Fish, Fiddle, and Flute;
F begins Fuchsia, Fowl, Farmer, and Fruit;
F begins Fortune, Flag, Frog, Foot, and Face;
F is always in office, but never in place.

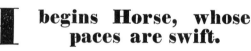

G stands for Gander, for Goose, and for Gift.

G begins Gander, Goose, Gosling, and Geese;
G is always in anger, but never in peace.
G begins Ginger, Grapes, Goat, Gate, and Gum;
G is always in finger, but never in thumb.
G begins Giant, Gun, Greyhound, and Gnat;
G ends stag, and ends dog, but it never ends cat.
G begins Gregory, Gertrude, and George;
G is never in anvil, but always in forge.
G is always in danger, and always in rage;
G is never in youth, but is always in age.
G begins Gentleman, Gimlet, and Gig;
G begins Grunter, and always ends pig.

H begins Horse, whose paces are swift.

H begins Hunter, Horse, Hire, Hunt, and Horn;
H is always in birth, but is never in born.
H begins Hollyhock, Henry, and Hand;
H begins Humble, but is never in grand.
H is always in might, but is never in power;
H is silent in Honour, in Herb, and in Hour.
H begins Harness, House, Hamper, and Hugh;
H is always in church, but is never in pew.
H is in riches, and H is in wealth;
H begins Happiness, H begins Health.
H begins Harvest, and finishes dearth;
H begins Heaven, and finishes earth.

I is an Infant, and dressed out in silk.

I begins Infant, and Image, and Inn;
I is never in stout, but is always in thin.
I begins Inkstand, and Ingle, and Ice;
I is never in once, but is always in twice.
I begins Isaac, Isabella, and Ire;
I is never in water, but always in fire.
I begins Idol, and Idle, and Irk;
I is always in holiday, never in work;
I begins Isa, and Island, and Isles;
I is never in frowns, but is always in smiles.
I begins Illness, and I is in pain;
I is never in losses, but always in gain.

J is a Jug, to hold water or milk,

J begins Jelly, Jam, Jar, Jug, and Joe;
J begins Journey, wherever we go
J begins Jacob, John, Jack, Jane, and James;
J begins Judy, and other fine names.
J begins Jewels, so sparkling and clear;
J begins Jesting, and J begins Jeer.
J begins Jingle, Juice, Justice, and Jew;
J begins Jalap; who likes it? Do you?
J begins Judge, but is never in thief;
J is always in major, but never in chief.
J begins Jumping, and comes after I;
J begins Jolly, Joy, June, and July.

K is a Kitten, that plays with a ball.

K begins Kitten, Knife, Kite, and Key;
K begins Knuckle, Knight, Kettle, and Knee.
K is always in pocket, but never in pouch;
K is always in blanket, but never in couch.
K begins Kitchen, Kine, Kestrel, and King;
K is always in talk, but is never in sing.
K begins Knocker, and Knowledge, and Kale;
K is always in bucket, but never in pail.
K begins Kerchief, and Kindness, and Ken;
K is always in chicken, but never in hen.
K begins Kangaroo, Kennel, and Keep;
K is always in waking, but never in sleep.

L is a Ladder, for climbing a wall.

L begins Ladder, Loaf, Ladle, and Light;
L is always in almost, but never in quite.
L begins Lamp-post, and Lion, and Lad;
L is always in fault, but is never in bad.
L begins Learning, and Laughing, and Lamb;
L is always in jelly, but never in jam.
L begins Lady, and Laurel, and Lake;
L is always in tremble, but never in shake.
L begins Leonard, and Lucy, and Lace;
L is always in allspice, but never in mace.
L begins Looking-glass, Laura, and Lawn;
L is always in twilight, but never in dawn.

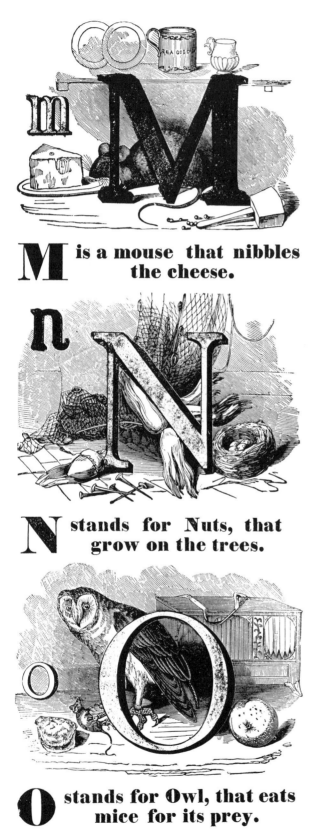

M is a mouse that nibbles the cheese.

N stands for Nuts, that grow on the trees.

O stands for Owl, that eats mice for its prey.

M begins Mallet, Mug, Mouse, Man, and Meat;
M is always in summer, but never in heat.
M begins Marble, Mind, Music, and Mince;
M is always in sometimes, but never in since.
M begins Mary, Maria, and Me;
M is always in bramble, but never in tree.
M begins Mason, Milk, Muslin, and Musk;
M is always in dimness, but never in dusk.
M begins Marion, Maud, Meg, and Maid;
M is always in commerce, but never in trade.
M begins Morning, March, Monday, and May;
M is always in ramble, but never in stray.

N begins Nannie, Nat, Nest, Nuts, and Nails;
N is always in England, but never in Wales.
N begins Nightingale, Needle, and Nurse;
N is always in money, but never in purse.
N begins Negro, and Nephew, and Niece;
N is always in goslings, but never in geese.
N begins Navy, Nile, Nelson, and Night;
N is always in conquer, but never in flight.
N begins Narrative, Nothing, and News;
N is always in stockings, but never in shoes.
N begins Nora, Nathaniel, and Name;
N is always in wrong, but is never in blame.

O begins Orange, and Organ, and Owl;
O is never in fish, but is always in fowl.
O begins Oyster, and Orchard, and Oak;
O is never in earnest, but always in joke.
O begins Oliver, Otter, and Ox;
O is never in watches, but always in clocks.
O is never in ship, but is always in boat;
O is never in music, but always in note.
O is in people, in country, in town;
O is never in black, but is always in brown.
O is in forty, in one, and in two;
O is never in me, but is always in you.

P stands for Parrots, some green and some grey.

Q stands for Quills, from the goose or the swan.

R stands for Rabbits, for Fanny or John.

P begins Parrot, Prop, Paint, Pot, and Pail ;
P is always in prosper, but never in fail.
P begins Pigeon, Plumes, Poles, Punt, and Pine ;
P is always in rope, but is never in twine.
P begins Parachute, Palings, and Perch ;
P is always in chapel, but never in church.
P begins Peter, and Philip, and Paul ;
P is always in topple, but never in fall.
P begins Phœbe, Priscilla, and Pope ;
P is never in fear, but is always in hope.
P begins Printer, Prince, Poet, and Peer ;
P is never in globe, but is always in sphere.

Q begins Quarto, Queen, Quill-pens, and Quart ;
Q is always in liquor, but never in port.
Q begins Question, and Quarrel, and Quay ;
Q is always in vanquish, but never in flee.
Q begins Quartern, and Quire, and Quilt ;
Q is always in lacquer, but never in gilt.
Q begins Quiver, and Quaver, and Quince ;
Q is always in marquis, but never in prince.
Q begins Quadruped, Quarry, and Queer ;
Q is always in squint, but is never in leer.
Q begins Quizzing, and this is Quite true ;
Q is always, when used in words, followed by u

R begins Rabbit, Rose, Roller, and Rake ;
R is always in terror, but never in quake.
R begins Robert, and Richard, and Ruth ;
R is never in falsehood, but always in truth.
R begins Raisins, Rice, Rook, and Roach ;
R is always in carriage, but never in coach.
R begins Roaming, and Raven, and Reap ;
R is always in shepherd, but never in sheep.
R begins Rattle, Robes, Reindeer, and Ring ;
R is always in prince, but is never in king.
R begins Railway, and River, and Road ;
R is always in burden, but never in load.

S stands for Snail, with its house on its back.

T stands for Tiger, striped yellow and black.

U stands for Urn, to hold water for tea.

S begins Swallow, Scythe, Spade, Snake, and
S is always in prison, but never in jail.   [Snail
S begins Sailor, Sea, Ship, Storm, and Steer;
S is always in mischief, but never in fear.
S begins Sparrow, and Struggle, and Strife;
S is always in husband, but never in wife.
S begins Summer, and Sunshine, and Steam;
S is always in horses, but never in team.
S begins Supper, School, Scholar, and Sprat;
S is always in this, but is never in that.
S begins Stable, Steed, Saddler, and Spice;
S is always in frost, but is never in ice.

T begins Tiger, Tent, Target, and Tower;
T is always in minute, but never in hour.
T begins Tinker, Trap, Top, Tree, and Tun;
T is always in father, but never in son.
T begins Timothy, Thomas, and Ted;
T is always in battle, but never in dread.
T begins Table, Tea, Turnips, and Tale;
T is always in porter, but never in ale.
T begins Thimble, and Tailor, and Toys;
T is always in youths, but is never in boys.
T begins Thousands, This, That, These, and Those
T is always in beating, but never in blows.

U begins Uncle, Umbrella, and Urn;
U is never in fire, but always in burn.
U begins Usurer, Urchin, and Urge;
U is never in billow, but always in surge.
U begins Urban, Unkindness, and Use;
U is never in gravy, but always in juice.
U begins Uppermost, Uproar, and Us;
U is never in comfort, but always in fuss.
U begins Unit, Untie, and Unite;
U is in courteous, but not in polite.
U begins Usher, Upholsterer, and Usk;
U is never in twilight, but always in dusk.

V begins Vulture, Verbena, and Vine;
V is always in cavern, but never in mine.
V begins Violet, Vintner, and Vest;
V is in jovial, but is not in jest.
V begins Violin, Verger, and Vane;
V is always in clover, but never in grain.
V begins Vinegar, Village, and Vale;
V is in travel, but never in rail.
V begins Viper, Venison, and Vow;
V is always in never, but never in now.
V begins Vicar, and Valley, and View;
V is always in mauve, but is never in blue.

V is a Violet, which here you may see.

W begins Windmill, Wheelbarrow, and Well;
W is in answer, but is not in tell.
W begins Walnut, Watch, Waggon, and Wed;
W is in Edward, but is not in Ned.
W begins William, Wheel, Window, and Wife;
W is in scowling, but is not in strife.
W begins Warrior, Wasp, Wallet, and Wane;
W is in railway, but is not in train.
W begins Wilderness, Water, and Wall;
W is in cowl, in fowl, and in bawl.
W begins Winter, and Writer, and Wing;
W is in towel, and vowel, and swing.

W is a Windmill, that turns with the wind.

X begins no English word, it is said.
X stands for 10, and as TEN it is read.
X begins Xenophon, famous of old;
X begins Xan-tip-pe; couldn't she scold!
X is in Exeter, axle, and axe;
X is found in excise, but is never in tacks.
X begins Xerxes, for valour renowned;
X in taxes, and boxes, and foxes is found.
X finishes Essex, and Sussex, and Ox;
X finishes lynx, sphinx, syntax, and box.
X finishes climax, and phœnix, and hoax.
X finishes borax, flax, flox, and coax.

X is a letter like this X, you will find.

Y is a Youth, who has many kind friends.

Z comes the last, and here it all ends.

Y begins Yew-tree, Youth, Yacht, and Yore ;
Y always ends many, but never ends more.
Y begins Yesterday, Yellow, and Yule ;
Y is always in donkeys, but never in mule.
Y begins Yeoman, Yoke, Yam, and Yarn ;
Y always ends granary, never ends barn.
Y finishes misery, folly, and day ;
Y begins Yea, and it finishes nay.
Y is in valleys, in chimneys, in drays ;
Y finishes flattery, but is not in praise.
Y finishes glory, and misery too ;
Y finishes beauty, and Y begins You.

Z begins Zebra, and Zouave, and Zone ;
Z is in grizzle, but never in groan.
Z begins Zany, and Zephyr, and Zinc ;
Z is always in puzzle, but never in think.
Z begins Zenith, and Zero, and Zeal ;
Z is always in razor, but never in steel.
Z begins Zealot, and Zion, and Zest ;
Z is always in crazy, but never in rest.
Z is in laziness—a bad thing it is ;
Z finishes buzz, and it finishes quiz.
Z begins Zo-e, and Zebra, and Zend ;
Z is, of the twenty-six letters, THE END.

The ABC Surprise Book. With Verses by Clifton Bingham. Pen-and-ink Illustrations by E. Stuart Hardy. London: Ernest Nister; New York: E. P. Dutton & Co., [1890?], inscribed March 15, 1900. Pp. [16]. 24.3 x 19.4 cm.

The

ABC SURPRISE BOOK

With Verses by
Clifton Bingham.

Pen-and-ink

Illustrations by
E. STUART HARDY.

London:
ERNEST NISTER

Printed in Bavaria.
458.

New York.
E. P. DUTTON & Co.

A IS for Apple so rosy and round,
That even our Baby enjoys,
As well as for Ark, which
is sure to be found
In the cupboard along with your toys.

B IS for Bellows, that make the fire blaze,
And B, you will see, is for Ball;
And B's for the Baby
who with the Ball plays,
Although she can only just crawl.

C IS for Chestnuts that grow on the trees,
That Children can roast by the fire,
And for Cradle where Baby
can sleep at her ease,
Whenever her pretty eyes tire.

D IS for Dustpan, and Dolly so Dear,
For Dog, and Dinner Service new—
The Dishes you take down
when Dinner-time's near,
And that very carefully too!

E IS for Elephant, seen at the Zoo,
And for Eagle, a very fierce bird;
And the Eye-glasses funny
that Grandma looks thro',
For without them she can't read a word.

F IS for Frying Pan, used when you cook,
And for Fan that will open and close;
And the Fine Fun you'll have
when you look at this book,
When you see the surprises it shows.

G IS for Goldfish so pretty and small,
And Guitar, that you wish you could play,
And for Games that
the little folks like one and all,
In the Garden with flowers so Gay.

H IS for Hammer, too Heavy for you,
And Hat, that you wear,
made of straw;
For the House that you live
in, and Happiness too—
And for Horses
who carriages draw.

I IS for Inkstand you use
when you write;
And J is for Jackdaw, and Jug,
And for Jane good and kind,
who at tea-time each night
Pours milk from it
into your mug.

K IS for Knife, and
for Kite that you fly,
And for Key that
will open a door;
For Kitty so playful, and Kiss when you cry,
And ever so many things more.

L IS for Looking-glass, and sister Loo,
For Lily, and Lion so strong;
For the Lessons you do, and for Lawn-mower too,
That cuts the green grass when it's Long.

M IS for Matchbox from
which you get light,
For Mother, and
Mousie, who'll steal
From his wee little hole
in the Middle of night,
And Make out of cheese a good Meal.

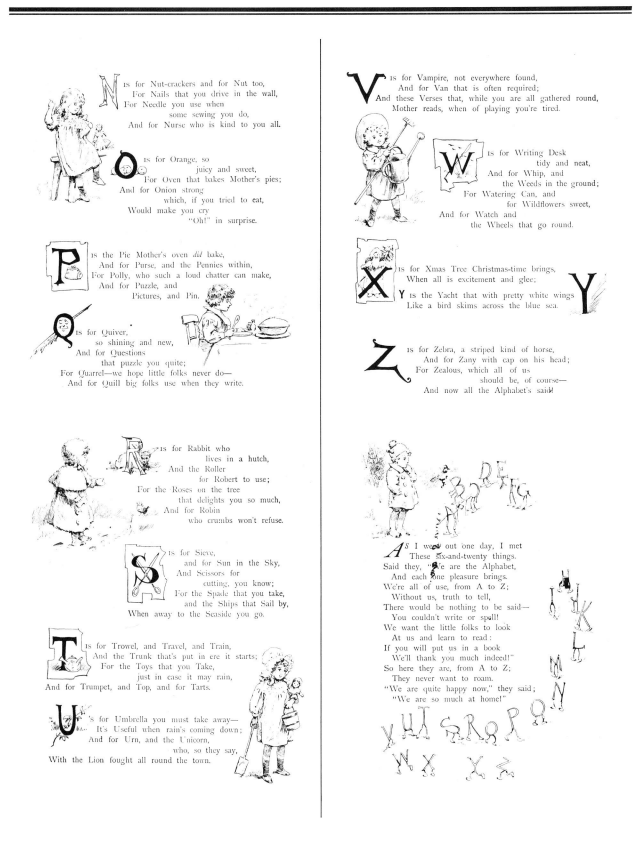

N is for Nut-crackers and for Nut too,
  For Nails that you drive in the wall,
For Needle you use when
      some sewing you do,
And for Nurse who is kind to you all.

O is for Orange, so
      juicy and sweet,
  For Oven that bakes Mother's pies;
And for Onion strong
      which, if you tried to eat,
Would make you cry
      "Oh!" in surprise.

P is the Pie Mother's oven *did* bake,
  And for Purse, and the Pennies within,
For Polly, who such a loud chatter can make,
  And for Puzzle, and
      Pictures, and Pin.

Q is for Quiver,
      so shining and new,
And for Questions
      that puzzle you quite;
For Quarrel—we hope little folks never do—
And for Quill big folks use when they write.

R is for Rabbit who
      lives in a hutch,
  And the Roller
      for Robert to use;
For the Roses on the tree
      that delights you so much,
And for Robin
      who crumbs won't refuse.

S is for Sieve,
      and for Sun in the Sky,
  And Scissors for
      cutting, you know;
For the Spade that you take,
      and the Ships that Sail by,
When away to the Seaside you go.

T is for Trowel, and Travel, and Train,
  And the Trunk that's put in ere it starts;
For the Toys that you Take,
      just in case it may rain,
And for Trumpet, and Top, and for Tarts.

U 's for Umbrella you must take away—
  It's Useful when rain's coming down;
And for Urn, and the Unicorn,
      who, so they say,
With the Lion fought all round the town.

V is for Vampire, not everywhere found,
  And for Van that is often required;
And these Verses that, while you are all gathered round,
  Mother reads, when of playing you're tired.

W is for Writing Desk
      tidy and neat,
  And for Whip, and
      the Weeds in the ground;
For Watering Can, and
      for Wildflowers sweet,
And for Watch and
      the Wheels that go round.

X is for Xmas Tree Christmas-time brings,
  When all is excitement and glee;
Y is the Yacht that with pretty white wings
  Like a bird skims across the blue sea.

Z is for Zebra, a striped kind of horse,
  And for Zany with cap on his head;
For Zealous, which all of us
      should be, of course—
And now all the Alphabet's said!

As I went out one day, I met
  These six-and-twenty things.
Said they, "We are the Alphabet,
  And each one pleasure brings.
We're all of use, from A to Z;
  Without us, truth to tell,
There would be nothing to be said—
  You couldn't write or spell!
We want the little folks to look
  At us and learn to read:
If you will put us in a book
  We'll thank you much indeed!"
So here they are, from A to Z;
  They never want to roam.
"We are quite happy now," they said;
  "We are so much at home!"

"Alphabet of the Old Testament" (12 pp., including 6 colored plates), from Routledge's Scripture Gift Book, Containing Alphabet of the Old Testament, Alphabet
of the New Testament, History of Joseph, History of Moses. With Ninety-Six Illustrations, Printed in Colours by Leighton. London and New York: George Routledge and Sons, [1866]. 27.5 x 23 cm.

AARON, the High Priest of the Jews, within the
Temple pray'd

And offer'd sacrifices, which were on the altar laid.

BALAAM the Prophet, on an ass, a visit went
to pay

To Balak: but an Angel stood to meet him on the way.

CAIN, the first son of Adam, full of jealousy and
pride,

Fiercely kill'd his brother Abel, and was wretched till
he died.

DANIEL, faithful, brave, and pious, was shut in
the lions' den

By the heathen King Darius, but came safely out
again;

For God, who made the Lions, watches over righteous
men.

ELIJAH, when he hid himself, had nothing left
to eat,

But the Lord's ravens daily brought the Prophet bread
and meat.

FINDING the infant Moses: who, left at the river's
side,

Was lying in a little ark, with fresh bulrushes tied;—

Great Pharaoh's daughter pitied as the child look'd up
and cried.

GOLIATH, of the Philistines the leader and the
pride,

Came forth and laugh'd, while all the host of Israel he
defied;

But David with a sling and stone so smote him that
he died.

HAGAR and **ISHMAEL** her son, out to
the desert fled,

With water in a bottle, and a little loaf of bread.

But, when they both had call'd to God, in safety they
were led.

JOB suffer'd many sorrows, but was patient to the end,

Knowing in all his troubles that the Lord was still his friend.

KING DAVID, once a shepherd boy, to Israel's throne was raised,

And, singing to his harp, in sweetest Psalms he pray'd and praised.

LOT, with his wife and daughters, left the Cities of the Plain,

Which for their wickedness God smote with storms of fiery rain;

But Lot's wife was destroy'd, because she would look back again.

MIRIAM the Prophetess, was Aaron's sister: she

Led forth the Jewish women who escaped from the Red Sea,

And danced and sang for joy that all her nation was set free.

NOAH alone of all the people hated evil and loved good,

And when the earth was drown'd by rain from heaven in a flood,

God taught him how to build a ship, or ark, of gopher wood.

OBADIAH sought from wicked men Elijah's life to save,

It was he who fed and hid a hundred prophets in a cave.

PHARAOH the King of Egypt would not let God's people go,

But made them slaves, till Moses wrought strange miracles, to show

That even Kings who disobey will suffer pain and woe.

QUEEN OF SHEBA. You have heard how she from her own country came,

And brought rich gifts to Solomon, whose wisdom, skill, and fame

Caused Kings and Princes to bow down in homage to his name.

RUTH was the youthful widow, of the tender, loving heart,

Who refused, in spite of poverty, from Naomi to part.

SAMSON, the man of mighty strength, who blind and captive lay

Within a house, in which his foes had come to drink and play,

Pull'd down the pillars, and the house fell on them all that day.

TUBAL CAIN was first of workmen who for useful metals sought,

And brass and iron into shape at the smith's anvil wrought.

VASHTI, the Queen, refused to go at her proud King's command,

And so was sent away, while Esther sat at his right hand.

WIDOWED and poor and hungry, the woman was who fed

Elijah, Prophet of the Lord, with a small cake of bread,

But God return'd a hundredfold, and kept her table spread.

X is the letter which is used to show the number ten.

And ten Commandments Moses gave from God to sinful men.

YOUNG JOASH, when a little child, was hidden from the sight

Of those who sought to slay him, and was kept both day and night,

Till priests and captains claim'd for him his own true kingly right.

ZEDEKIAH, King of Judah, lived to see his sons both slain,

Then blind and captive went away, never to see again.

For he led an evil life, which brings both misery and pain.

"The Railway Alphabet" (12 pp., including 6 colored plates), from *The Little Folks' Gift Book,* Containing Forty-eight Pages of Pictures, Printed in Colours with Letterpress Descriptions. London: Frederick Warne & Co., [1885]. 18.6 x 16.4 cm.

THE RAILWAY ALPHABET.

A stands for the ARCH that's thrown over a stream,
On which the bright sun throws its earliest beam.

B's for BOOKING OFFICE, where tickets we buy;
Here, to learn when our train will come in, we apply.

C is for CHARING CROSS. This is the station
At which trav'llers gather from every nation.

D stands for the DRIVER, who looks out for Danger;
To this District Railway we hope he's no stranger.

B

E stands for the ENGINE, and "Empire," its name;
Along an Embankment this large Engine came.

F stands for FOG-SIGNAL; great danger there'd be
If the driver its light in fogs did not see.

G stands for the GUARD, who takes care of the train,
By his aid our station in safety we gain.

H stands for HIGH LEVEL. Above and below
The trains on their journeys by day and night go.

I stands for INSIDE of the Carriage you see;
The passengers seem very happy to be.

J stands for the JUNCTION where many lines meet;
We pass it in safety, the plan's so complete.

K stands for KING'S CROSS, with the trains coming in;
At stations so large there's a terrible din.

L is for LONDON BRIDGE; and Luggage that's waiting;
Here passengers often the porters are rating.

M stands for MIDNIGHT MAIL: swiftly it goes,
And Moonlight around it its silver ray throws.

N stands for NEWS-BOY who the papers supplies;
"Times! Standard! and Telegraph!" loudly he cries.

O stands for OFFICIALS, the porters and guard;
To keep the trains safe they all work very hard.

P stands for PULLMAN'S CAR, Pulling up by a Pond;
You may travel asleep, if of bed you are fond.

Q stands for the QUEEN, who here travels by train;
We hope that to Windsor she'll soon come again.

R stands for the RAILS of which Railways are made;
They all are of iron most carefully laid.

S stands for SIGNAL, and the Signal-box near,
Where warnings of danger must sometimes appear.

T stands for the TRAIN and the Tunnel as well,
In which for some minutes in darkness we dwell.

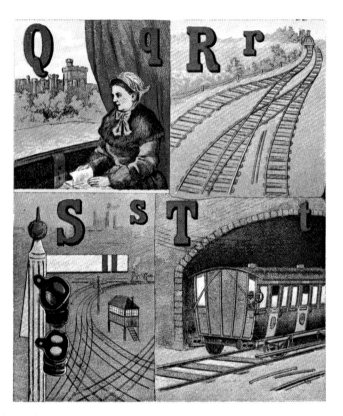

U stands for the UNDERGROUND RAILWAY, below,
By which to their business the Londoners go.

V stands for a VIADUCT, built with great pains,
To carry us over the rivers and plains.

W stands for the WATER TANK, that we require
To boil up for steam, or to put out a fire.

X for 'XCURSION TRAIN, when in fine weather,

Y, YEOMEN, Z, ZOUAVES, go travelling together.

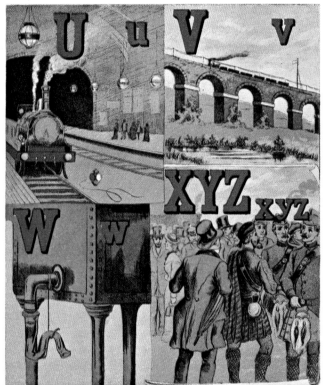

Picture Alphabet of Nations of the World. London & Edinburgh: T. Nelson & Sons, [1874]. Pp. [8], including 4 pages of colored plates. 28.4 x 22 cm.

THE ABYSSINIANS.[1]

A fierce and powerful race of old,
In their wild mountain land,
Against the arms of Britain they
Were all too weak to stand.

THE DYAKS.[4]

Beneath the palms of Borneo
The Dyak women rest;
While by their side the warriors stand,
In martial colours drest.

THE BEDOUIN.[2]

But seldom from his faithful steed
Will Arab parted be;
Courageous, grave, and stern of mood,
He loveth liberty

THE EGYPTIANS.[5]

Where rolls the famous river Nile
Its waters to the main,
The Egyptian leads a simple life,
And tills the sandy plain.

THE CHINESE.[3]

Long have the Chinese race been famed
For their mechanic skill;
Reserved and proud, they follow out
Their old traditions still.

THE FEEJEES.[6]

The Feejee Islands form a group
Within the sunny zone;
Their people are a savage race,
To strife and bloodshed prone.

[1] *Abyssinia* is on the western shore of the Red Sea.
[2] The *Bedouins* dwell in the wildernesses of Arabia.
[3] The *Chinese* inhabit the empire of China in Eastern Asia.

[4] The *Dyaks* are a race of Malays, living in the Island of Borneo.
[5] *Egypt* is a country of Africa, bounded on the north by the Mediterranean.
[6] The *Feejee Islands* are situated in the South Pacific Ocean.

THE GREEKS.[1]

A handsome people are the Greeks,
Who own a classic land;
But restless, wayward, and disposed
To spurn a ruler's hand.

THE JAPANESE.[4]

In far Japan, a patient race
Is famed for arts of peace;
And still their wealth and still their power
Through industry increase.

THE HINDOO.[2]

The Hindoo juggler's fame has spread
For strange and wondrous skill;
Unhurt he grasps the venomed snake,
And plays with it at will.

THE KAMTSCHADALES.[5]

A land of frost, and ice, and snow,
A sky all cold and drear;—
Well may the peaceful Kamtschadales
Their coats of sable wear.

THE ITALIANS.[3]

Beneath a bright transparent sky
The blithe Italian lives,
And joys in all the wealth of flowers
And fruit that Nature gives.

THE LAPLANDER.[6]

With furs and skins all warmly clad,
And snow-shoes on his feet,
The Lapp skims o'er the frozen plains
With motion light and fleet.

[1] *Greece* is a country of Europe, washed by the Mediterranean.
[2] *India* is a large territory in Southern Asia, belonging to England.
[3] *Italy* is a country in the south of Europe.

[4] The islands included in the empire of *Japan* lie off the east coast of Asia.
[5] *Kamtschatka* is situated in the extreme north-east of Asia.
[6] *Lapland* is a country of Northern Europe.

THE MEXICANS.[1]

A golden land is theirs; a land
  Where Nature's gifts abound;
But idle, ignorant, and proud
  The Mexicans are found.

THE PERSIANS.[1]

A powerful race were they of yore,
  Now fallen to decay;
Yet flowery Persia still can show
  A people free and gay.

THE NORWEGIANS.[1]

Among old Norway's piny woods
  They dwell, a people brave;
The reindeer is their wealth, their friend,
  Their playmate, and their slave!

THE RUSSIAN.[1]

Russia to one of England's sons
  Has given a charming bride;
Her people in their country feel
  A just and noble pride.

THE OTAHEITIANS.[1]

Where waves the palm-tree's leafy crest,
  Where Southern waters smile,
The graceful Otaheitians till
  Their Heaven-favoured isle.

THE SPANIARDS.[1]

The Spanish dame around her form
  The rich mantilla draws;
The Spanish cavalier his sword
  Wields in his country's cause.

[1] *Mexico* occupies the southern portion of North America.
[1] *Norway* is one of the countries of Northern Europe.
[1] *Otaheite* is a beautiful Island in the South Pacific Ocean.

[1] *Persia* is a country in Asia bordering on British India.
[1] *Russia*, a vast extent of country in Europe and Asia.
[1] *Spain* occupies the south-west corner of Europe.

THE TURK.[1]

Composed and calm the Moslem smokes
  His pipe, and bows to Fate;
And even in the battle din
  Preserves his mien sedate.

THE WALLACHIAN.[1]

The fierce Wallachian keeps his herds
  On many a marshy plain,
Or on the sunny mountain slopes
  Gathers the golden grain.

THE UNTERWALDER.[1]

The Unterwalders climb the rocks,
  And there themselves conceal,
Until the foemen pass, when loud
  Rings out their rifles' peal.

THE YANKEE.[1]

Quick and acute, with active brain,
  And ever nimble mind,
In life's great race the Yankee ne'er
  Will linger far behind.

THE VENETIAN.[1]

The gay gondola o'er the wave
  Of Venice lightly floats,
While each Venetian minstrel fills
  The air with silver notes.

THE ZEALANDER.[1]

In far New Zealand's fertile isles
  Lives a courageous race;
But ev'n the bold Maori soon
  To white men must give place.

[1] *Turkey* lies in the south of Europe and Asia.
[1] *Unterwalden* is a mountainous district of Switzerland.
[1] *Venice*, a city of Italy, on the Adriatic.

[1] *Wallachia*, a province of Turkey in Europe.
[1] The *Yankee*, a nickname for an American of the United States.
[1] The *Zealander*, or Maori; that is, a native inhabitant of New Zealand.

Aunt Louisa's The Globe Alphabet. London: Frederick Warne & Co., [1880]. Pp. [12], including 6 pages of colored plates. 26.2 x 23 cm.

THE "GLOBE" ALPHABET.

A stands for the Anchor we cast
    in the sea,
To hold the ship fast where we
    wish it to be.

B stands for the Baker who makes
    men their bread,
The great staff of life on which
    nations are fed.

C stands for a Chinaman; here
    one you see
Walking amidst his plantations
    of tea.

D for Dromedary; o'er deserts
    he strays,
And goes without water for many
    long days.

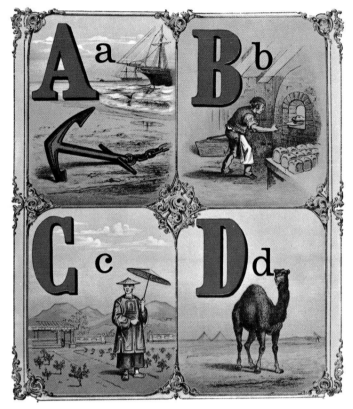

E stands for Elk, in cold countries
    he's found;
With Elks the American forests
    abound.

F stands for the Fruit that in
    summer we eat,
And find so refreshingly cooling
    and sweet.

G stands for Giraffe, which is able,
    you see,
To eat the top leaves from the
    branch of a tree.

H for Hippopotamus, savage
    and strong;
By African rivers he wanders
    along.

I's for Italian, an organ he grinds.

J is for Jewels of various kinds.

K stands for Kangaroos, sitting and leaping;
Hunters to kill them a keen watch are keeping.

L stands for the Lion, of forests the king;
With terrible roaring he makes the woods ring.

M stands for the Mill, where by water's great pow'r
The wheat is ground down to a very fine flour.

N stands for a Nabob, a lord of the East,
Who likes on strong coffee and sweetmeats to feast.

O stands for the Organ, delightful the sound
In church when its music floats solemnly round.

P stands for the Peacock, a bird very vain
Of feathers he sweeps on the earth like a train.

Q stands for Quadrille, which the little ones dance
As well, we all think, as the children in France.

R stands for Reindeer, very swiftly
it goes
Carrying the Laplander over the
snows.

S stands for the Sculptor, who
statues can make,
And portraits with chisel and
mallet can take.

T stands for the Tiger, a terrible
beast,
That lives in the jungles and woods
of the East.

U stands for the Uniform, in
which are seen
The soldiers who fight for their
country and Queen.

V stands for the Vulture, a great
bird of prey.
W for the Waggon that carries
the hay.

X for the Xylographer, cutting
on wood
A picture, which printed he thinks
will be good.

Y stands for the Yacht, that
bounds o'er the sea:
A prettier cutter you don't often
see.

Z stands for a Zebra, whose ele-
gant shape
The sculptor, we think, for his model
might take.

London Alphabet. Aunt Louisa's London Toy Books. London: Frederick Warne & Co., [1866]. Pp. [12], including 6 pages of colored plates. 26.4 x 22.8 cm.

APPLE-STALL.

The *Apple-Stall* stands at the end of the street,
 With piles of ripe apples, bright, rosy, and sweet;
Old Sarah is honest, and civil to all,
So, Arthur, my dear, we will buy at her stall.

BAZAAR.

The *Bazaar* is full of such beautiful things,—
Of dolls, carts and horses, and toys upon springs;
The children are puzzled to know what to buy,
And George at its wonders does nothing but pry.

CABMAN.

We have lost our way, Sister Mary and I,
So good *Mr. Cabman*, we beg you will try
And carry us home;—if you wish to know where—
'Tis the corner house of a very fine square.

DUSTMEN.

We are only poor *Dustmen* of this great town;
On our labour people are apt to look down;
But if nobody carried the rubbish away,
I think very few in the City could stay.

ENGINE.

Here comes the great *Fire Engine* rushing along,
With seven brave Firemen, bold, daring, and strong;
The smoke rises thickly, the sky is quite red;
If they don't put it out soon, the fire will spread.

FOG.

There's a yellow *Fog* in the City to-day,
We can scarcely see there, an inch of our way;
But the little link-boy will lend us his light,
And lead puzzled people all through it quite right.

GUNS.

BANG! go the *Guns* with a terrible noise,
But they do not frighten brave little boys;
And Johnny would wish for no better fun
Than to try if *he* couldn't fire off a gun.

HORSE-GUARDS.

The *Horse-Guards* are coming,—I see the shine
Of their swords, as they trot in stately line;
In war they fight bravely, as people know
Who remember the great war, long ago.

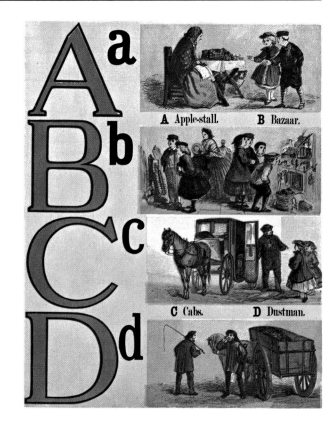

A Apple-stall.　　B Bazaar.
C Cabs.　　D Dustman.

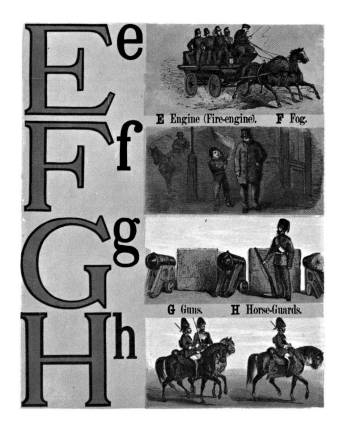

E Engine (Fire-engine).　　F Fog.
G Guns.　　H Horse-Guards.

IDLERS.

These *Idlers*, who loiter about all day,
Are quite a disgrace to the Queen's highway;
For laziness only has made them poor,
And reduced them to beg from door to door.

JAIL.

The *Jail* too often becomes the last home
Of beggars, who through the streets idly roam;
For that "idle hands find mischief to do,"
Is a proverb found to be always true.

KING WILLIAM'S STATUE.

King William's Statue looks calmly down
On the busiest street of this great town,
Where all is hurry, and bustle, and noise,
Of men and women, carts, horses, and boys.

LAMPLIGHTER.

The *Lamplighter* hastens the gas to light,
That streets may be cheerful and safe at night;
How prettily in a long twinkling line—
Growing smaller and smaller—the bright lamps shine!

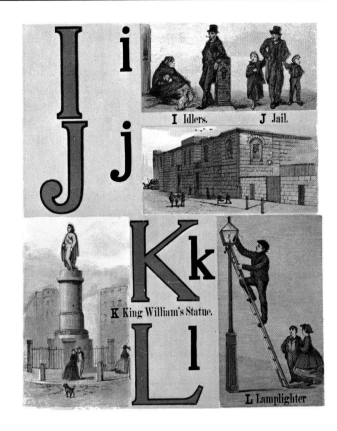

I Idlers. J Jail.

K King William's Statue.

L Lamplighter

MONUMENT.

The *Monument* stands on the very spot
Where the Great Fire (never to be forgot)
Broke out, in the days when gay Charles was King,
And burnt and destroyed almost everything.

NEWS-BOY.

The *News-Boy*, though little, does a good trade;
Morning and evening his pennies are made;
"The Times" and the "Standard" you hear him cry,
Or "Daily Telegraph,"—which will you buy?

OMNIBUS.

Omnibus, Ma'am?—just a-going to the Zoo':
There's room inside for the children and you;
Step in, if you please, Miss; we cannot wait;
We will set you down quite close to the gate."

PUNCH.

Our friends "*Punch*" and Toby display their feats
At the corner of many London streets;
The tricks of the puppets all of us know,
Yet we always laugh at the funny show.

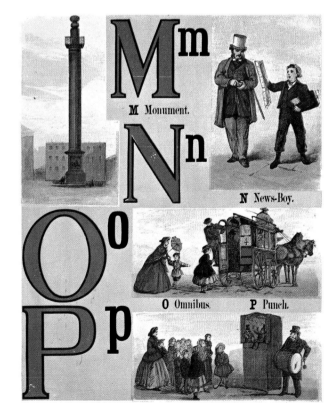

M Monument.

N News-Boy.

O Omnibus. P Punch.

QUEEN.

Queen Victoria now sits on the throne,
A better *Queen* England never has known;
Though the nation owed much, we must confess,
To the brave wise rule of our good Queen Bess.

RIVER.

The *River!* the River sparkles and plays,
As if it rejoiced in the sun's bright rays.
"Mamma, if you love your little daughter,
Please let me go on the shining water."

STEAMER.

The *Steamer* puffs out a long cloud of steam,
As it cuts its way through the rippling stream.
"Mamma, dear, I wonder how I should feel
If I were the man who stands by the wheel?"

TOWER.

The *Tower* of London is dark, grey, and old,
Sad tales of its dismal towers are told;
The two little Princes in it were slain,
That cruel King Richard the Third might reign.

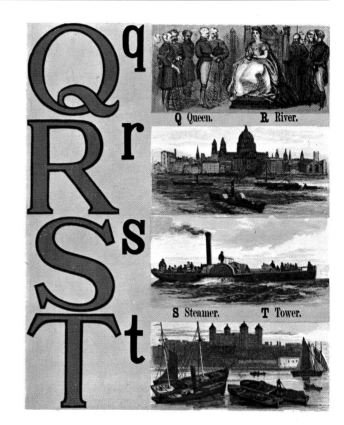

Q Queen.   R River.   S Steamer.   T Tower.

UNDERGROUND RAILWAY.

Into the darkness, and out of the light,
The *Underground Railway* carries us quite;
They have taken a lesson from the moles,
And burrow, like them, in underground holes.

VOLUNTEERS.   WESTMINSTER.

The brave *Volunteers* in St. James's Park
Go to drill in the ev'ning before it is dark,
Past the Parliament Houses at *Westminster*, where
The Lords and the Commons make laws just and fair.

X, Y.

These are Policeman, their numbers, *X, Y:*
How that boy laughs as he sees them march by!
If they should look round, away he would run,
Though he is not naughty,—'t is only fun.

ZOOLOGICAL GARDENS.

The *Zoological Gardens* to-day
Are full of happy young creatures at play;
But the tiger seems thinking, "What a treat
Such nice little morsels would be to eat!"

U Underground Railway. W Westminster.
V Volunteer.
X Y Policemen's No. Z Zoological Gardens.

The Picture Alphabet. Inscribed 1863 as Christmas gift. Pp. [8], in color. 20.2 x 17 cm.

295

M is the Moon with its calm silver light,
N is its season of shining, the Night.

O is the Orphan that at the door sat,
P is the Penny we dropt in his hat.

Q is the Queen in her majesty drest,
R is her Reign, which we pray may be blest.

S is the Shepherd-boy feeding his sheep,
T the tall Trees beneath which they sleep.

U is the upland where blows the wild heath,
V is the Violet sighing beneath.

W the Waterfall down in the glen,
X is the Numeral Letter for Ten.

Y is the Year gliding swiftly away,
Z is the Zenith where rests the noon-day.